The

Principles of Light
and Color

(1878)

Edwin D. Babbitt

ISBN 0-7661-0537-7

Kessinger Publishing's Rare Reprints
Thousands of Scarce and Hard-to-Find Books!

.   .   .
.   .   .
.   .   .
.   .   .
.   .   .
.   .   .
.   .   .
.   .   .
.   .   .
.   .   .
.   .   .
.   .   .
.   .   .
.   .   .
.   .   .
.   .   .
.   .   .
.   .   .

We kindly invite you to view our extensive catalog list at:
http://www.kessinger.net

THE
PRINCIPLES
OF
LIGHT AND COLOR

EDWIN D. BABBITT

1828-1905

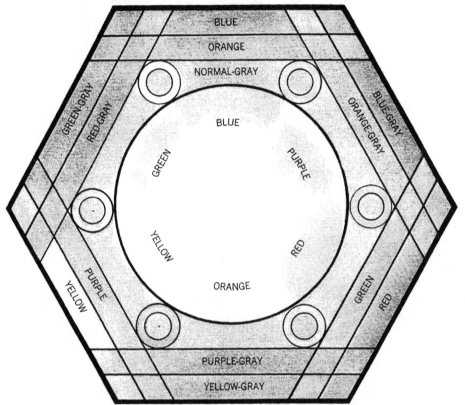

CHROMATIC HARMONY OF GRADATION AND CONTRAST.

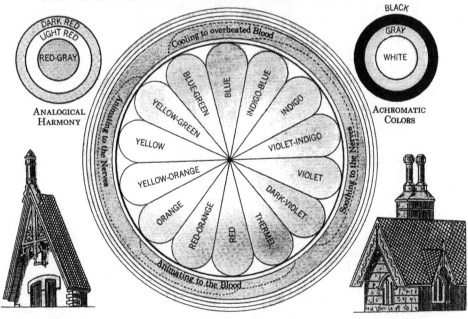

ANALOGICAL HARMONY

ACHROMATIC COLORS

CONTRASTING HARMONY

CHROMATIC COLORS PLACED OPPOSITE THOSE WHICH FORM A CHEMICAL AFFINITY WITH THEM

ANALOGICAL HARMONY

PREFACE

The preface of my work is like a Hebrew book; it begins at its very end. Having spent several years in developing this large volume, what is my excuse for thrusting it out upon mankind? None at all unless human knowledge and upbuilding can be enhanced thereby.

Am I laboring under a vain delusion when I assert that no science whatever, excepting pure mathematics, has thus far reached down to basic principles—that in spite of the wonderful achievements of experimental scientists, no definite conceptions of atomic machinery, or the fundamental processes of thermal, electric, chemical, physiological or psychological action have been attained, and that because the correlations of matter and force have been misapprehended? If I am deluded and cannot depend upon the thousand facts that seem to sustain me and clear up so many mysteries, it is certainly a sad matter, for then no one will be made the wiser for my labors; if I am right, and so many scientists are wrong in their conceptions of force, then too there is a melancholy side to the question, for great will be the trouble of having to pull up old stakes and put down new ones, and some opinionated persons will be so indignant at having dear old beliefs attacked, that if unable to demolish my facts in fair discussion will present one-sided views of them, or attack the author himself. I hope and pray that I may be duly abused, however, by all such crystallized conservatives, otherwise it will show that my efforts to advance this great cause of truth have been but feeble. After all, if this work shall develop some new and better foundations of scientific truth, scientific men themselves should rejoice at it even if it does cause a little trouble to adjust themselves to new conditions, for the more truth they get, the more luminous and triumphant will their pathway of progress become, and they will be able to build a superstructure upon these new foundations that is far more magnificent than any which my own limited efforts could achieve.

My discovery of the form and constitution of atoms, and their working in connection with etherial forces to produce the effects of heat, cold, electricity, magnetism, chemical action, light, color, and many other effects, was announced during our centennial year, 1876, in some New York and Chicago papers, and my ideas have been brought to still further maturity since. Having acquired this knowledge, it seemed quite possible at last to crystallize the subjects of Light, Color, and other Fine Forces into a science, and learn their chemical and therapeutical potencies as well as many of their mystic relations to physical and psychological action.

Before reaching out into the unknown and invisible it was important to establish briefly the laws of the known and visible, the misapprehension of which has led scientists into various errors, as it seemed to me, hence my first chapters. Before being able to understand Light and Color, with any exactness, it was absolutely necessary to investigate the working of atoms, and the general laws of the fine forces, so that we may not always have to move in the dark when considering them. Hence my chapter on the Etherio-atomic Philosophy of Force. Whatever may be thought of my details of atoms, it seems quite impossible that a thoughtful mind should dispute the corrrectness of their general features, so absolutely capable are they of being demonstrated by facts.

It is quite time that the wonderful world of light and color which is invisible to the ordinary eye, and which is capable of being demonstrated by spectrum analysis and otherwise, should be made known, especially as so many mysteries of nature and human life are cleared up thereby, and such marvelous powers of vital and mental control are revealed.

I would especially ask one favor of all critics, which is, that they will examine and weigh well all departments of the work before they condemn, for it has cost too much thought and careful investigation to have it rudely and hastily passed upon. Comprising, as it does, so large a field of heretofore untrodden ground, there certainly must be some errors in spite of all my great care and desire for exact truth.

I have chosen a diluted sky-blue tint for my paper, not only because it is soothing to the nerves of the eye, but as I deem it, handsome. Calendered white, or yellowish paper is known to be irritating to the retina.

The beautiful engravings of this work, many of which have the steel plate finish, have been executed by the sun under the control of the Photo-Engraving Co., 67 Park Place, N.Y. For the very careful and conscientious labors of this company I am greatly indebted. The Superintendent, Mr. J. C. Moss, was the first, I believe, to bring these finest solar relief plates into practical use.

I owe a word of acknowledgment also to Mr. John Fahnestock, of 25 Rose St., N.Y., for the colored plates, which for beauty I have not seen surpassed on either side of the ocean.

Science Hall, N.Y.   EDWIN D. BABBITT

Lower New York in Dr. Babbitt's time

THE

PRINCIPLES

OF

LIGHT AND COLOR:

INCLUDING AMONG OTHER THINGS

THE HARMONIC LAWS OF THE UNIVERSE, THE
ETHERIO-ATOMIC PHILOSOPHY OF FORCE,
CHROMO CHEMISTRY, CHROMO THERA-
PEUTICS, AND THE GENERAL PHIL-
OSOPHY OF THE FINE FORCES,
TOGETHER WITH NUMER-
OUS DISCOVERIES AND
PRACTICAL APPLI-
CATIONS.

ILLUSTRATED BY 204 EXQUISITE PHOTO-ENGRAVINGS, BESIDES FOUR
SUPERB COLORED PLATES PRINTED ON SEVEN PLATES EACH.

By EDWIN D. BABBITT.

" Study the Light ; attempt the high ; seek out
The Soul's bright path."—*Bailey.*

NEW YORK:
BABBITT & CO.,
SCIENCE HALL, 141 EIGHTH STREET.
1878.

CONTENTS

THE
PRINCIPLES
OF
LIGHT AND COLOR

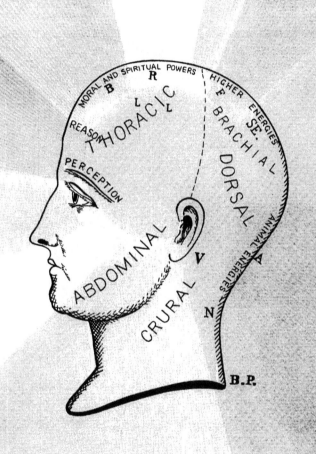

CHAPTER FIRST

HARMONIC LAWS OF THE UNIVERSE

THIS first chapter is as broad (and vague) as its title. He added Victorian fringe and tassel to an otherwise remarkable book on color healing. The text does much circumnavigating of the central theme—color—and seems very old-fashioned today. What is reprinted verbatim from Chapter First are a few paragraphs of Babbitt's comments on the fundamentals of color. While they will hardly be found original or enlightening to any student of color and art, they are pertinent to the later and vital chapters.

TRIAD OF PRIMARY COLORS.

A few words may be appropriate as to the threefold division of representative *Colors*. We have
RED, an exciting color at nearly the centre of heat.
YELLOW, the medium color and centre of luminosity.
BLUE, a fine color which is cold, soothing, electrical.
Practically all colors can be made out of these or could be if we could get a supply of the invisible red to assist in forming violet and indigo and could find pigments of absolutely pure red, yellow and blue. We have also

A TRIAD OF SECONDARY COLORS.

ORANGE composed of equal parts of red and yellow.
GREEN   "   "   blue and yellow.
PURPLE   "   "   blue and red.

A Triad of Achromatic or Neutral Colors. Pl.II, 4.

BLACK composed of equal parts of red, yellow and blue.

WHITE composed of five parts of red, three parts of yellow, and eight parts of blue.

GRAY *(normal gray)*, composed of black and white.

This is given from the formula of eminent artists and would seem to prove that after all "black is white, and white is black," but not quite. It cannot be verified entirely in practice from the impurity of pigments. When we call them *neutral* we mean neutral, chromatically speaking, as they have no especial hues, but white is the most positive of all colors as to luminosity. The folly of calling black the absence of colors is now done away with among the intelligent, although it is really caused by the absorption of all colors. Normal gray is the most neutral of all colors and does not make discord with any.

A Triad of Primary Grays.

RED GRAY, or RUSSET, composed of normal gray and red.

YELLOW GRAY, or CITRINE, of normal gray and yellow.

BLUE GRAY, or OLIVE, of normal gray and blue.

A Triad of Secondary Grays.

ORANGE GRAY, composed of normal gray and orange.

GREEN GRAY,   "   "   "   green.

PURPLE GRAY,   "   "   "   purple.

Orange Gray and *Red Gray* are sometimes called BROWN.

Trinal Division of Tints and Shades.

1st. *Light tints of a color* in which some white is introduced, as light yellow, light blue, light green, light gray, light green-gray, light blue-gray, etc.

2d. *Medium grades of color,* such as ordinary yellow, purple, red-gray, green-gray, etc.

3d. *Dark Shades of Color,* in which some black is introduced, as dark yellow, dark blue, dark green, dark red, dark gray, dark red-gray, etc. These are said to have a lower tone.

TRINAL DIVISION OF HUES.

The three basic colors, red, yellow and blue, should have a definite meaning and for this reason it is not so correct to say green-blue, orange-red or green-yellow, as it is to say blue-green, red-orange, yellow-green, for the great central colors are not to bend to the secondaries but the secondaries to them. From the imperfection of language, however, we sometimes are forced to say reddish-blue, yellowish-blue, bluish-red, etc., and by these terms we mean blue with a very slight tint of red, blue with a slight tint of yellow, red with a slight tint of blue, etc. A general threefold division of the secondaries may be made as follows:

ORANGE, combination of red and yellow.

RED-ORANGE, red and yellow combined, with red in excess.

YELLOW-ORANGE, red and yellow combined, with yellow in excess.

GREEN, combination of yellow and blue.

YELLOW-GREEN, yellow and blue, with yellow in excess.

BLUE-GREEN, yellow and blue, with blue in excess.

PURPLE, combination of red and blue.

BLUE-PURPLE, red and blue, with blue in excess.

RED-PURPLE, red and blue, with red in excess.

For further study of the colors see plate II., 1, in which the part of purple nearest the blue is blue-purple, that nearest the red is red-purple, that between these points near the periphery is deep medium purple, that near the centre, light purple, and so with the other hues, which may also be represented in fig. 3 of same plate. As I have said violet cannot be exactly represented by any two pigments combined, but I have had a blue-purple placed on the plate as the nearest representation of the violet.

INSUFFICIENCY OF THE PRESENT THEORIES OF LIGHT AND FORCE

In this second chapter, Babbitt is again verbose. He writes regarding: Science and Philosophy should be Combined, Basic Principles not yet Reached, Cohesion, Chemical Affinity, Gravitation, and the like. When Babbitt becomes involved with the physiology of color, with undulatory and corpuscular theories of color energy, he is confused—just as were the other scientists of his day. However, Chapter Second in its final paragraph presents one of Babbitt's favorite topics, the atom, and is well worthy of reproduction, complex though the text may seem.

New Worlds of Light and Color.

Finally *there are new and surpassingly beautiful worlds of color* which seem to be almost entirely unknown to our writers on Optics, but which can be demonstrated on scientific principles and by abundant facts and observations. These colors reveal the very dynamics of nature and man, and the most exquisite and interior principles of force which reach far into the mysteries of mind and matter. They help to make a science out of what would otherwise be guess work, broader than mere *physics*, broader than mere *metaphysics*, and combining both on nature's great law of duality to form the grander science of Psychophysics.

Summation of Points.

To *review* our ground, then, we see, that notwithstanding *all the brilliant achievements of science, the fundamental principles of Cohesion, Chemical Affinity, Electricity, Magnetism, Diamagnetism, Gravitation, Physiology, Psychology, Light, Color and other departments of knowledge are unknown—that the cause of this deficiency is the failure of scientists to ascertain the atomic constitution of things and their ignoring of the dual nature of the universe in their efforts to divorce matter from force, or force from matter, or at least in their swinging to the extremes of the dynamic theory on the one hand, or the material theory on the other, while the whole known mechanics of nature teach this great lesson, that all force must act through relatively static and fluidic conditions of matter, the finer fluidic conditions vitalizing the more stationary conditions, and the more stationary conditions reacting upon and answering as a base work for the fluidic conditions. In closing I will simply add that there are many grades of fluidic and also of relatively static conditions, the coarser grade of the static being acted on by the coarser grade of the fluidic, a still finer grade of the static by a finer grade of the fluidic, and so on upward toward the infinitely fine. A slower fluidic force may also be vitalized by finer and swifter fluidic forces.*

CHAPTER THIRD

THE ETHERIO–ATOMIC PHILOSOPHY OF FORCE

ONE of Babbitt's most proud enthusiasms concerned a unique theory of the atom.

Babbitt theorized about atom "spirals" and "spirallae." For some seventy pages he expounded on the Heat End of Atoms, Nature of Atom Spirals, Ethereal Forces, Different Grades of Ether, Magnetism, and such, but tended to confuse the scientific findings of his day with the mystical qualities of his own fertile and fervent imagination.

There were to Babbitt thermal or positive colors, such as red, orange, yellow. As the spirals for these colors grew smaller, thermal energy shifted into the electrical or negative colors, such as green, indigo, violet. He attempted to make all this clear in a diagram herein reproduced, and what he had to say about all this will follow.

He ended Chapter Third with a long and a short paragraph which to the writer of these notes seems incredible! One wonders with amazement how Babbitt in 1878 anticipated that an atom bomb would be the size of a man's head! How could he conceive that if it were released in the midst of New ' 'k it would raise such havoc!

Let the reader be his own witness to Babbitt's prescience.

GENERAL FEATURES OF ATOMS.

1. Years of investigation of what the general form and constitution of atoms must be to harmonize with and furnish a key to
the facts discovered by the scientific world, aided by many more
years of inquiry into the fundamental principles of nature, have
led me to a very positive conclusion that fig. 135 is the general
outline of an ordinary atom, especially of one by means of which
all the colors can be made manifest. The hundreds of points to
prove it correct cannot be given here, but they will appear more
and more all through this work in the mysteries which are cleared
up thereby, especially in Chapter V. as well as in this chapter.
Although the modification of tints, hues and other forces which
are manifested through atoms is almost infinite from the fact
that atoms of the same substance must vary within certain limits
in the size of their spirillae of the same kind, yet facts seem to
indicate seven intra-spirals (4) on the outside of atoms for the
warm or thermal colors, and which are properly the *thermo-
lumino* group, whereas the same spirals form the principle of the
electrical colors while passing through the axis of atoms. These
are all named and located in fig. 135, commencing with the
largest spirilla for the hot invisible solar rays called *thermal,* after
which is the slightly smaller spirilla for red, another for red-
orange, etc. Passing around the atom and becoming smaller and
finer, the same spirillae form the channels for the electrical colors
by passing into the vortex and through the axis, thermal being
converted into blue-green, red into blue, red-orange into indigo-
blue, orange into indigo, yellow-orange into violet-indigo, yellow
into violet, and yellow-green into dark violet. The group of
thermospirals at 3, 3, are called *positive,* because the spirillae
that surround them are larger and the heat greater than the portion of the same group at 5, 5, which are therefore called *negative* thermo-spirals. The group 2, embraces the positive color-
spirals, but as they are concealed by gliding into the contiguous
atoms, it is only the same group at 4 that are vis'' '- as thermo-

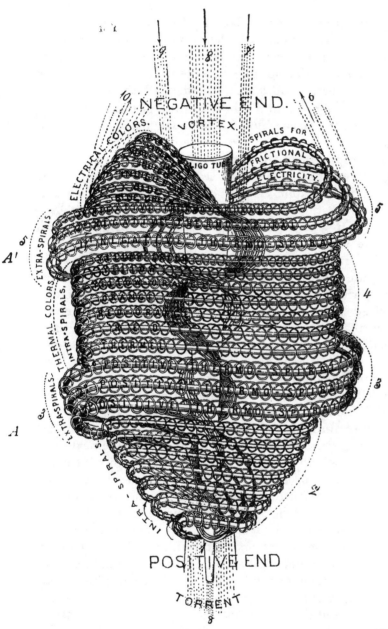

The general Form of an Atom, including the spirals and 1st Spirillae, together with influx and efflux ethers, represented by dots, which pass through these spirillae. The 2d and 3d spirrilae with their still finer ethers are not shown.

color spirals, or at the vortex above as electro-color spirals. 9 and 10 represent minute streams of ether, which are simply combinations of much finer atoms, that flow from the thermo spirillae and the thermo-lumino spirillae into the same grades of spirillae in the atom above; 7 and 9 are axial ethers which flow from the

atom above into the axial spirillae of this atom; 8 represents ethers which flow through the *ligo tube,* and these and other ethers are represented as passing on through their appropriate channels until they emerge at the torrent end. These ethers sweep through the atom and quicken its spiral wheel-work into new life, just as the winds move a wind-mill, or the waters a water-wheel, while the atom itself, armed as it is with its vortical spring-work, must have a great reactive suction which draws on these ethereal winds.*

Atoms joined.

2. Why are ethers drawn from spirillae of one atom to the same kind of spirillae in a contiguous atom, and why does a certain grade of ether exactly harmonize with, and seek out, a certain size of spirilla? For the same reason that a tuning fork or the cord of a piano will be set into vibration by a tone made in its own key. In the case of a piano, a cord vibrates to tones of its own pitch, or in other words, to tones whose waves synchronize with its own vibrations. Let us apply this principle to atoms. The vibratory action of the red spirilla throws the current of ether which passes through it into the eddy-like whirl which just harmonizes in size and form to the red spirilla of the next atom above it with which it comes in contact, and which must necessarily draw it on. This second atom passes it on to the red spirilla of the third, the third to that of the fourth, and so on through millions of miles, so long as there is a spirilla of the right grade to conduct it onward. The same process applies to the orange, or yellow, or any other spiral, and, constituting as it does a fundamental principle of chemical action, the reader should note this point well. The same principle applies to the axial spirals whose lines of force, reaching the positive end at 1, make a sudden dart to the outside and thus in part *jolt* their contents into the answer-

---

* As will be shown hereafter, there must be still finer atmospheres within the ordinary atmosphere, so fine doubtless that they permeate solids and fluids, and form a base-work for fluidic action which may assist the spiral eddies and vortical suctions of the larger atoms.

ing spirals of the next atom, the blue ethers of this plunging into the blue spirilla of the next, the violet ethers of this into the violet spirilla of the next, and so on.

3. The ethers are *efflux* as they flow out of one atom or series of atoms, and *influx* as they flow into an atom or series of atoms. Thus 9 and 7 are influx, and 6 and 10 efflux ethers. The ethers at the torrent end are powerfully efflux, and have momentum not only from the projectile force of this atom, but from the suctional force of the next, into whose vortex this atom is inserted.

4. It should be noticed that the same spirillae which wind around the outside of atoms on the expansive law of thermism, pass on through the axis on the contracting law of cold, and after becoming the most contracted and intense at the positive end of the atom, suddenly plunge to the outside and again become thermal. Thus the very intensity of the interior cold forces may develop intensity of heat, and we at once see why it is that an object which is so cold as to be 60° F. below zero is said to have an effect similar to that of red hot iron.

5. The *First Positive Thermo-Spiral* at *A* projects beyond the intra-spirals below and forms a regulating barrier to determine just how far this atom shall be inserted into the vortex of the next atom: in other words, this atom becomes sheathed in the next as far as *A,* while the atom above becomes encased in this precisely the same distance, and so on, which accounts for the great regularity of form in crystallizations, etc. In chemical affinity, as I shall show hereafter, the atom glides into a wide mouthed atom up to its *shoulders* at *A'* where the second circuit of these same thermo-spirals is seen. By this means the color-spirals are hidden in the encasing atom, and this explains some mysteries of color change which puzzle the chemist, and which will be explained in Chapter V.

6. The *Ligo* is supposed to exist only in solids, such as rocks, metals, fibrous substances, etc., in which it forms the leading element of cohesion and hardness, while in liquids, gases and ethers it is wanting, which accounts for their flowing qualities. This tube probably has spiral convolutions with openings in the sides something like those Chimney pieces, the object of which is to cause a draft.

7. The seven thermo-lumino spirals which become the electro-lumino spirals on reaching the vortex and axial portion of the

atom, naturally grow somewhat smaller, from the smaller space in which they move, and receive a finer grade of ethers from the axis of the atom above at 9 and 7 than those which course through them in their thermal portions on the outside. As they progress through the axis they become narrower, more nearly straight and consequently more keenly electrical until they reach the torrent end. The reason the dark violet is the coldest of all the colors is, because from its position it must circulate with a more narrow and interior course through the axis, as being the highest (See fig. 135), it reaches the vortex and enters before the others, next to which comes the violet, then the violet-indigo, the indigo, the indigo-blue, the blue, and warmest and least electrical of all in the electrical group, the blue-green. My reasons for calling these the electrical group of colors will be fully shown in XXIX of this chapter. *All axial forces move on the law of electricity of some kind, while the coarser grades of electricity impart the ruder sensations of cold, which are so distressing. The finest grades of electricity, while producing the phenomena of cold, such as contraction, do not impart the chilling sensations of cold at all, to most persons.* To compose all the colors which constitute white light, both the electrical and thermal colors must be combined and carried along side by side through conversely polarized lines of atmosphere, or other media, through which they are conveyed.

8. The axial spirillae doubtless fill up the whole interior of their atoms from their elasticity, which fact the artist has not quite expressed.

Thus is an atom an epitome of the universe, having a gradation of elliptical and spiral orbits in imitation of those of the solar system; having its axial center of unity around which its external spirals revolve as a principle of diversity; having its positive end at which repulsion rules, and its negative end at which attraction is the dominant principle; constituting the most marvelous of machines with wheels within wheels driven by water; even the water of ether, some of which is much swifter than the lightning; resembling also an animal with veins, arteries, nerves, spine, viscera, blood, nerve-force, etc. In general form it resembles the egg, which at one time was thought to be the starting point of all life, Harvey having written *"omne vivum ex ovo."* Atoms indeed are the eggs out of which the whole universe is built, though on quite another principle. Their activities are so amazing that if one of them could be enlarged to the size of a man's head, constructed of some material millions of times stronger than anything known upon earth, and the tremendous whirl of forces set to revolving through their spirals which at their ordinary speed vibrate several hundred trillion times a second, what must be the effect? If such an atom should be set in the midst of New York City, it must create such a whirlwind that all its palatial structures, ships, bridges and surrounding cities, with nearly two millions of people, which be swept into fragments and carried into the sky.

If the reader has become familiar with the foregoing chapters and gained possession of the atomic key, I think we shall be able to go hand in hand through many hidden pathways of power and open new doors in the infinite temple of knowledge.

CHAPTER FOURTH
THE SOURCES OF LIGHT

IN this chapter, Babbitt discussed such subjects as World Formations, Nebulous Matter, The Sun, The Moon, Comets, Terrestrial Forces, Lime Light, Electric Light. Little need be repeated except a section on How Color Effects are Produced.

HOW COLOR EFFECTS ARE PRODUCED.

1. We have already seen in Chapter Third, how different colors are formed by different sized spirillae in connection with the different grades of ethers which pass through these spirillae. But what causes gold to appear yellow, or coal black, or snow white, for instance? Gold is yellow because it has a spirilla of the right grade to *repel* or *reflect* the yellow-forming ether while it has other spirillae which receive the other color ethers more or less within themselves and thus hide them. If all of the spirillae had such an affinity for the other color-ethers, and their atoms could become polarized in such a way that these ethers could be transmitted entirely through them, it would be transparent like the air or nearly like clear glass. If its spirillae should briskly repel all of the color-ethers into our eyes it would give us the

effect of *white;* if they affinitize with them sufficiently to draw them all within its surface, the effect would be *black;* if they should absorb a part of each color-ether and reflect a part, the effect would be *normal gray;* if a majority of each color-ether is reflected, *light gray* would result, and if a majority absorbed, *dark gray* would appear. If the red and part of the other colors should be reflected it would cause red-gray, and the same principle applies to the other grays. If nearly the whole of the red or the blue should be transmitted, while the other colors were absorbed, reflected, or slightly transmitted, we should have the effect of red-glass, or blue-glass, or any other colored glass according to which color predominates.

2. Let us see, then, how rays of luminous ether can produce the effect of light. Take the yellow ray, for instance, the center of luminosity. Sodium, magnesium, iron, and other substances, when under the terrific heat at or near the burning surface of the sun have a tremendous repulsive action upon all yellow-forming ethers including fine particles of their own substance, and project them into space. Before getting entirely away from the solar atmospheres, however, the coarser part of these ethers is strained off while the finer part proceeds through space and strikes our atmosphere. According to the principles of chemical affinity already explained (Chapter Third, XXXVII, 10), the atoms of both nitrogen and oxygen must have an especial affinity for the principal yellow-forming ethers, as they are strong in violet, and thus become ignited as they pass through, aided in this ignition by proximate particles of hydrogen, which are so quick to take fire, and which constitute an ingredient of vapor. So far the globules of vapor are the principal sources of light, but that is not sufficient. All luminelles of materials like themselves, such as sodium, magnesium, etc., must be repelled at their touch, ignited by their impact against them, and many of them driven on to the earth before their power. Violet-colored luminelles having a chemical affinity for them will transmit them freely and become incandescent thereby, and luminelles of various colors will be met and penetrated in the same way, for, as Isaac Newton has shown, all styles of matter, however opaque or however colored, become more or less transparent to light, in case they are in very minute masses. The same principle holds true with reference to the other color-forming ethers, the violet ethers sweeping

with special ease through luminelles of sodium, magnesium, etc., in which yellow is active, the blue ethers sweeping with especial ease through the hydrogen of vapor luminelles, in which the red principle in the spectrum is active, as well as through many other substances, such as carbon, lithium, nitrogen, etc., and so on with all the other colors, each of which drives before it certain ethereal atoms like itself in a common tide to the earth, and each does its part in setting the whole atmosphere on fire and thus filling the world with light.

CHAPTER FIFTH

CHROMO–CHEMISTRY

BABBITT developed his concept of color therapy from a rather fanciful extension of ideas, centering around the colors of metals and elements discovered after the spectroscope was invented in 1814. At that time various metals and gases were found to produce characteristic lines when their emissions were passed through a prism. The spectrum of magnesium, for example, was chiefly green; that of hydrogen, red; that of calcium, violet; that of common table salt, yellow. It was an easy step, therefore, for Babbitt to assume that different colors had different chemical and therefore therapeutic properties. He did not hesitate to construct a highly complex science of Chromo-Chemistry, Chromo-Therapeutics and Chromopathy.

Chapter Fifth elaborates all this and deals with such topics as Spectrum Analysis, the Spectra of Metals, Chromatic Repulsion and Attraction, and the Materials of Colors. This serves as a firm basis for Babbitt's work in color therapy, and leads directly to the true sum and substance of his book.

There follows a brief summary and account of the Materials of Colors in Babbitt's own words.

I will draw up a list of the *materials of colors* so far as contributed by 20 important elements, including 16 metals which the spectroscope has discovered in the sun's atmosphere, and the four metalloids, oxygen, hydrogen, nitrogen and carbon, which have so much to do with light, and which must certainly form a part of the solar ethers from their universality. The names of the metals are sodium, calcium, barium, magnesium, iron, chromium, nickel, copper, zinc, strontium, cadmium, cobalt, manganese, aluminum, titanium, rubidium. Hydrogen also exists in vast quantities in the solar atmosphere, as has been seen. Doubtless many more, if not all of the elements, have something of their finer emanations represented in light. Carbon we know forms a part of light and is imparted to plants by the sun's rays.

Materials of Red-light:—Nitrogen, oxygen, barium, zinc, strontium, cadmium, rubidium.

Materials of Red Orange Light:—Hydrogen, oxygen, nitrogen, calcium, barium, iron, copper, strontium, cadmium. This color, in common parlance, would pass for red, and constitutes a refined grade of that color.

Materials of Orange Light:—Oxygen, calcium, iron, nickel, zinc, cobalt, rubidium, aluminum, titanium.

Materials of Yellow-Orange Light:—Carbon, nitrogen, sodium, nickel, zinc, cobalt, manganese, titanium. This would often pass for yellow with those who are not discriminative.

Materials of Yellow Light:—Carbon, nitrogen, oxygen, calcium, barium, iron, chromium, nickel, copper, zinc, strontium, cadmium, cobalt, manganese, aluminum, titanium.

Materials of Yellow-Green Light:—Carbon, nitrogen, oxygen, sodium, calcium, barium, magnesium, chromium, nickel, copper, strontium, cadmium, cobalt, rubidium, aluminum, titanium.

Materials of Blue-Green Light:—Carbon, nitrogen, hydrogen, sodium, iron, nickel, copper, zinc, cobalt, manganese, titanium.

Materials of Blue Light:—Oxygen, nitrogen, barium, magnesium, chromium, nickel, copper, zinc, strontium, cadmium, cobalt, manganese, aluminum, titanium.

Materials of Indigo-Blue Light:—Oxygen, nitrogen, iron, calcium, manganese, titanium.

Materials of Indigo Light:—Oxygen, hydrogen, carbon, iron, chromium, copper, strontium, titanium.

Materials of Violet-Indigo Light:—Oxygen, nitrogen, carbon, iron, calcium, cobalt, rubidium, manganese, titanium.

Materials of Violet Light:—Nitrogen, oxygen, barium, iron, strontium, manganese.

Materials of Dark Violet Light:—Hydrogen, calcium, aluminum.

There is a great intensity, as well as quantity of reflecting power in the range of the yellow and its kindred yellow-green and yellow-orange as the leading principle of luminosity, by means of which the universe is revealed to the eye of man. It occurs to me that the reason why the yellow is the most luminous of colors is that its luminelles are of that golden medium size which are not so coarse that the solar ethers fail to make them incandescent, as in the case of the trans-red, nor so fine as to give out waves too small to make an impression upon the sensorium, like the trans-violet. The blue principle, including the indigo, is also strong and intense as the most prominent realm of chromo-electricity, or in fact of the other electricities which tend to manifest themselves in some hue or shade of blue. Magnetic substances are always strong in the blue as well as the still finer grades of electricity represented by the indigo or violet, as in iron, oxygen, cobalt, manganese, chromium, etc. The *red*, especially the finer grade of red, more properly called red-orange, is not imparted by as many substances as some other colors, but by those which are ever and everywhere abounding, such as hydrogen, oxygen, nitrogen, etc., so we are not left to perish with the cold. The trinity of colors, the red, yellow and blue, finds representation in the three great elements of Hydrogen, Carbon and Oxygen, which constitute so much of the world, including the whole or a large portion of the sugars, gums, starches, ethers, alcohols, many acids and much of the substance of the vegetable world.

CHAPTER SIXTH.

CHROMO–THERAPEUTICS, OR CHRO–MOPATHY.

I. The Healing Power of Color.

This must be quite evident to the reader by this time, especially as, in the last chapter, we saw the wonderful power of color repulsions and color affinities, and saw also that all things manifest their potencies by means of color. This being true, then, we may construct a more exquisite and exact *Materia Medica*, and erect a standard of medical practice based on principles of almost mathematical precision. Not only may we, by means of the principles already laid down, judge of the medical potencies of the coarser mineral elements, but of the finer potencies of the vegetable world, of water, air, electricity, and magnetism, and the still finer forces of the sunlight. Sunlight constitutes a truly *celestial materia medica* which, according to principle XV of Chap. First, must be more safe, effective and enduring than the cruder elements, in case we know how to control it.

II. Comparative Fineness of Healing Elements.

Minerals are at the bottom of nature's scale of forces, being so crude that the most of their particles are unable to float in the atmosphere, and consequently are held down in the midst of earthy substances. The vegetable world which constitutes the direct food of man, is sifted of the coarser mineral elements by a beautiful and ingenious process, the carbon and some other of the finer elements of the sunlight and atmosphere being received into the plant or vegetable from the sky, while the elements that come from the earth are strained of their coarser ingredients by the spongioles of the root and absorbed only in a liquid state. It may readily be seen why cereals and fruits, growing, as they do, above ground and drinking in the refined elements of the sunlight so freely, constitute a higher grade of food or food-medicines than the roots, tubers, and bulbs, such as radishes, potatoes, onions, etc., which grow under ground. Water owes its healing power, 1st, to its cleansing character, and 2dly to its electricity, combined also with a goodly amount of thermism. The electro-magnetic machine also presents similar grades of fine elements, inasmuch as, like water, it combines galvano, magneto and other grades of electricity. Pure air furnishes a somewhat more ethereal combination of elements than water, as it includes those which are sufficiently volatile to float, and presents fine ethers, which during the day-time are so constantly under the action of sunlight. But the finest potency of all, of which we can avail ourselves in the external world, comes from the sunlight, the only known element which transcends it in fineness, being the psycho-magnetic radiation from highly organized human beings. By understanding the etherio-atomic law we see at once how all things must incessantly radiate their peculiar essences and ethers, all ethers partaking more or less of the substances through which they pass, the finest substances having the finest emanations.

III. The Healing Power of Red.

1. According to principles XIX and XX in the last chapter, red must stimulate and increase the action of the warm red principle in the human system, as for instance, the *arterial blood,* and also act as the harmonizing affinitive element of the cold blue principle, which causes blueness of veins, paleness of countenance, etc. Examples have already been given, but a few examples quoted a little more minutely in the exact words of the U. S. Dispensatory and other recognized authorities, will help the better to establish the principles of not only the red but other colors, so far as drugs are concerned; having established which, we may be sure from the unity that reigns throughout nature, that the same principle in sunlight and every where else must produce similar results, the difference being that fine elements like the sunlight are more penetrating, safe, and enduring than coarse drugs.

2. The *Balsam of Peru* (Balsamum Peruvianum) "is of a dark reddish brown color, a warm bitterish taste, leaving when swallowed a burning or prickling sensation in the throat," "is a warm stimulating tonic and expectorant."

3. *Cayenne Pepper* (Capsicum) Flowers white, "fruit smooth and shining, of a bright scarlet, orange or sometimes yellow color." "Powdered capsicum is usually of a more or less bright red color;" "is a powerful stimulant, producing a sense of heat in the stomach and general glow over the body;" "an arterial stimulant and rubefacient."

4. *Cloves* (Caryophyllus) "are externally deep brown, internally reddish, their taste hot"—"among the most stimulant of aromatics."

5. *Bromine.* "A red liquid," "caustic and irritant,"—"when diluted, tonic and diuretic." (Waring.)

6. *Iron.* *Ferric Oxide* (Fe_2O_3) "is of a reddish color and forms salts which, for the most part, have a reddish color." *Ferrous Trioxide* (FeO_3) "wine red color." "The preparations of iron are powerfully tonic, raising the pulse, promoting the secretions, and increasing the coloring matter of blood."

7. *Red Cedar* (Juniperus Virginiana), "stimulant, emmenagogue and diuretic."

8. *Musk.* "Powder, reddish brown, is a stimulant and antispasmodic, increasing the vigor of the circulation."

9. *Ammonium Carbonate* ($N_4H_{16}C_3O_8$). Powerful in the red principle of hydrogen. "An arterial stimulant."

10. *Alcohol* (C_2H_6O). Red predominates strongly from its Hydrogen. "A diffusible stimulant of heart and arteries—exciting to the nervous and vascular system, succeeded by equal depression."

11. The power of *oxygen* to develope the red principle of the blood and thus by reaction to harmonize and animate the system which has become too cold and sluggish, under a predominance of the bluish venous blood, is well known. The power of *red glass* and a red chamber to excite, cheer and cure the cold morbid condition of two despondent lunatics, as proved by the experiments of Dr. Ponza, has already been spoken of in Chap. Fifth XX, 20.

IV. Healing Power of Red Light.

Red light, like red drugs, is the warming element of sunlight, with an especially rousing effect upon the blood and to some extent upon the nerves, especially as strained through some grades of red glass which admit not only of the red but the yellow rays, and thus prove valuable in paralysis and other dormant and chronic conditions. The following facts are quoted from Dr. S. Pancoast's new work, entitled *Blue and Red Light:*—

1st Case.—Paraplegia (Paralysis of both Legs).

" Master F., aged 8 years, had a tedious convalescence from a severe attack of diphtheria, which was suddenly interrupted by a very severe attack of paraplegia ; the paralysis was almost complete ; he could not walk and could stand only when supported by a table or chair. We had him arrayed entirely in white and placed in strong *red* baths from one to two hours at a time ; soon after being placed in the red light he would fall asleep, and a profuse perspiration burst forth, saturating his underclothing ; in three weeks he was walking firmly, and in two months was perfectly well. More than two years have since elapsed and he has continued in perfect health."

2d Case.—Consumption in the Third Stage.

" Mrs. H., aged 35 years. This was a case of *consumption in the third stage, with both lungs involved,* the left hepatized with mucus râle through the upper third, and crepitation in the apex of the right lung ; sputa copious, amounting to half a pint in twenty four-hours ; her expectoration was a yellowish, ropy and frothy mucus and pus, a portion of which sank in water ; she had severe night-sweats, and chills or creeps regularly at 11 o'clock, A.M., followed by fever with flushed cheeks." Dr. Pancoast proceeds to show that her parents and most of the family had died with consumption. He continues :—" I placed Mrs. H. under red baths regulated by the effects produced. In two weeks improvement began to manifest itself in all her symptoms ; in another week the mucus râle became a sub-mucus, then successively a crepitant and a bronchial ; soon respiration was resumed through the entire left lung, and the crepitation at the apex of the right lung disappeared ; expectoration improved and the cough became less frequent and less distressing ; with the improvement in these symptoms the chills and fever and the dyspnœa disappeared and her strength rapidly increased ; in two months and a half, the only remaining trouble was a slight hacking cough arising from an irritated throat." Dr. Pancoast proceeds to state that she remained well between one and two years, and then, from assuming extra duties, caught a severe cold which developed into pneumonia and finally led to her death. He says that " in an active and extensive practice covering more than 30 years, we have never known or heard of a case of consumption at so advanced a stage successfully treated. Her recovery was entire."

If in the above case a deep blue glass had been used for her head, and beneath this some red, and then yellow, and then red for the limbs, it would doubtless have been a still more potent combination.

3d Case.—Complete Physical Exhaustion.

" Mr. R., 45 years of age, an overtaxed and prematurely worn out man of business became involved in financial troubles, * * mind and body were continuously on the rack, he could neither eat nor sleep normally, and at last complete physical exhaustion and nervous prostration naturally came upon him, for nature could endure no more. The first warning was severe pains in the back of the head, soon followed by shortness of breath, flutterings of heart, compressible pulse, loss of appetite, constipation and phospatic urine. * * We determined to try the red light treatment, especially as his prostration was unattended by any indication of morbid irritability, and in all our experience as a physician, we have never witnessed more remarkable beneficial results than were at once produced by the red ray in this case. The very first bath had the most encouraging effect: it acted as a tonic both upon mind and body, dispelled his gloomy apprehensions and gave vigor to his physical functions. Commencing with small doses, we gradually increased them until assured that we had reached the most effective dose in proportion of red to plain panes and in length of bath. Mr. R. rapidly improved, notwithstanding his continued attention to business. From the first he slept more refreshingly, ate with better relish, his bowels became regular, and the secretions of his kidneys recovered the healthy appearance. Three weeks treatment sufficed, and there have been no signs of relapse."

4th CASE.—UTERINE AND NERVOUS PROSTRATION.

" Mrs. S., 45 years of age, had naturally a frail constitution, was from youth weak and delicate, with a tendency to nervous prostration ; easily despondent, and ready to give up when ill. Her natural weakness had resulted in and been augmented by uterine difficulties which had continued for ten years, and had at last broken down her entire system, when she called on us for professional advice. Her condition was such that the slightest exertion completely overcame her and sent her to bed for days at a time; the influence of ' the change of life,' had brought on the crisis in an illness that kept her bedfast, which was directly attributed to a brief visit to the Centennial Exhibition ; but this last was but a feather in the balance—the attack was impending and the excitement of the visit only hastened it. We applied the blue and red light treatment, alternating not at equal intervals, but according to variations in her symptoms. Her recovery was rapid and permanent—a whole day at the Centennial some time afterwards did not over fatigue her. She has enjoyed better health uniformly since the treatment than ever before."

V.   WHEN THE RED IS INJURIOUS.

1. Red is injurious, of course, when there is already too much of the red, or inflammatory condition of the system, such as the predominance of red hair, very rubicund countenance, or feverish and excitable condition generally.

Iron,   the preparations of which abound in the red, is "contra-indicated in inflammatory diseases, producing, when injudiciously employed, heat, thirst, head-ache, difficulty of breathing and other symptoms of an excited circulation ; " " contra-indicated in the sanguine temperament generally."

2. The same is true of the other red elements, or of elements in which red abounds in the spectrum, but the principle is too obvious to need further examples. The exciting effect of red

objects on various animals is also well known. That red light has exactly the same exciting effect is well known. I quote the following from a letter of a thoughtful observer, Edwin M. Hale, M. D., to the Chicago Tribune :—

3. "In one of the French Insane Asylums, not only the blue ray but others were tried, and the effect was very interesting. The red ray caused results which confirmed the popular belief in its exciting, maddening influence. When violent and maniacal patients were placed in rooms where the red ray predominated, they became worse. All the violent symptoms were aggravated. If these patients were removed to a room where the blue ray predominated, they become calm and quiet. It is related that one patient, a woman, whose delirium was greatly aggravated by the red ray, immediately said on going into the blue room—'how soothing that is,' and shortly after, when left alone, fell asleep."

4. *Thermel* must naturally produce an effect somewhat similar to that of red, so far as its heating qualities are concerned, but being invisible cannot, of course, affect one through the optic nerve.

5. Dr. Pancoast speaking of the red light says that "if employed to excess, as to amount or time, the red light over-excites the nervous system and may produce dangerous fevers or other disorders that may prove as troublesome as the evil we are seeking to correct. We seldom employ red light to the exclusion of the other rays, and it should never be so employed, except in extreme cases, when prompt action is the first consideration."

The danger of the above "exclusive red light," which Dr. Pancoast deems so great as to require "a skilful physician," may be averted by using the red glass only a few minutes at a time at first, taking the precaution when the system becomes too hot, to put blue glass in its place, or a wet bandage over the head. For general cases, however, it would be better to have blue glass over the head and red and clear glass over the rest of the body in conditions of lethargy. A better arrangement still is the instrument devised by the author called the CHROMOLUME, in which both physiological and chemical laws are complied with in the harmonic arrangement of glass. See explanation in XXIII and XXIV of this chapter.

VI. The Healing Power of Yellow and Orange.

We have seen in the last chapter (XIX, 3) the law by which the *nerves* become stimulated, more especially by the yellow color, and to some extent by the orange and even the red, these principles being included in the substance of the nerves themselves. We have seen that the more violent nerve stimuli include something of the red or orange as well as the yellow, that drugs taken internally, when sufficiently active and exciting and working, no doubt, to some extent upon the vascular as well as the nervous tissues of the stomach, cause that quick repulsive action which is termed EMETIC; that those drugs whose yellow principle works somewhat more slowly, do not exert their expansive and repulsive action until they reach the bowels and thus constitute LAXATIVES, or when sufficiently active, PURGATIVES; that certain drugs which have an affinity for the liver and bile, causing them to act, are called CHOLAGOGUES; that those which stimulate the kidneys are called DIURETICS; those which stimulate the uterus, from some special affinity they may have for that organ, are called EMMENAGOGUES; those which stimulate the nerves of the skin and to some extent the vascular glands in a way to cause perspiration are called DIAPHORETICS; those which stimulate the nerves of the skin and call the blood outward until the surface becomes reddened are called RUBEFACIENTS. In all cases yellow is the central principle of nerve stimulus as well as the exciting principle of the brain which is the fountain head of the nerves, although, as we have seen, the more violent elements of stimulus approach the red, especially where vascular action is called forth. Those elements which act more directly to excite the brain, are called CEREBRAL STIMULANTS. I will give a few examples of the different drugs and foods which belong to the various departments of nerve action :—

VII. Emetics, Yellow with some Red and Orange.

1. *Indian Hemp* (Apocynum Cannabinum). The root is of " a yellowish brown while young, but dark chesnut (red brown) when old, with a nauseous acrid taste." " The internal ligneous part is yellowish white." " Powerfully emetic and cathartic, sometimes diuretic."

2. *Lobelina.* " The active principle of lobelia is a yellowish liquid." " Lobelia is emetic, occasionally cathartic, diaphoretic," etc.

3. *Tartar Emetic* ($KSbC_4H_4O_7$, H_2O), " a white crystalline salt," with the yellow, orange and red all strongly developed in the spectra of its elements. " According to the dose it acts variously as a diaphoretic, diuretic, expectorant, purgative and emetic."

4. *Bloodroot* (sanguinaria). " The whole plant is pervaded by an orange colored sap. The color of the powder is brownish red." The leaf " is yellowish green on the upper surface, paler or glaucous on the under, and strongly marked, by orange-colored veins." " Sanguinaria is an acrid emetic, with stimulant and narcotic powers."

5. The fact that emetics deal so much in the red as well as in the yellow principle shows that they act more or less upon the blood and muscular tissues as well as the nerves. " The action of an emetic is directly or indirectly upon the nerve centres that supply these muscles. * * All emetics acting through the blood produce more or less depression." (Hartshorne). Emetics act principally upon the pneumogastric nerve.

VIII. Laxatives and Purgatives—Yellow the principal color, or red in Drastic Purgatives.

1. *Podophyllum* or *May Apple*. "Yellowish green petioles." " The fruit is lemon yellow, diversified by brownish spots." " The powder is light yellowish gray." " An active and certain cathartic. In some cases it has given rise to nausea and vomiting." " A hydragogue and cholagogue." The office of a cholagogue is to cause a flow of bile, which is of itself a yellow or yellow green fluid that has a laxative effect as it passes into the duodenum and lower bowels.

2. *Senna*, (Cassia Marilandica). " Flowers beautiful golden yellow ; the calyx is composed of five oval yellow leaves ; the stamens are ten, with yellow filaments and brown anthers." " An efficient and safe cathartic."

3. *Colocynth* (colocynthis). " Flowers are yellow." " Fruit yellow when ripe." " Contains a white spongy medullary matter." " A powerful hydragogue cathartic."

4. *Copaiba.* "A transparent liquid of a pale yellow color." It is "stimulant, diuretic, laxative."

5. *Gluten, phosphate of lime,* etc., which constitute the hard yellow portion of grains near the external portion, are somewhat laxative.

6. *Figs* (Ficus). "The best are yellowish or brownish." "Figs are nutritious, laxative and demulcent."

7. *Magnesia* (MgO). The yellow-green principle strongest in the spectrum of magnesium. "Antacid and laxative."

8. *Magnesium Carbonate* ($MgCO_3$). The yellow strong in both carbon and magnesium. "Laxative."

9. *Castor Oil* (Oleum Ricini). "Yellowish." "A mild cathartic."

10. *Olive Oil* (Oleum Olivæ). "Pale yellow or greenish yellow." "Nutritious and mildly laxative, given in case of irritable intestines."

11. *Sulphur* is "pale yellow * * laxative, diaphoretic," etc.

12. *Magnesium Sulphate* (Epsom salt, $MgSO_4$), has the strong yellow principle of magnesium and sulphur, but is toned down by the cool blue of oxygen, so it is called "a mild and safe cathartic," a "refrigerant," etc.

13. *Eggs* (Ovum). "The yolk in its raw state is thought to be laxative."

14. *Prunes* (Prunum). Yellowish brown or orange brown. "Laxative and nourishing."

15. *Peaches* have a yellowish pulp. Gently laxative.

16. *Cape Aloes* (Aloe). "Powder greenish yellow." "Cathartic."

17. Many more similar examples could be given, but these are quite sufficient to establish the potency of yellow as connected with the nerves of the bowels. I will quote the following, however, to show that when we appeal more to the red principle with drugs we reach the coarser elements of blood and thus produce a more severe and drastic effect than when dealing more exclusively with the finer elements of the nerves :—

18. *Gamboge* when broken "is of a uniform reddish orange, which becomes a beautiful bright yellow." "Gamboge is a powerful drastic hydragogue cathartic, very apt to produce nausea and vomiting, when given in the full dose."

19. *Black Hellebore* (Helleborus niger). " The flower stem is reddish toward the base," has " rose like flowers."   The petals are of a white or pale rose color with occasionally a greenish tinge."   The root is "externally, black or deep brown, internally white or yellowish white, producing on the tongue a burning and benumbing expression, like that which results from taking hot liquids into the mouth."   " Black Hellebore is a drastic hydragogue cathartic possessed also of emmenagogue powers. The fresh root applied to the skin produces inflammation and even vesication."   A good example of the burning qualities of black and red.

20. *Croton Oil* (Oleum Tiglii), " varies from a pale yellow to a dark reddish brown.   Its taste is hot and acrid—it is a powerful hydragogue cathartic, in large doses apt to excite vomiting and severe pain."

21. *Senna* (Cassia acutifolia, etc.).   " The leaflets are yellowish green color, the flowers are yellow, the fruit grayish brown." " The infusion is of a deep reddish brown color.   When exposed to the air a short time, it deposits a yellowish insoluble precipitate.   It is a prompt and safe purgative.   An objection sometimes urged against it is that it is apt to produce severe griping pain."

22. *Rhubarb* (Rheum).   " Good rhubarb is yellow, with a slight reddish brown tinge ; "—" unites a cathartic with an astringent power, the latter of which does not interfere with the former, as the purgative effect precedes the astringent ; * * appears to affect the muscular fibres more than the secretory vessels.   It sometimes occasions griping pains in the bowels."

23. Why it is that a substance like *potassium tartrate*, and other saline substances may have the rubific element of potassium, and yet be but a " mild refrigerant cathartic," is easily explained by noticing the amount of oxygen ($C_4H_4K_2O_6$) which moderates and cools the thermal and expansive qualities of the other substances, and acts somewhat as it does in acids.

IX. HEALING POWER OF YELLOW LIGHT AIDED BY SOME RED AND ORANGE :—LAXATIVE, ANIMATING, ETC.

1st CASE.—COSTIVENESS.

In a case of costiveness at my office, during the month of June, I let the sunlight pass through some yellow-orange glass of a hue which is usually termed yellow, and over which I had placed a lens to concentrate the rays the better at certain points. I gradually moved the focus of the yellow light over the whole bowels but especially over the descending color on the left lower side. Commencing at 2 P.M., I continued the process for 10 minutes. The perspiration was started over the whole body, although the thermometer stood at only 70° F. In 5 minutes after receiving the light, the bowels commenced the rattling motion similar to what is experienced with physic, and in 18 minutes a gentle passage was caused, and that wholly without pain. Some persons would require 2 or 3 times as long an application as the above. I have caused the same results with the chromo-disc to be described hereafter. Any deep yellow glass would act in the same way, but the yellow-orange hollow lens which, the author has devised, is more prompt and effective than any other instrument, and charges the water within for internal use while it is being used externally.

2d CASE.—BRONCHIAL DIFFICULTY.

In a case of Chronic bronchial irritation, I used the chromo-disc over the breast, straining a hot sunlight thus concentrated by reflection, through yellow glass. In less than a minute I was able to rubricate the skin. I used it about 15 or 20 minutes each day for several days. The patient felt uncommonly animated and clear in his mental perceptions, and his bronchial difficulties gradually decreased. The same result would, of course, be produced by means of yellow glass without the chromo-disc, by taking a longer time, or even by hot sunlight, by taking a still longer time. The Chromo Lens to be hereafter described is entirely unequalled in the rapidity and power of its action.

3d CASE.—COSTIVENESS CURED BY CHARGED WATER, etc.

Knowing as I did the power of the yellow and orange light to act upon the system directly, I concluded at once that it must have the power of so charging other substances that they would act upon the system in the same way, and as ordinary lamp light and gas light abound in the yellow-orange principle of carbon, etc., I was confident that they might be used with yellow glass to good advantage.

Having been costive for a few days I held a small half-ounce amber colored vial of water close to a kerosene lamp for 7 minutes, before retiring, and then drank it. In the morning I had two gentle passages without any pain, and for weeks experienced no return of costiveness. This is a good example to show the enduring character of the cures wrought by the finer elements.

4th CASE.—ANIMATING AND LAXATIVE EFFECT of Do.

The following letter from Mr. E. Norris, Artist, 59 Columbia st., Albany, N. Y., will explain itself :—

"Dr. Babbitt: My Dear Sir :—I have tried the novel experiment of the yellow light and have been astonished at the results. I have found water charged with the sun's rays through yellow glass to be an absolute and to me unfailing cathartic ; in small doses a gentle laxative, and in all cases exhilarative to the spirits. What its qualities are beyond these effects I do not know, but this much seems certain and it is marvelous. To me it is a great blessing, and I shall remember you with kind feelings. I am quite well, made, and kept so, by the yellow light."

5th CASE.—DO.

A lady of East Tennessee, who had suffered with constipation and feeble health for many years, was advised to drink water charged in yellow bottles. She wrote me that she was drinking water charged in yellow wine bottles, and asked me to send her bottles of the right shade of color, remarking as follows : "My bowels have been acted upon now five successive days. I am so delighted that I can scarcely wait the intervening time before receiving yours." I had not then got my yellow chromo lenses ready, and so had to recommend the poor substitute of yellow bottles.

6th Case.—Costiveness and Hemorrhoids.

Mrs. C. A. von Cort, of New York, author of " Household Treasure and Medical Adviser," and a lady of considerable medical experience, received from me a bottle of sugar of milk which I had charged with yellow-orange light, and the usual dose of which was an amount as large as one to three peas. Concerning its effects she wrote me the following letter, speaking of her experience in giving to Mrs. VanKeuren, of Morrisania, and enclosing a note from the latter :—

" Mrs. VanKeuren has suffered with hemorrhoids so severely that all ordinary purgatives which her physicians have given her, cause intense pain, and prove very prostrating. Your medicine charged with the yellow-light is elegant, and works gently and admirably." C. A. von Cort.

The following is Mrs. Van Keuren's letter :—

" Mrs. von Cort :—Please tell the doctor that the medicine you gave me has had the desired effect. The first needed a little assistance, the last one after 24 hours relieved me without help almost free from pain. I feel easier to-night than I have been for months."

The first dose was doubtless too small, on account of her great costiveness. In severe cases it would be well to take two to four teaspoonfuls of charged water before each meal, until the bowels move, or even every hour in an emergency. The water can be charged somewhat in a few minutes of bright sunlight, but I allow my lenses to lie out of doors on the window ledge where the light can strike them constantly, meantime putting in fresh water every two or three days in hot weather to keep it pure. I have tested the power of water charged in these yellow-orange lenses in a great number of cases, and uniformly with the same effect, excepting with two or three persons whose bowels were already in a positive and active condition. With these no change was discovered. I also had a patient whose bowels were so very much constricted as to resist all ordinary medicine, and which resisted a single dose or two of the charged yellow water, but I feel confident that if the water had been taken hourly the proper result would have been accomplished during the day.

I use deep blue lenses for water to check diarrhœa, or inflammation, or sleeplessness, as will be seen hereafter. I have also a few purple lenses in which I charge water for indigestion, although I may not be able to supply the public yet, excepting a few physicians, to whom it is highly important, as their manufacture for a small number is troublesome.

The above examples, and all of my experience with the yellow-charged water, or blue-charged water, go to prove the *gentle*, safe and *enduring* effect of these refined elements, and their influence on the mind, in harmony with principle XV of Chapter First, and the reason of this deep and radical influence is that they deal directly with the nerve-forces which lie at the seat of power, instead of the blood, or muscles, or other subsidiary functions, and that, too, without clogging the system with coarse and poisonous elements, such as is too commonly done with drugs.

X. DIURETICS, DIAPHORETICS, EMMENAGOGUES, ETC. :—

YELLOW AIDED BY A CONSIDERABLE RED.

Several of these have already been given. A few more will suffice to settle the principle.

1. *Dandelion* (taraxacum). "It has a golden yellow flower. The fresh, full grown root is of a light brown color externally, whitish within, having a yellowish ligneous cord running through its center. Taraxacum is slightly tonic, diuretic and aperient ; and it is thought to have a specific action upon the liver."

2. *Pure Carbonate of Potassium* (CO_3K_2. $2 \times H_2O$). Red and yellow principle modified by the blue in the spectrum. "Antacid, alkaline and diuretic."

3. *Potassium Nitrate* (Salt Petre, NO_3K or NO_2 (OK): The red, yellow and blue principles all strong in the spectrum. "Refrigerant diaphoretic."

4. *Sassafras Oil* (Oleum Sassafras). "Yellowish, becoming reddish by age." "A mild diaphoretic."

5. *Seneka* (Senega). "Externally brownish, internally yellowish." "An active, stimulating expectorant, acting in overdoses like squill, as a harsh emetic, and also having some tendency towards the kidneys.

6. *Buchu* (Leaves of Barosma). "Brownish yellow," etc.

"Gently stimulant, with a particular tendency to the urinary organs, producing diuresis, and like all similar medicines, exciting diaphoresis when circumstances favor this mode of action."

7. *Oil of Savine* (Oleum Sabinæ $C_{10}H_8$). "Colorless or yellow," has also the red principle of hydrogen, " is stimulant, emmenagogue and actively rubefacient."

8. *Mustard* (Sinapis). "Black mustard seeds are of a deep brown color, slightly rugose on the surface, and internally yellow. White mustard seeds are of a yellowish color and less pungent taste." "Mustard seeds act as a gentle laxative." Its powder made into a poultice, or sinapism, "is an excellent rubefacient."

XI. Cerebral Stimulants:—Yellow with some Red and Orange.

1. *Opium* is "reddish brown or deep fawn—when pulverized, a yellow-brown powder. Opium is a stimulant narcotic ; it increases the force, fulness and frequency of the pulse, animates the spirits and gives new energy to the intellectual faculties. Its operation is directed with peculiar force to the brain, the functions of which it excites even to intoxication or delirium." After this comes the reaction in the form of sleep, then "nausea, headache, tremors—all the secretions, with the exception of that from the skin, are either suspended or diminished ; the peristaltic action of the bowels is lessened," etc.

2. *Saffron* (Crocus), "has a rich deep orange color." "In small doses it exhilarates the spirits and produces sleep ; in large doses gives rise to headache, intoxication, delirium, etc.

3. *Valerian* (Valeriana). "The powder is yellowish gray. It is gently stimulant with an especial direction to the nervous system. In large doses it produces a sense of heaviness, pain in the head," etc.

4. *Ether is* a colorless fluid, but strong in the yellow principle of carbon and the red principle of hydrogen ($C_4H_{10}O$). "Ether is a powerful diffusible stimulant, possessed also of expectorant, antispasmodic and narcotic properties." "Its effects are increased arterial action with delirium and diminished sensibility, followed by unconsciousness," etc.

5. *Water, charged with yellow and some red light* through a yellow chromo lens, is stimulating to the brain and nerves,

as signified in IX of this chapter, and leaves no bad after effects, as is the case with drugs.

XII. Tonics :—Yellow and Red Predominant.

1. Tonics are substances which gently and persistently stimulate and invigorate the human system, especially the nutritive and blood-making functions. I have already given several of them in the preceding matter and will mention but few here. Some of the best tonics have a fair share of the electrical colors also. Vegetable tonics are generally bitter and appetizing. Quinine and Iron are called the most important tonics.

2. *Quassia*, yellowish, flowers sometimes red. " Highly tonic."

3. *Gold thread* (Coptis). Roots of a golden color. " Tonic bitter."

4. *Gentian* (Gentiana), " yellowish powder." " Tonic."

5. *Peruvian Bark* (Cinchona). Pale, yellow and red varieties. " Excites warmth in the epigastrium," etc. " Nausea and vomiting," also " purging " sometimes caused. " Frequency of the pulse is increased." Its action upon the nervous system is often evinced by a sense of tension, or fulness, or slight pain in the head, singing in the ears and partial deafness." Its most important extract is *Quinine* or *Quinia*, whose component parts are as follows, $NC_{20}H_{12}O_2$.

6. *Iron*, already described, see III of this chapter.

7. *Myrrh* (Myrrha), " reddish yellow or reddish brown." " Tonic and stimulating, with a tendency to the lungs and uterus."

8. *Ginger* (Zingiber), " yellowish brown." " A powerful stimulant."

9. *Black Pepper* (Piper Nigrum). " Piperin the active principle of pepper is in transparent crystals—as ordinarily procured it is yellow." Formula of piperin, according to Wertheim, $N_2 C_{70}H_{37}O_{10}$. " Black pepper is a warm, carminative stimulant, capable of producing general arterial excitement."

XIII. When Yellow is Injurious.

1. Yellow is injurious and over exciting to a system which

has the nervous condition already very active and perhaps irritable.   Dormant, paralytic, costive, cold, chronic and stupid conditions, inert tumors, etc., are greatly relieved by the yellow, aided
by the red principle, but in fevers, acute inflammations, delirium,
diarrhœa, neuralgia, palpitation of the heart, and over excitement
of any kind, it is evident enough that these colors are contra-
indicated.   I will quote briefly again from Dr. Hale :—

2. " Green is a quieting color, if not too green.   A dark green
is like a dark blue, it seems to lose its calmative power.   Nor
must the green have a suggestion of yellow in it, for yellow, like
red, irritates the nerves of the insane.   I have had patients who
begged to have the yellow shades removed from the windows, it
' irritated them so.'   In the asylum to which I have alluded, there
were a number of patients afflicted with melancholy.   Some of
them were placed in the blue rooms, others in the green.   In
both instances their malady seemed aggravated, or at least not
benefited.   Those placed in the yellow rooms complained that
it made them feel badly.   They become morose.   All were benefited, however, by being placed in the red room, or in rooms
lighted by ultra violet rays.   The extreme violet rays, which some
would call purple, are very stimulating to the nervous system.
Children become exceedingly nervous from the bright sunlight,
containing an excess of red and yellow rays.   When ill from
teething, from fever, and especially when the brain is affected,
they instinctively turn from these rays, and seem to be soothed
by a pale blue, or gray light."

3. These remarks show a thoughtful study of the subject on
the part of Dr. Hale, but should be modified slightly to prevent
readers from being misled.   Dark green and dark blue are spoken
of as not being *calmative* in their nature.   The doctor is evidently speaking of those persons who are melancholy and are already
overstocked with the blue venous blood.   To such ones these
colors would simply be adding sombreness to sombreness, and of
course they would not calm them.   All the electrical colors must
be more or less calmative to an excited human system as will be
shown hereafter.   All the circumstances with reference to the
inmates of the asylum, show that their melancholy was due to
a considerable extent to an excess of venous blood, from their re-
pugnance to blue, and to an excess of nervous sensibility from

their being injured by the yellow. Whenever they were under the chemical affinity of the yellow, namely the violet, they were benefited, not because the ultra violet is stimulating to the nerves, as the doctor supposes, but just the contrary as already shown (Chap. Fifth, XX, 18). Their nerves were already over excitable. A red purple is stimulating, especially to the blood. The stimulus which they most needed was in the red to offset the excess of blue in the veins, and this is the reason that the red was so useful to them. My own experience has shown me that persons with the erysipelas or an excitable nervous condition, cannot endure much of the strong sunlight without harm. The red, orange and yellow rays prove too exciting for them. A lady patient who inherited something of an erysipelatous condition, and was also neuralgic and otherwise excitable until she had spells of insanity, always became worse after taking baths of white light and found even blue and white light too exciting for her. Blue glass was far more soothing, but the glass which she used being mazarine, admitted so many of the other more exciting rays, that she could not use that very long at a time without feeling their exciting effect. I advised two thicknesses of the blue and the exclusion of all other rays.

4. One great reason why yellow rules in the most violent of *poisons*, such as *Prussic acid* and *strychnine*, is because of the prominence of the yellow principle as a stimulus of the nerves combined with the red principle as a stimulus of the blood. Thus *strychnine*, according to Liebig, is composed as follows : N_2C_{44} $H_{23}O_4$, which shows a decided predominance of the yellow principle in the carbon, much power of the red in the hydrogen, and not enough of the electrical oxygen to balance the irritating and fiery action of these thermal elements. " Next to Prussic acid, strichnia is perhaps the most violent poison in the catalogue of medicines." Prussic acid is constituted as follows :— CNH, which gives great power of the yellow principle in carbon, and even in nitrogen, predominating red in the hydrogen and no decided electrical element to balance all this thermism, although the nitrogen may be considered slightly more electrical than it is thermal when in combination. " Strichnine acts especially as an excitor of the motor filaments of the spiral cord, causing tonic muscular contractions." " Hydrocyanic (prussic) acid, in poison-

ous doses, acts conjointly on the cerebrum and spinal cord. All the animals I have seen killed by this agent, utter a scream, lose their consciousness and are convulsed. These are the symptoms of epilepsy. * * * The phenomena of epilepsy are eminently congestive. While the cerebral functions are for the time anni-hilated, the spinal ones are violently excited." (Bennett.) When prussic acid is taken in large amounts, the patient may fall almost as if struck by lightning."

5. The yellow principle then being so powerful in its action on the nerves, we may easily understand why large doses of yel-low drugs are said to cause convulsions, delirium, vomiting, dras-tic purging, etc. Even so mild a substance as *coffee* with its yellow brown principle is said to be "contra-indicated in acute inflammatory affections," causing "nervous excitement" and a "disposition to wakefulness." Of *dandelion* it is said that "an irritable condition of the stomach and bowels, and the existence of acute inflammation contra-indicate its employment." Other even more active drugs with yellow, and especially with yellow and orange, or yellow and red potencies predominant, such as mercury, jalap, opium, alcohol, etc., must be still more disastrous to a sensitive nervous or sanguine system, especially when taken in large amounts. Coffee, though yellowish brown and laxative in some of its elements, has an astringent principle in its tannin. Those who wish to escape some of the worst effects of coffee, should not let it steep more than five to ten minutes, when the coffee grounds should be removed from the liquid to prevent the tannin from escaping into it. Under such circumstances I have found coffee laxative than otherwise.

XIV. HEALING POWER OF BLUE AND VIOLET.

NERVINE, ASTRINGENT, REFRIGERENT, FEBRIFUGE AND SEDATIVE.

1. We come now to the cold, electrical and contracting poten-cies, which are very fine and penetrating, and also very soothing to all systems in which inflammatory and nervous conditions predominate. As we have seen in the last chapter, substances combine in a harmonizing union with those substances whose colors form a chemical affinity with their own and thus keep up that law of equilibrium which is the safety of all things. This

law having been so abundantly explained, it is obvious beyond
all guess work, that if the red arterial blood should become over
active and inflammatory, blue light or some other blue substance
must be the balancing and harmonizing principle, while again,
if the yellow and to some extent the red and orange principle of
the nerves should become unduly excited, the violet and also the
blue and indigo would be the soothing principles to have applied.
This applies to the nerves of the cranium, stomach, bowels, and
kidneys, as well as elsewhere, in which the heating and expansive
action of these thermal principles may beget the condition of
delirium, emesis, diarrhœa, diuresis, etc., that can be assuaged
only by the cooling and contracting influences of substances
possessing the electrical colors. Can this law, which thus
stands out clearly and simply like a mathematical demonstration,
be shown to have a basis in actual practice in harmony with the
experience of the medical world for ages back? The following
are a few of the many facts that settle these principles and assist
in crystallizing them into a chromo-therapeutical science. In
considering them, the reader, who has become familiar with the
working of atoms (Chap. Third), will readily understand that the
electrical blue and violet forming atoms of substances, being the
interior ones which are encased more or less by thermal atoms,
must have their colors in part or wholly concealed at times by
the encasing atoms, or at other times subject to the law of met-
achromism which reverses the usual order of things especially in
binary compounds (See Chap. Fifth, XX, 19, and XXII, 4, which
the reader should be familiar with before proceeding farther).
The law as a whole stands out in prominent light :—

2. *Aconite* (Aconitum napellus). "Flowers dark violet blue."
"A powerful nervous sedative and anodyne." "Applicable to
cerebral inflammations."

3. *Belladonna*, or Deadly night-shade, "has purplish stems,"
leaves "ultimately of a deep purple color, with violet colored
juice." "The root is reddish brown, internally whitish." "Has
sometimes been mistaken for a parsnip." "Soothes irritation and
pain particularly in nervous maladies ; " "is a powerful narcotic,
possessing also diaphoretic and diuretic qualities," "causes
dilatation of the pupil," "a powerful poison." Belladonna, from
its large amount of yellow and red principle in its carbon and

hydrogen, is stimulating, and from its electrical principle is soothing, thus combining both styles of force.

4. *Foxglove* (Digitalis purpurea). "Beautiful purple flowers ;" "Powder of a fine deep green," "a red coloring principle,
chlorophyl, albumen, starch, etc. Digitalis is narcotic, sedative
and diuretic." In large doses a strong poison, leading to "convulsions, vomiting," etc.

5. *Ergot* (Ergota), "is in solid grains of violet brown color
externally, yellowish white or violet white within." "Ergot has
been much used for promoting contraction of the uterus." Dr.
Müller found it to check the bleeding from large divided arteries
(applied externally), and Dr. Wright states that "either in powder or infusion it has a prompt effect in arresting hemorrhage."

6. *Cranesbill* (Geranium). "Large purple, often spotted
flowers." "Our best native astringent."

7. *Logwood* (Hæmatoxylon). "The flowers have a brownish
purple calyx, and lemon yellow petals." "Of itself it is not a
coloring substance, but affords beautiful red, blue and purple
colors by the joint action of an alkaline base and the oxygen of
the air. It is a mild astringent." "Contains tannin,—blue black
variety."

8. *Purple Willow Herb* (Lythrum salicaria). "Showy purple
flowers." "Is demulcent and astringent."

9. *Indigo.* "The complaints in which it has been employed
with supposed advantage are epilepsy, infantile convulsions,
chorea, hysteria and amenorrhœa."

10. *Phosphoric Acid* (PO_4H_3), the blue principle of Oxygen
predominant. "When diluted is deemed tonic and refrigerant,"
"allaying spasms," etc.

11. *Sulphuric Acid* (SO_4H_2). Blue, indigo, and violet very
strong. "Diluted, it is tonic, refrigerant and astringent."

12. *Nitric Acid* ($N_2O_5.OH_2$). Blue, indigo, etc. "Tonic
and antiseptic." "Largely diluted with water, forms a good acid
drink in febrile diseases."

13. *Hydrochloric Acid* (HCl). Blue-green, blue and indigo, of
chlorine, and blue-green, indigo and dark violet of hydrogen,
giving some preponderance of electricity. "Tonic, refrigerant
and antiseptic."

14. *Tartaric Acid* ($C_4H_6O_6$). Blue and violet strongest.
"Refrigerant."

15. *Tannic Acid* ($C_{27}H_{22}O_{17}$). In this important compound the powders of which are *light bluish yellow*, it may be supposed that the thermal principle rules from the amount of Carbon and hydrogen, but when we remember that it takes two atoms of hydrogen to balance one of oxygen as in water, and that hydrogen and even carbon are strong in the electrical colors, it may easily be understood why electricity as a whole has the mastery in this substance, although a part of the electrical atoms are encased in the yellow atoms of carbon. " The chief principle of vegetable astringents." " Used for hemorrhages," etc.

16. *Galls* (Galla). " The best are externally of a dark bluish or lead color, sometimes with a greenish tinge, internally whitish or brownish." " Astringent."

17. *Sulphate of Copper* (Cupric Sulphate, or blue vitroil SO_4 Cu. 5(OH_2). " Deep blue." " In small doses astringent ; in large ones an emetic," from its yellow and orange principle.

18. *Ferrous Sulphate* (Green Vitriol, Fe SO_4). " Pale bluish green." " Astringent and tonic."

19. *Blackberry* (Rubus villosus). Violet colored juice. "Astringent."

20. *Chloroform* ($CHCl_3$). Strong blue and indigo, and some violet from preponderance of Chlorine. " A direct sedative to the nervous system, used as an anæsthetic by inhalation ; but it frequently causes death by paralysis of the heart."

21. *Chloral hydrate* ($C_2HCl_3O. H_2O$). Predominance of blue, indigo and violet, but better balanced by thermism than chloroform. For the promotion of sleep as an anodyne, it is much inferior to opium. Generally its after effects are less disagreeable than those of opiates. " Considerably used in delirium tremens and tetanus." " Poison."

Green Tea (Thea viridis). " Green tea is characterized by a dark green color, sometimes inclining to blue or brown. Its infusion has a pale greenish yellow color." " Tea is astringent and gently excitant, and in its finer varieties exercise a decided influence over the nervous system," causing " exhilaration, wakefulness," etc. " Long continued in excessive quantity, it is capable of inducing unpleasant nervous and dyspeptic symptoms, the necessary consequence of over-excitement of the brain and nervous system. Green tea is decidedly more injurious in these respects than black." Green tea has 17.8 per cent of tannic acid. The reader will readily see that the double quality of producing excitement and astringency comes from the yellow and blue which combine to produce the green.

XV. Healing Power of Blue or Violet Light. :—

NERVINE, ANTI-INFLAMMATORY, COOLING, ETC.

In other words blue, indigo and violet light heal on exactly the same principles as do the drugs already named, only in a more exquisite, penetrating and less harmful way, from the superior refinement of the elements thus received. To show that this is not mere theory, I will quote a few actual facts.

1st Case.—Sciatica, Inflammation, etc.

" An elderly lady on Hospital Place, off Lockwood street, has been afflicted with a sciatic difficulty for 11 years, and has not been entirely free from pain a single day during that time. Her age was 59, though she seemed to be 70. The disease was confined to the left limb, and the knee, ankle and foot would be swollen, to twice their natural size. A week ago, 3 panes of blue glass were inserted in a west window, and the first bath was applied to the ankle where the pain and soreness were located. In two or three hours a large lump on the ankle the size of a hen's egg and of a purplish color, entirely disappeared, as did also the pain and soreness. During the following night, the pain reappeared in the foot, and the light being poor during the following two or three days, this point was not so easily relieved, but under a bath of strong light soon drove the peace destroyer away. But the most remarkable effect of blue glass sun baths on this patient was witnessed on Sunday. The disease attacked her knee Saturday night, and she suffered the most excruciating agony. Sunday morning the knee was very much swollen, and the least weight upon her affected parts nearly threw her into spasms. As soon as possible the blue glass bath was taken, and in less than three quarters of an hour the pain had left, the swelling and soreness had disappeared, and the limb was to all appearance as healthy as it ever was. Yesterday she walked about the house as lively as a girl of 16. Another remarkable feature in this case is that for over a year the toes of the left foot have been entirely useless, being benumbed ; but the blue glass sun-baths have restored to her the full use of those members.—*Providence Press, Feb. 14, 1877.*

2d Case.—Violent Hemorrhage of the Lungs.

" A lady of my family, about six weeks ago, had a violent hemorrhage of the lungs, and for ten days raised more or less blood daily. She was very much weakened by the loss of blood, and considerably frightened withal. I obtained some blue glass and placed it in the window where she was in the habit of sitting, the blue glass constituting one-half of the lower sash of the window. The lady sat daily in the associated lights, allowing the blue rays especially to fall upon the nerves of the back of the neck for about an hour a day. The second day, the sun's rays being unusually strong, she got ' too much blue glass,' and at night felt peculiar sensations in the back of the neck, among the nerves, and an unpleasant fulness in the head. These sensations wore off next day, and since then she has not remained so long at a time under the blue glass. But from the first she began to grow stronger, her face soon gained its natural fulness, and in a week she was, to all appearances, as well as ever. Of course, she was not cured of the trouble in her lungs in so short a time, but the soreness in her chest has passed away, and she begins to feel well again. After sitting in the associated light for a week, a large number of red pimples came out on her neck and shoulders, an indication that the treatment was bringing out to the surface the humors of the blood." *From " Dutton," N. Y., Jan. 12, 1877, in Correspondence of Chicago Tribune.*

The expression in the above " she got too much blue glass " is incorrect. It should have been *too much blue and transparent glass*, as the stimulating white rays of the sun were totally wrong for such a case. She had too little blue glass. Even the mazarine blue glass alone lets in too much of the other warmer rays to make it safe to take them on the head or upper spine for an hour at a time if the patient has a very sensitive brain or nervous system. This mistake results from the incorrectness of conception which would make one method a panacea for everything.

3d Case.—Cerebro-Spinal Meningitis.

General Pleasanton received a letter from a lady in Cairo, Illinois, who had been afflicted with a dreadful case of spinal meningitis, and after suffering four years was cured by the blue light process. *Condensed from N. Y. World.*

4th Case.—Neuralgic Headache.

A merchant on Broadway informed the author that he came home from church one Sunday with a severe neuralgia and headache, and although he had no special faith in the blue glass, concluded he would try it. By sitting under mazarine blue glass 30 minutes he was entirely relieved.

5th Case.—General Nervousness.

A benevolent lady physician of Vineland, New Jersey, informed me that she placed a large sheet of blue glass over one of her windows, and then set an easy chair in front of it, into which she invited her visitors. A feeble, nervous, elderly lady, who called frequently, was placed in the chair under the blue light. She immediately commenced improving, and after awhile concluded to ask the object of the blue glass in the window. After being told, she admitted that something had been making her feel much better, but could not tell before what it was.

6th Case.—Rheumatism.

The Hartford Post gives the account of a Mr. W. W. Larabee, proprietor of the Brower House, who was confined to his room with a severe attack of Rheumatism. A short course of blue sun baths gave him health and power to attend to business in a way which the paper calls "astonishing."

7th Case.—Rheumatism.

Dr. Robert Rohland of New York, in a letter to Gen. Pleasanton says : " I exposed, about a year ago, a man suffering with severe rheumatism to the influence of blue light through two glass panes. He felt, after 15 minutes, much relieved, and could move about without pains, but complained of a nasty metallic taste on his tongue."

Dr. Rohland speaks of another gentleman, a patient of Dr. Fincke, of Brooklyn, who, when his hand was placed in the blue light, experienced a taste like verdigris on his tongue. We have seen, Chapter Fifth XXI, 10, that copper, zinc and other metals must exist in blue light, although in that refined condition which prevents the poisonous effects of the crude metal.

8th CASE.—TUMOR ON AN INFANT.

" In a little girl one month old, was found a hard resisting tumor about the size of a robin's egg, in the sub-maxillary region of the left side. I had it placed in such a position that the rays of light through a blue glass should impinge upon it, one hour at least each day. This tumefaction disappeared entirely within 40 days. The child has developed astonishingly; is now seven months old; is exceedingly bright and happy; has not known an hour's sickness or discomfort. Its peculiar freedom from infantile ills, I attribute, at least in some degree, to the influence of the Blue Light. WM. M. McLAURY (M. D.), *to Gen. Pleasanton in " Blue and Sun-Lights."*

If a lens had been used in the above case to concentrate the rays in one place, and yellow orange glass, which has the rousing power of yellow and red, to animate the nerves and blood, alternated at times with blue, the cure would doubtless have been performed several times as soon.

9th CASE, OR SERIES OF CASES.—COLORS FOR LUNACY.

The following treatment of lunacy in an Italian Asylum, I copy from a condensed report. The ideas are somewhat vague, but mainly correct as far as they go :—

Dr. Ponza, director of the lunatic asylum at Alessandria (Piedmont), having conceived the idea that the solar rays might have some curative power in diseases of the brain, communicated his views to Father Secchi of Rome, who replied : " The idea of studying the disturbed state of lunatics in connection with magnetic perturbations, and with the colored, especially violet light of the sun, is of remarkable importance." Such light is easily obtained by filtering the solar rays through a glass of that color. " Violet," adds Father Secchi, "has something melan-

choly and depressive about it, which, physiologically, causes low
spirits ; hence, no doubt, poets have draped melancholy in violet
garments.   Perhaps violet light may calm the nervous excitement
of unfortunate maniacs." He then, in his letter, advises Dr.
Ponza to perform his experiments in rooms, the walls of which
are painted of the same color as the glass panes of the windows,
which should be as numerous as possible, in order to favor the
action of solar light, so that it may be admissible at any hour of
the day.   The patients should pass the night in rooms oriented
to the east and the south, and painted and glazed as above.   Dr.
Ponza, following the instructions of the learned Jesuit, prepared
several rooms in the manner described, and kept several patients
there under observation.   One of them affected with morbid
taciturnity, became gay and affable after three hours' stay in a
red chamber ; another, a maniac who refused all food, asked for
some breakfast after having stayed twenty-four hours in the same
red chamber.   In a blue one, a highly excited madman with a
strait waistcoat on was kept all day ; an hour after, he appeared
much calmer.   The action of blue light is very intense on the
optic nerve, and seems to cause a sort of oppression.   A patient
was made to pass the night in a violet chamber ; on the following day, he begged Dr. Ponza to send him home, because he felt
himself cured, and indeed he has been well ever since.   Dr.
Ponza's conclusions from his experiments are these : " The violet
rays are, of all others, those that possess the most intense electro-
chemical power ; the red light is also very rich in calorific rays ;
blue light, on the contrary, is quite devoid of them as well as of
chemical and electric ones.   Its beneficent influence is hard to
explain ; as it is the absolute negation of all excitement, it
succeeds admirably in calming the furious excitement of maniacs."

The soothing power of blue as tested in a French Insane
Asylum, is shown in this chapter, IV. 3.   The idea that blue
light is devoid of " chemical and electrical rays " shows the pre-
vailing ignorance on the subject.

10th Case.—-Sun-Stroke.

Dr. Rohland has called my attention to a remarkable cure
published in the N. Y. Evening Post.   A Mr. E., of Englewood,

and doing business in New York City, had suffered severely for two years from the effects of a sun-stroke, and by merely wearing a blue band on the inside of his hat was entirely relieved. This is a refutation of the absurd idea which some still entertain, that color has no potency excepting when the sun shines upon it. Sunlight stimulates all colors into greater activity, but all substances have their potencies according to their colors quite independent of light.

11th CASE.—SCIATICA, etc.

" Mrs. L., a widow aged 32, had been a severe sufferer for several years from *Sciatica*, with extreme tenderness in the lumbar region. We instructed her to sit daily for about two hours in a bath of all blue panes, with her back bared to the light. After the third sitting, the tenderness along her spine was almost entirely gone, while the distress and pain sensibly abated. This treatment continued but for ten days, when all symptoms disappeared." *Dr. Pancoast's Blue and Red Light*, p. 274.

12th CASE.—CHOLERA INFANTUM AND MARASMUS.

" Master H., aged 18 months. This was a severe case of *cholera infantum* and *marasmus* brought on by teething in extremely warm weather; he had been under treatment by an excellent physician for some time, but was steadily declining. As the last faint hope we determined to try the *blue* treatment ; he had been exceedingly irritable, but the blue light immediately soothed him into a gentle sleep and he came out of the bath calm and refreshed. Two months' treatment of him made him a fine healthy-looking child, with full, rosy cheeks and happy temper. We are confident that but for the blue ray this child must have died—no ordinary treatment could have saved him." *Blue and Red Light.*

13th CASE.—NERVOUS IRRITABILITY.

Mr. T., aged 35. In consequence of long continued excessive physical and mental exertion, his nervous system was entirely disordered ; the derangement manifested itself in nervousness, and trying irritability ; he could not sleep at night, was disturbed by frightful dreams ; his appetite was variable, sometimes ravenous, at others, the very sight of food was an annoyance ; his bowels varied, too, at times constipated, at others lax ; he had frequent pains in his head, the least excitement unnerved him, and he was inclined to extreme despondency. His irritability forbade red light, and we determined to administer blue light with red light medicine. The beneficial results were immediate ; his entire system improved rapidly ; five baths actually restored a healthy tone to his nervous system, and he has since experienced nothing even of " nervousness," though his life is one of constant physical and mental activity." *Blue and Red Light*, p. 280.

XVI. HEALING POWER OF BLUE AND WHITE SUNLIGHT.

This combination, of course, is more rousing and animating than blue or violet light alone, as it contains the electrical power of the latter, and the healing power of all the rays combined in the ordinary white light. Gen. Pleasanton, who has demonstrated to the public the efficiency of combined blue and sunlight in vegetable growth and human healing, seems quite unacquainted with the principle by which this is done, as most persons must be who do not understand atomic law and the principles of chemical affinity. He concludes that, as the rays of the sun come 186,000 miles per second and are all intercepted excepting the blue by the blue glass, their impact upon the glass produces negative electricity, " while the electrical condition of the glass is opposite, or positive, and heat is therefore evolved by their conjunction. This heat sufficiently expands the pores of the glass to pass through it and then you have within the apartment electricity, magnetism, light and heat, all essential elements of vital force." With reference to the above, I would say, 1st, that we would have the electricity, light, heat, etc., if there were no glass used ; the same effects being produced by thin blue curtains, etc. ; 2dly, the meaning of the terms positive and negative electricity, as commonly used, being entirely unknown, their use tends principally to blind one by means of words which smack of science but signify nothing ; 3dly, the more the glass becomes heated by this action of sunlight, the more the

heat rays will fail to pass through, as heat is repellant. The
diathermancy of blue glass is exceedingly small, while the blue
substance, sulphate of copper, is said to shut off all heat as shown
by experiment, although the substance itself becomes warm by
absorbing the heat rays, and this is a substance which makes
perhaps the purest blue glass, especially when ammonia is added,
and constitutes *cupro-diammonium sulphate* $(N_2H_6Cu) SO_4$.
Melloni has shown that plate glass shuts off over half of the heat
rays of artificial light, while the mazarine blue glass must shut
off more, and the cupro-sulphate blue the whole or nearly the
whole. The blue should be understood to be of itself a cold
electrical ray, so cold that when the thermometer stands at 56°
F. in the blue rays of the spectrum, the yellow light will raise it
to 62°, and the thermal to 79°, or nearly half as high again as the
blue rays. How then does a mass of blue rays produce action
when combined with a mass of white rays? We have seen in
the Third and Fifth chapter that the blue color has a chemical
affinity for the red, which being true, the blue rays of light must
seize upon and combine with the red portion of the white
light. I shall present facts a little farther on to show that
while a small amount of blue with a larger proportion of white
light will produce a greater heat than white light alone, yet an
equal amount of blue and transparent glass placed side by side,
is much more cooling than the ordinary transparent glass alone.
In the following cases, which I quote mainly from General
Pleasanton's work on " Blue and Sun-Lights,"* the blue light
is probably in a considerable predominance so far as actual
contact with the persons of the patients is concerned, and the
effects already attributed to blue, are, as might be expected, the
ones which generally appear. While the great error of General
Pleasanton's book, therapeutically considered, is the one-sided-
ness of recommending blue and white light for everything, yet if
we were to take one combination only, this is perhaps as good
as any that could be selected, as it gives the penetrating, calming principle of blue, and the warming animating principle of
white light, enabling one to take both at a time, with the head
or any other warm and sensitive portion of the body under the

* I think the grammar of his title would have been better under the name of
Blue and White Sunlight, for both colors belong equally to the Sunlight.

blue glass, while the colder portions are under the clear glass, or in case of fever or extra nervousness, to use the blue glass almost solely, while in case of a cold, dormant and chronic condition, the clear glass, or pure sunlight, should be used almost solely. In proving the advantage of the blue or violet combined with white light, in vegetable and animal life, Gen. Pleasanton has done a good thing for the world, and in spite of all his crude theories merits far more commendation than many of his critics who seem to have tried to offset his *facts* by their *prejudices*

1st Case.—Sciatica.

"About this time (Sept. 1871), one of my sons, about 22 years of age, a remarkably vigorous and muscular young man, was afflicted with a severe attack of sciatica, or rheumatism of the sciatic nerve, in his left hip and thigh, from which he had been unable to obtain any relief, although the usual medical as well as galvanic remedies had been applied. He had become lame from it and he suffered much pain in his attempts to walk. I advised him to try the associated sun and blue light, both upon his naked spine and hip, which he did with such benefit, that at the end of three weeks, after taking the first of these baths of light, every symptom of the disorder disappeared, and he has had no return of it since, a period now of three years." *Gen. Pleasanton's Blue and Sun-Lights, p. 14.*

2d. Case.—Two Cures of Rheumatism.

"Some time since, two of my friends, Major Generals S. and D. of the United States regular army, were on duty in this city. On making them a visit at their official residence, I saw on the window ledge, as I entered the room, a piece of blue glass of about the size of one of the panes of glass in the window. After some conversation, General D. said to me, Did you notice that piece of blue glass on the window ledge? I said I had observed it. 'Do you know what it is there for? ** S. and I have been suffering very much from rheumatism in our fore-arms, from the elbow joints to our fingers' ends ; sometimes our fingers were so rigid that we could not hold a pen—we have tried almost every remedy that was ever heard of for relief, but without avail ; at last I said to Gen. S., suppose we try Pleasanton's blue glass, to which he assented—when I sent for the glass and placed it on the window-ledge. When the sun began about ten o'clock in the morning to throw its light through the glass of the window, we took off our coats, rolled up our shirt sleeves to the shoulders, and then held our naked arms under the blue and sunlight ; in three days thereafter, having taken each day one of these sun-baths for 30 minutes on our arms, the pains in them ceased, and we have not had any return of them since. We are cured.'

" It is now more than two years since the date of my visit to these officers. Two months ago Gen. S. told me that he had not had any return of the rheumatism, nor did he think that Gen. D. had had any. Gen. S. in the mean time had been exposed to every vicissitude of climate from the Atlantic Ocean to Washington Territory, on the Pacific, and from the 49th degree of north latitude to the Gulf of Mexico, and Gen. D. was then stationed in the far north." *Blue and Sun-Lights, p. 15.*

The foregoing and other examples illustrate the durability and power of the fine forces according to Chap. First, XV.

3d CASE.—NERVOUS PROSTRATION.

Statement made by a lady patient of Dr. Fisher, N. Y.:
" Having been an invalid for nearly three years, and for the last half of that time confined entirely to my rooms on one floor, I became so reduced by the long confinement, and my nervous system seemed so completely broken down, that all tonics lost their effects, sleep at nights could only be obtained by the use of opiates, appetite, of course, there was none, and scarcely a vestige of color remained either in my lips, face or hands—as a last resort I was placed, about the 19th of January, 1874, under the influence of the blue glass rays. Two large panes of the glass, each 36 inches long by 16 inches wide, were placed in the upper part of a sunny window in my parlor, a window with a south exposure, and as the blue and sunlight streamed into the room, I sat in it continuously. I was also advised by Dr. Fisher to make a regular sun bath of it ; at least, to let the blue rays fall directly on the spine for about 20 or 30 minutes at a time, morning and afternoon ; but the effects of it were too strong for

me to bear; and as I was progressing very favorably, by merely sitting in it in my ordinary dress, that was considered sufficient.

"In two or three weeks the change began to be very perceptible. The color began returning to my face, lips and hands, my nights became better, my appetite more natural, and my strength and vitality to return, while my whole nervous system was most decidedly strengthened and soothed.

"In about six weeks I was allowed to try going up and down a few stairs at a time, being able to test in that way how the strength was returning into my limbs, and by the middle of April, when the spring was sufficiently advanced to make it prudent for me to try walking out, I was able to do so.

"The experiment was made a peculiarly fair one by the stoppage of all tonics, etc., as soon as the glass was placed in the window, allowing me to depend solely on the efficacy of the blue light." *Blue and Sun-Lights, p. 25.*

In the above case the lady had a mass of blue glass sufficiently great to cover almost if not entirely the whole of her body which was very proper, as much of the white light would have been too exciting for so sensitive a person. A proper kind of blue would not have been thus "too strong" on the bare skin.

4th CASE.—NEURALGIA, RHEUMATISM, NERVOUS EXHAUSTION.

"In the latter part of August, 1871, I chanced to visit a physician of this city, of my acquaintance, whom I found to be in great distress, and plunged in the lowest despondency. On inquiring the cause he told me he feared he was about to lose his wife, who was suffering from a complication of disorders that were most painful and distressing, and which had baffled the skill of several of the most eminent physicians here, as also others of equal distinction in New York. He then stated that his wife was suffering great pains in the lower part of her back, and in her head and neck, and also in her lower limbs; that she could not sleep; that she had no appetite for food and was rapidly wasting away in flesh; and that her secretions were all abnormal." [Here is given an account of her commencing the use of blue and white light, her husband having placed alternate blue and clear panes of glass in one window.]

"Six days after this interview, I received a note from the doctor, asking me to send him some copies of my memoir on blue light, etc., which he wished to forward to some of his distant friends, and at the close of it he had written : 'You will be surprised to learn that since my wife has been under the blue glass, the hair on her head has begun to grow, not merely longer but in places on her head where there was none, new hair is coming out thick.' This was certainly an unexpected effect, but it displayed an evident action on the skin, and so far was encouraging. Two days after the receipt of this note, I called to see the doctor, and while he was giving me an account of the experiment with the blue light, his wife entered the office, and coming to me, she said, 'Oh, General ! I am so much obliged to you for having recommended to me that blue light !' 'Ah !' said I, 'is it doing you any good ?' 'Yes,' she said, 'the greatest possible good. Do you know that when I put my naked foot under the blue light, all my pains in the limb cease ? * * My maid tells me that my hair is growing not merely longer on my head, but in places which were bald, new hair is coming out thick.' She also said that the pains in her back were less and that there was a general improvement in the condition of her health.

"Three weeks afterward, on visiting them, the doctor told me that the arrangement of blue and sunlight had been a complete success with his wife ; that her pains had left her ; that she now slept well ; her appetite had returned, and that she had already gained much flesh. His wife a few moments afterward, in person, confirmed this statement of her husband, and he added :—'From my observation of the effects of blue and sunlight upon my wife, I regard it as the greatest stimulant and the most powerful tonic that I know of in medicine. It will be invaluable in typhoid cases, cases of debility, nervous depressions and the like.'" *Blue and Sun-Lights, p. 10.*

The above mentioned physician is Dr. S. W. Beckwith, Electrical Institute, 1220 Walnut St., Philadelphia. I have not space here for his letter confirmatory of the above, and speaking enthusiastically of General Pleasanton's theory for the improvement of vegetable, animal and human life by these arrangements of colors.

5th Case.—Infantile and Animal Growth.

The following is a part of a letter from Commodore J. R. Goldsborough, of the U. S. Navy, dated Mound City, Ill., May 31st, 1872, and addressed to Gen. Pleasanton. After speaking of the extraordinary growth of plants which he had caused by alternate blue and plain glass, he speaks of two broods of chickens hatched on the same day, one of which was reared under an ordinary coop and the other " partly covered with blue and plain glass." " The chickens of each brood," he continues, " were fed at the same times, and with equal quantities of similar food. Those under the blue glass soon began to display the effects of the stimulating influence of the associated blue and sunlight by their daily almost visible growth, increase of strength and activity, far exceeding in all these respects, the developments of the chickens of the other brood which were exposed to the ordinary atmospheric influences.

" I will also relate to you what I imagine to be another remarkable circumstance having relation to this subject.

" On the 29th of January, 1872, the wife of one of the gentlemen on the station gave birth prematurely to a very small child, which weighed at the time only 3½ pounds. It was very feeble, possessing apparently but little vitality. It so happened that the windows of the room, in which it was born and reared, were draped with blue curtains, through which, and the plain glass of the windows, the sunlight entered the apartment. The lacteal system of the mother was greatly excited, and secreted an excessive quantity of milk, while at the same time the appetite of the child for food was greatly increased, to such an extent indeed that its mother, notwithstanding the inordinate flow of her milk, at times found it difficult to satisfy its hunger.

" The child grew rapidly in health, strength and size ; and on the 29th of May, 1872, just four months after its birth, when I saw it, before I left Mound City, it weighed 22 pounds." *Blue and Sun-Lights, p. 7.*

With reference to the above I would simply remark that a thin, somewhat gauzy, blue curtain would doubtless be desirable, for in case a curtain is too thick it would become nearly opaque, and thus absorb the blue rays before they reach the patient. Glass, when convenient, is doubtless best.

6th Case.—Partial Paralysis in a Child.

" Sometime since, Mrs. C., the wife of Major-General C., a distinguished officer of the U. S. regular army, told me that one of her grandchildren, a little boy about 18 months old, had from his birth had so little use of his legs that he could neither crawl nor walk, and was apparently so enfeebled in those limbs that she began to fear that the child was permanently paralyzed in them. To obviate such an affliction, she requested the mother of the child to send him with his two young sisters, to play in the entry of the second story of her house, where she had fitted up a window with blue and plain glass in equal proportions. The children were accordingly brought there, and were allowed to play for several hours in this large entry or hall under the mixed sun and blue light. In a very few days, Mrs. C. told me that the child manifested great improvement in the strength of its limbs, having learned to climb by a chair, to crawl and to walk, and that he was then as promising a child as any one is likely to see." *Blue and Sun-Lights, p. 22.*

Parents, especially those whose children are somewhat nervous and feeble, should take a hint from the above and have their nurseries arranged accordingly. Some blue and violet glass in the windows would tend to quiet the brains and stimulate the nutritive functions of children, who in our climate tend rather to over activity of brain and nerves.

7th Case.—Spinal Meningitis and Baldness.

Gen. Pleasanton relates an agreeable incident which occurred to him but a few weeks since. " A lady and her daughter called to see him, and announced that they had come from Corning, N. Y., to Philadelphia, for the express purpose of thanking him for saving the daughter's life.

" Four years ago she was afflicted with a violent attack of spinal meningitis. Her sufferings were indescribable but continuous. Every conceivable remedy had been resorted to during these four years, but the patient received no benefit. Her nervous system at last became so disordered that the slightest sound, or the most gentle agitation of the air, threw her into the most agonizing suffering. She was wasted away in flesh, could not

sleep at night, had no appetite, and her life was despaired of.
Hearing of Gen. Pleasanton's discovery in associated lights, her
parents determined to try it. A bay window was fitted with alternate panes of blue and plain glass, and the young lady sat daily
in the light which streamed through them. Her physicians, of
course, laughed at the idea, pronounced the whole thing a hum-
bug, etc., as is the habit of professional gentlemen whenever any
new idea is broached. The physician was dismissed, and the
young lady relied wholly upon the blue-glass treatment for her
restoration to health. The lady says that on entering the room
thus lighted, the pains from which she was suffering almost immediately ceased. They would return in a modified form on
leaving the room, but grew less from day to day. Very soon her
condition began to improve, her appetite returned, and with it
her strength ; she began to gain flesh, her sleeplessness disappeared, and in short, she was speedily restored to health.

"A singular feature of this young lady's case was that her
hair all came out and she became as bald as an egg. Her physician examined the scalp with a microscope, and declared that
there were no roots of hair remaining, and that, consequently, she
would never again have a natural head of hair. This announce-
ment, to a young lady, was worse than would have been the
reading of her death-warrant. Better the cold grave and its attendant worms than to go through life with a wig. Under the
blue-glass treatment, however, the hair did begin to grow, the
young lady discarded her wig, and when she called upon Gen.
Pleasanton she showed him a luxuriant growth of hair, which any
young lady might envy. She was profusely grateful to the General for having restored her hair, and incidentally saved her life.
So much for examples and illustrations. These and numerous
others which I might cite if you had space to print them, show
that the blue associated with the sunlight has a wonderfully
stimulating effect upon both vegetable and animal life." *Correspondence of the Chicago Tribune, dated Jan. 12, 1877, by Dutton.*

An account of the same case was given in the New York
Tribune. I have caused a new and rich growth of hair in several persons by manipulating the scalp with the ends of my fingers, and thus animating it with vital force. How much safer to
use these finer forces for the head than the many preparations

which poison the system and sometimes induce paralysis and insanity.

8th Case.—Concussion and Inflammation.

The following is a portion of a letter dated Jan. 23, 1877, to the
Chicago Tribune by General Pleasanton and relates to a severe
fall which he received in alighting from his carriage :—

" My right shoulder, right dorsal muscles, and right lumbar
region received the shock of the fall.   Fortunately, my head did
not strike the pavement.   The concussion knocked the breath
out of my body, and it was a considerable fraction of a second before I could have an inspiration of air.   Some gentlemen kindly
picked me up, and assisted me into the nearest store.   At the
expiration of an hour I was sufficiently recovered to be enabled
to call upon my family physician, who lived about a square distant, by whom my body was carefully examined.   He said that
there had been no fracture of ribs or bones, but that I had received a very severe contusion, the effects of which I would feel
for some time at my age.   I knew that such an opinion meant
long protracted suffering with very little hope of relief from any
process *secundum artem*.   He prescribed soap liniment to soften
the muscles of the injured parts ; it afforded no relief.   The
pains were very great and constant, and, in a paroxysm of coughing, I experienced the most intense pain in the back part of my
right lung, which I thought had been brought into contact with
the inside of my ribs when I fell.   Inflammation of the lung, with
its consequent attachment to the inside of the ribs, immediately
recurred to my imagination, and the doctor was again invoked.
He prescribed a porous plaster to confine the muscles, so that, in
the act of coughing or sneezing, the pain might be mitigated, but
it afforded no relief.   The next day there was a bright sunshine
and a clear atmosphere.   In my bathroom I have a window with
a southern exposure, arranged with alternate panes of blue and
plain, transparent glass.   I determined to try the efficacy of a
sun-bath with blue glass.   Accordingly, uncovering my back, I
sat with it to the blue and sun lights, which were streaming
through the window into the bathroom.   As soon as these lights
began to fall upon my back the pains began to diminish, and

at the end of half an hour they had ceased altogether. Towards evening the pains returned ; but they were much less than they had been before I had taken the blue-light bath, and during the night I was easier than I had been previously. The next day we had again a brilliant sunshine, clear atmosphere and low temperature ; and, intending to take another bath of blue and sunlight, I sent for my physician, that he might witness the effect for himself. He is the very eminent surgeon, Dr. D. Hayes Agnew, Professor of Surgery and Anatomy in the University of Pennsylvania.

"He arrived while I was taking this bath, and was shown up into my bath room. On coming into the room I said to him, ' Doctor, I am glad you have come at this time. I am taking a bath of blue and sun lights.' He replied, with a smile of incredulity as to its effect, ' I see you are ; ' and I said, ' It is doing me great good ; it is relieving all my pains ; and I wish to give you some information that you should know. Will you be good enough to place your naked hand on that pane of transparent glass, through which the sunlight is streaming into the room ? You will find it as cold as the outer atmoshere, which is at freezing temperature.' He placed his hand on it, and said, ' Yes, it is very cold.' ' Now,' said I to him, ' put the same hand on the next pane of glass, which is blue ; you will find it hot.' He did so, and, in the greatest surprise, said, ' Why, I never knew that ! ' ' Of course you did not,' I replied ; ' that is one of my discoveries, that I have been trying to pump into you doctors for the last fifteen years, but without effect.' He then said, ' This is very wonderful ; I had no idea of it before.' Then he said. ' This room is very warm ; have you any fire to heat it ? ' I answered, ' No ! The windows and the southern and western walls are in contact with the outer air. The adjoining chamber on one side, and the staircase on the other, are each without artificial heat.' ' Then,' said he, ' how do you make it so warm ? ' ' That,' I said, ' is another of my discoveries, and is produced by the conjunction of the opposite electricities of sunlight and blue glass ! ' "

The fact that so learned a gentleman as Dr. Agnew was not aware that blue glass under the influence of luminous rays is warmer than clear glass, shows how uninformed our medical men are concerning some very simple facts in connection with these fine potencies, and for Gen. Pleasanton to say " that is one of my discoveries," shows that he is not very familiar with the principles of optical science as already developed.

9th CASE.—RHEUMATISM, ETC.

Dr. Robert Rohland having referred me to Mrs. William Proessel, of No. 20 East 42d st., N. Y., as a very remarkable cure by sunlight, I was led to make a personal and careful examination of the same. She has been a severe sufferer from rheumatism for eight years as a reactive effect of uterine difficulties, her knees were badly swollen and hardened at the joints, limbs made crooked, finger joints enlarged, and fingers badly contracted by the flexor muscles, left arm and shoulder seemingly paralyzed, and she altogether so helpless as to have to be carried to different parts of the room by her friends. She tried nearly every style of treatment in vain, as nothing but the blue and white sunlight combined has ever succeeded in bringing her steadily and thoroughly forward. Her windows are prepared with about half a pane of blue glass set up against one side of each pane of clear glass. This she found to be more soothing than when set up in the middle of a pane of clear glass, each kind of light thus being made to come in larger masses. She has blue-green shades by which she regulates the quantity and locality of the light. She has been in the habit of taking the light not only on the knees, but on the whole spine including a little of the cerebellum. Although taking it upon the bare skin even in winter, she did not suffer with the cold after getting the light fairly upon her. When the blue light struck her, its immediate effect was to make her feel cold, but almost instantly a reaction would give her warmth. She says it would often seem as though flies were touching her skin where the blue and white light joined. This shows the electrical and chemical action evolved by the two styles of light.

She has already used the above for 8 or 9 months, commencing early in the Autumn of 1876, and extending onward during the good days of the following winter and spring, and can now walk freely with only a slight limp, the knees have assumed their usual size, the arm and shoulder are well, the fingers have become straight and the joints nearly their proper size, and although not yet a strong person, she is like a transformed being as compared with her past.

I have pointed out to her what, as it seems to me, have been mistakes in her method of using the light, 1st, that which comes from following Gen. Pleasanton's rule of having equal amounts of blue and clear glass, which, in her very sensitive and nervous condition, caused too much excitement, pain, and sometimes sleeplessness, leading her at times to resort to quieting drugs which have a bad after effect. In the process of arousing a dormant system, deadened by chronic diseases, all thorough radical treatment must arouse more or less of acute pain and bring up perhaps old symptoms which for the time being lead the uninformed to think they are growing worse, but in such a case when the pain becomes too severe, a resort for a time to nothing but the blue or violet light would give relief; 2dly, as soon as her arm and shoulder had been relieved, it would have been well not to have taken the light so near her brain, as it often caused pain in the head : when she first commenced, she could not endure the light thus over ten minutes at a time, but afterwards she came gradually to use it several times as long; 3dly, she has wholly neglected to use the light on her liver, stomach, lungs and bowels, consequently her vital processes have not been as greatly animated and strengthened as might have been done.

MISCELLANEOUS CASES.

I will merely mention the following cases, given in *Blue and Sun-Lights* by Gen. Pleasanton, as treated by blue and clear glass :—

1. *Major-General Chas. W. Sanford's invalid daughter* " materially benefited."

2. *Henry H. Holloway*, of 5 South 10th st., Philadelphia, cured of *rheumatism* of nearly two months' standing by 3 or 4 sunbaths of blue and white light. His mother, also, relieved of severe sickness.

3. Two *lambs*, newly born, weighing respectively 3½ and 4 pounds, were placed in a pen fitted with blue and uncolored glass, "fed alike with skimmed cow's milk," and at the end of 3 months weighed, respectively, 55 and 51 pounds.

4. Several cases given which show that *flies and hurtful insects* are killed under blue glass or blue gauze.

5. Remarkable increase of *vegetable growth* caused, which will be noticed in the next chapter.

6. A mule cured of *deafness and rheumatism* by having its head and neck illuminated by the blue and white light which came through transoms.

7. The hatching of *silk-worms* greatly facilitated by violet glass.

8. Marvelous development of an *Alderney calf*, which was supposed at first by the keeper, to be too feeble to live.

XVII. WHEN BLUE AND VIOLET ARE INJURIOUS.

1. All the electrical colors, including the various shades of blue, indigo, violet, and even blue green, are too cooling and constricting in general cases of paralysis, costiveness, chronic rheumatism, and gout, consumption (the acute forms excepted), and all cold, pale, and dormant conditions of the system, although the brain, especially its upper portion, may, quite generally, even in these conditions be put under blue glass to advantage. In all cases of melancholia, and depression, these electrical colors are contra-indicated, as a person who has what is called *the blues*, is already sufficiently supplied with that article without having any more of it.

2. Dr. Pancoast, of Philadelphia, who has a considerable experience in healing by means of colored lights, speaking of blue light, says: "Its action is as pronounced in reducing, as that of the red is in producing, nervous excitement. If administered in small doses, it acts as a gentle sedative, creating a disposition to sleep, but as soon as this effect is reached, the bath should cease. In cases of extreme nerve tension, when prompt action is imperatively demanded, we employ a pure blue bath, but this is rare, and as there is always danger in so large a dose, we are very careful to note the momentary effects, lest the patient be reduced to a condition of extreme prostration—sometimes the lapse from intense excitement to as extreme prostration is sudden. As a general rule, a dose in ordinary cases would be a bath of about two hours, through a window containing alternate blue and plain glass." Dr. Pancoast has thus made his bath much longer,

I think, than most persons could comfortably endure, especially if their heads were to be exposed to the full light of clear glass in the mid-summer of our American climate. In England, Russia, or Prussia, a sun-bath could be taken with impunity for a much longer time than in Italy, Greece, India, Spain, or even in France or Austria, and in winter perhaps twice or thrice as long as in summer. I once took a seven hour sun-bath on the upper deck of one of our steamers as it passed through the New York Bay, and a short distance into the ocean, during a hot July day, but the electricity of a constant breeze sustained me, and the only damage I received was that the skin of my hands and face became somewhat burned, but was soon relieved by the use of blue glass and a little glycerine. The new animation of body and mind canceled this little drawback many times over.

XVIII. HEALING BY MEANS OF SUBSTANCES CHARGED WITH BLUE LIGHT.

1. Light being an actual substance moving with peculiar styles of vibrations according to the particular colors which compose it, and at a rate of nearly 186,000 miles a second, it is easy to see that it must have great power, and that the substances receiving it must partake of this power. The fact that the whole world, mineral, vegetable, and animal, is ever being transformed into new and beautiful growths, forms and colors under its magic touch, shows its almost omnific power.

2. Reichenbach proved by many experiments upon persons of very delicate sensibilities, whom he called *sensitives*, the great and peculiar power of sunlight. Sometimes he would carry a long copper wire, one end of which they held in a dark room, and without their knowledge, would place a plate of metal attached to the other end directly in the rays of the sun. The sensitives would feel it immediately and powerfully as an icy cold principle, so cold in fact that it would stiffen their hands. Baron Reichenbach took this as a proof that the finer elements of sunlight are cold. This is true so far as its electrical rays are concerned, but the cold which they felt so powerfully may be accounted for on the principle that thermo-electricity was evolved

by the heating power of the sun's rays, the natural tendency of electricity being always to move from a hot to a cold portion of an object.

3. Reichenbach had water stand in the sunlight five minutes, when Miss Maix, on drinking it without knowing what was done, said immediately that it was magnetized. " It produced the peculiar pepper-like burning, well known to the sensitive, on her tongue, palate, throat, down to the stomach, at every point arousing spasmodic symptoms." Water which stood twenty minutes in the sunshine, was found to be as strongly magnetic as it could be when charged with a large nine layered magnet. " I allowed Miss Reichel to become used to the feeling of my hand, and then went out into the sunshine. After ten minutes had elapsed, during which time I had exposed myself on all sides to the sun's rays, I went back and gave her the same hand. She was much astonished at the rapid alteration in the great increase of force which she experienced in it, the cause of which was unknown to her. The sun had evidently impregnated me in exactly the same way as a magnet had charged the body of a man " (in a previous experiment). Reichenbach further affirms that Miss Maix could not bear the increased power of persons coming out of strong sunlight, and that iron, glass, or any other object could be charged with a power which affected her like a magnet, while a magnet which had become weak was made strong by being placed in the sun, thus confirming the observations of Barlocci, Zantedesschi and others concerning solar magnetism.

4. A substance called *Od-sugar* or *Odo-magnetic sugar* has been devised and used with remarkable success as a curative agent by Adolph von Gerhardt, M.D., of Germany, and also prepared and supplied by Robt. Rohland, M.D., of 429, 2d Ave., New York. It consists of the sugar of milk charged by certain rays of the sun through a prism, being called *od-sugar* from the fact that a certain amount of *odic* or *od* force is brought into action by means of the sunlight, although the sunlight itself must be the more immediate potency. When the sugar is charged by the thermal rays it is called *positive odo-magnetic sugar;* when charged by the electrical rays, *negative odo-magnetic sugar,* or *negative od-sugar,* terms which are not very accurate, as the word

positive naturally means strong or aggressive, while *negative* means weak or yielding. Surely the wonderful chemical potencies of blue and violet cannot be called negative in their character, for in many combinations the red and yellow are most feeble in comparison. Thermo-od-sugar and electro-od-sugar would discriminate better. In Dr. Rohland's pamphlet he says, " If a part of the sugar becomes placed within the solar spectrum in the *red* and *yellow* rays, and another part in the *blue* and *violet* rays of the sunlight, and a sensitive tastes them after some time of exposure, the first will taste tepid and nauseous, and the latter cool and refreshing." This admirably confirms what we have already seen to be the true potencies of color, the red and yellow drugs being more warming and nauseating and including the emetics, while the blue and violet ones are cooling and soothing to the nerves. I will quote from Dr. Rohland's pamphlet a little of the testimony of physicians, some of whom I am acquainted with and know to be eminent in their profession. This testimony is with reference to the electro-od-sugar, and shows its quieting, cooling, soporific character according to the principles which I have already given.

CASE 1st.—PHTHISIS PULMONALIS, SLEEPLESSNESS, etc.

" The patient was very weak, very sallow, and the eyes looked strained and staring ; sleepless, expectoration of purulent taste. After " Od," one dose,* reports : Slept well, feels better and stronger than he has for a month, looks fresher in the face and eyes, the expectoration tastes salty—cough unchanged." S. SWAN, M.D., 13, West 38th St., N. Y., Nov. 8, 1870.

2d CASE.—NASAL AND BRONCHIAL CATARRH, NERVOUSNESS, etc.

" A young lady from Philadelphia, * * was much reduced in strength and vitality, extreme excitability of the nervous system—raised blood and pus from the bronchia or lung ; could not sleep. First night, gave her pulsatilla—no relief ; then nux vomica—no better. I then, the third night, gave her one odo-magnetic sugar powder. Result : sound sleep all night — the first she had had for more than two months—much refreshed in

* A dose is half a grain or about what would lie on the point of a knife. Double this amount I have found to be more effective.

the morning." O. R. GROSS, M.D., 273, *West 52d St., N. Y.,* *Aug.* 28, 1870.

3d CASE.—CONVULSIONS.

" The child of Mr. Mailander, a mechanic near Jena, $1\frac{1}{2}$ years old, had been lying with the most fearful attacks of cramps for four hours, so that the parents as well as the physician declared it hopelessly lost. Good luck happened to make me pass near his house; I was called in and saw the child lying in terrible convulsions. I chanced to have a flask of od-negative (electro-od) milk-sugar with me, so I poured a blade's end full of it into his mouth. Scarcely 15 minutes elapsed when the cramps, to my great surprise and that of every one else, ceased altogether and the child became perfectly well again." ADOLPH VON GERHARDT.

4th CASE.—MENORRHAGIA AND TOOTHACHE.

" On the 4th of Aug. 1870, I gave Dr. St. Clair Smith, Physician of the " Five Points House of Industry," two doses of my odo-magnetic milk-sugar. Yesterday (Sept. 12, 1870), he bought a flask of the sugar, and on this occasion told me the following :

" One of his lady patients suffered from profuse menstruation ; another from violent toothache, and each was completely cured 15 minutes after the odo-magnetic sugar had been taken. The two patients themselves could not comprehend it ; but as Dr. Smith, having had two doses only, could not continue the medicine, the sufferings returned next day." ROBT. ROHLAND, M.D.

Dr. Rohland says that " every physician, without one exception, who has tried this odo-magnetic milk-sugar, even with great reluctance and caution, has had to report some great results ; some in *intermittent fever* with China, when the latter had failed by itself; others in *headache, toothache;* some in *diarrhœa,* or other disorders of the *digestive organs,* in *fits* and *hemorrhages ;* and every one in *nervous debility, nervousness, weakness, sleeplessness, depression of mind,"* etc. etc.

In IX of this chapter, the reader will see a simpler method of gaining the potencies of blue and violet light in connection with water, which the author has devised, and also a number of examples in which the yellow and red principles have been developed in connection with water and given with marked success for animating the system, acting as a laxative, alterative, etc. Dr. Von Gerhardt did not seem to have ascertained the potencies of the thermal colors, although they are perhaps more practical and valuable than those of the electrical colors taken all in all.

5th Case.—Diarrhœa cured with blue–charged Water.

Although the blue and violet principles are especially valuable for checking nervous and inflammable conditions, I have in several instances checked the too free action of the bowels by light strained through blue glass placed over the bowels, or by water charged in blue bottles, or blue chromo lenses.

Miss K., formerly a patient of mine, living on Broadway, was becoming haggard in her appearance from diarrhœa which had lasted five weeks. I handed her a blue bottle which I had filled with water, and had standing in the sun for a part of a day. She drank something like a tablespoonful of this two or· three times a day. In one or two days her diarrhœa ceased, and up to this time, several months having elapsed; it has not returned. A favorable symptom in the case is that she did not swing to the other extreme of constipation, as would very likely have occurred under an opium treatment. It should be remarked that she took only an occasional sip of the water after the first day or two. The blue chromo lens, to be described hereafter, is still better.

XIX. Healing Power of Pure Sunlight.

Pure white light, as nature gives it to us, is of course far more desirable for man than any one color of sunlight, for in this we get all colors and all potencies combined. While many conditions of disease and perhaps imperfections of climate may be improved by a predominance of some one or more colors as brought about through prisms or colored glass, the combined rays, as in white light, are the ones which man and nature must generally depend upon, and which most of all they require. *Although sunlight combines both the thermal aud electrical rays, covering every variety of power, yet as a whole, especially in warm weather, it is powerfully heating and stimulating in its nature, kindling into action dormant systems and proving to be over-exciting especially when falling on sensitive brains.* By exposing any portion of the body to the sun not to an undue extent, the skin becomes somewhat darker, clearer and more rosy in its general character, having on the whole a richer effect than the waxy whiteness of bleached indoor faces. The darker and more rubicund appearance comes from the carbon which is driven into the skin by the light, and being of the right color to stimulate the nerves of the surface, the blood is more or less drawn there and thus a more rosy appearance is developed. This gives an activity and toughness to the cuticle which enables it to resist many external influences of the atmosphere, and often prevents the *taking of cold*, while it also withdraws heat and inflammation from the internal organs. Light which has passed through glass must be somewhat softer and more refined than the full glare directly from the sun, as it is strained of some of its coarser elements and some of the intensity of its heat. This, of course, makes it less desirable when the greatest external power is required. I will quote a very few cases of sun-healing.

1st Case. Prevention of Colds, etc.

The toughening power of the sun was well illustrated some years since in the case of a lady patient of the author. She was very feeble and negative, and every little exposure would cause her to take cold. She took a course of sun-baths on the skin over the lungs and other parts of her body, since which she rarely if ever takes cold. In this respect she has become permanently strong, as years have elapsed without a recurrence of her old conditions.

2d Case, or Series of Cases. Cure of Tumors, Mother's Marks, etc.

The following, taken from the N. Y. " Herald of Health," is from the pen of Augustus Barnes, who remarks that he has studied the hygienic properties of light for 38 years :

" I can remove cancers in their earlier stages, tumors, *nævus maternus* (or mother's marks). It matters not whether the latter are red, black, purple, brown, or other color, or whether they cover the entire side of the face, or large protuberances appear, I remove all by a lens and the simple rays of the sun, without starting a drop of blood, or leaving a scar but for a short time. There is less pain attending this operation than by common surgery. Uncomely moles that disfigure the face of many persons can be made to disappear and leave the face as fair as Nature intended it, nor do they ever reappear. This treatment produces no ill effects, for there is no mineral or chemical poison in the rays of the sun.

ADVANTAGES OF THE SUN'S RAYS OVER ALL OTHER CAUSTICS AND THE LANCET.

1. There is no mutilation of any part, nor is a drop of blood ever drawn. The sun's rays will cauterize a vein or an artery so as almost instantly to stop their bleeding.

2. There is no after dressing needed, except for cancers.

3. There are no bad effects resulting from poisoning, for the sun's rays are not poisonous.

4. There is no scar left, after a sufficient time has elapsed for the healing process ; and the redness caused by the burning will disappear in from one to six months.

5. Those who have been subjected to both systems express themselves as feeling less than half the pain under the sun's rays.

6. No detention from business is required.

7. There is no fainting under the operation.

8. Anæsthetics are rarely required.

9. The quickness and permanence of the treatment and the simplicity of the operation are remarkable. It is easily controlled, and the operator can burn to a considerable depth, or so slightly as to only destroy the cuticle, stopping the cauterization at whatever stage he pleases.

10. The remedy is to be found wherever the sun shines, requiring no preparation, no grinding, no mixing, but is ready every day and free to all."

With reference to the above it should be remembered that the blue is the balancing principle where too much of the red or inflamed condition exists, while the yellow-orange is the great animating principle in hard tumors or other dormant conditions, for which reason the blue chromo-lens and the yellow-orange chromo-lens, to be described hereafter, would be superior to one which is transparent, in certain cases.

3d. Case.—Complication of Diseases.

" A very remarkable instance of recovery from disease has been related by the late Baron Dupuytren, the eminent French surgeon. A lady, residing in Paris, had suffered for many years from an enormous complication of diseases, which had baffled the skill of all her medical advisers, and her state appeared almost hopeless. As a last resource, the opinion of Dupuytren was requested upon her case, and he, unable to offer any direct medical treatment essentially differing from all that had been previously tried in vain, suggested that she should be taken out of the dark room in which she lived, and away from the dismal street, to a brighter part of the city, and that she should expose herself as much as possible to the daylight. The result was quickly manifest in her rapid improvement, and this continued until her recovery was complete. An equally singular instance has been related by Southey, in the case of his own parent."
Dr. Forbes Winslow's " Influence of Light," p. 171.

XX. Disastrous Effects of a Lack of Sunlight.

1. Sir James Wylie says that " the cases of disease on the dark side of an extensive barrack at St. Petersburgh, have been uniformly, for many years, in the proportion of 3 to 1 to those on the side exposed to strong light."

2. Dr. Forbes Winslow in his volume entitled " Light ; its Influence on Life and Health," uses the following language :—

" It may be enunciated as an indisputable fact, that all who live and pursue their calling in situations where the minimum of light is permitted to penetrate, suffer seriously in bodily and mental health. The total exclusion of the sunbeams induces the severer forms of chlorosis, green sickness, and other anæmic conditions depending upon an impoverished and disordered state of the blood. Under these circumstances the face assumes a death-like paleness, the membranes of the eyes become blood-less, and the skin shrunken and turned in a white, greasy, waxy

color ; also emaciation, muscular debility and degeneration, dropsical effusion, softening of the bones, general nervous excitability, morbid irritability of the heart, loss of appetite, tendency
to syncope and hemorrhages, consumption, physical deformity,
stunted growth, mental impairment and premature old age. The
offspring of those so unhappily trained are often deformed, weak
and puny, and are disposed to scrofulous affections."

3. Dr. Ellsworth, of Hartford, says : "Take a rabbit and shut
him from the sunlight, and he will die of consumption in a few
weeks. The tubercles will be just as perfectly formed in his
lungs as in the human species, and the symptoms in every respect will be the same."

4. Many persons keep themselves pale and sickly by means
of parasols, unbrellas, shaded rooms, and in-door life generally.
Parasols should be dispensed with excepting in the hottest seasons. Sailors who are ever in the pure air and sunlight, and
children who play much out of doors, generally present a ruddy,
healthy appearance. The following severe cut on our American
house-keepers, from an editorial of the Chicago Tribune, is well
merited :—

"In this country, there seems to be an implacable feud between people and the sun—the one striving vigorously and even
fiercely to get into the houses, and the other striving just as
fiercely and vigorously to keep him out. The average American
housekeeper does not think she has fulfilled her whole duty until she has made the rounds of the whole household, shut all the
doors, closed all the shutters, and drawn all the curtains on the
east and south sides of the house. This is the morning's job.
In the afternoon she makes the same grand round on the west
side of the house. She is not quite happy and contented until
the sun has gone down and darkness sets in. She is substan-
tially aided in her raid against the sunlight by the heaviest of
shades, curtains and lambrequins. Thus the fight goes on day
by day and season by season. In summer she shuts out the
sun because it is too hot. In winter she shuts it out because it
will spoil her carpets. In spring and fall she has other reasons.
She has reasons for all seasons. Thus she keeps the house in
perpetual shade, in which the children grow up sickly, dwarfed,
full of aches and pains, and finally have to be sent off into the

country post-haste so that they may get into that very sunlight which they have been denied at home, and in which the country children run and are glorified."

5. Our *Street-Car and Railroad Conductors* are too often most careful to shut out the sun from their vehicles, even in weather when it would be especially delightful and animating to have its rays. In fact this glorious orb of heaven is frequently treated as if it was man's deadliest enemy, instead of being the dispenser of power and beauty in all directions, as it really is.

6. The ancients often had terraces, called *Solaria*, built on the tops of their houses, where they were in the habit of taking their solar air baths. Pliny says that for 600 years Rome had no physicians. Using such natural methods of retaining or gaining physical power as vapor baths, manipulation, sunlight, exercise, etc., they became the mightiest of nations. By this remark I throw out no slur against true and wise physicians, who are blessings to a community, but would call their attention more to nature's finer methods rather than to the use of so many drugs, blisters, moxas, bleedings, leechings, and other violent processes which so weaken and destroy the beautiful temple of the human body.

7. " Who has not observed the purifying effect of light," says the beloved Florence Nightingale, " and especially of direct sunlight upon the air of a room? Go into a sick room where the shutters are always shut (in a sick room or bed-chamber there should never be shutters shut), and though the room has never been polluted by the breathing of human beings, you will observe a close, musty smell of corrupt air, *i. e.* unpurified by the effect of the sun's rays. The mustiness of dark rooms and corners, indeed, is proverbial. The cheerfulness of a room, the usefulness of light in treating disease, is all-important. ' Where there is sun there is thought.' All physiology goes to confirm this. Where is the shady side of deep valleys, there is cretinism. Where are cellars and the unsunned sides of narrow streets, there is the degeneracy and weakliness of the human race, mind and body equally degenerating. Put the pale, withering plant and human being into the sun, and if not too far gone, each will recover health and spirit." *Notes on Nursing.*

8. The lack of pure light and pure air in mines tells seriously

upon the health of miners. " Fourcault affirms that where life is prolonged to the average term, the evil effects of the want of light are seen in the stunted forms and general deterioration of the human race. It appears that the inhabitants of the arondissement of Chimay, in Belgium, 3000 in number, are engaged partly as coal miners, and partly as field-laborers. The latter are robust and readily supply their proper number of recruits to the army ; while among the miners it is in most years impossible to find a man who is not ineligible from bodily deformity or arrest of physical development." *Forbes Winslow's Influence of Light.*

9. Dr. Andrew Winter in the *Pall Mall Gazette,* London, says : —" When the St. Martin's national school, leading out of Endell street, was built some years ago, we noticed with pleasure that a play-ground was built at the top of the school, where light and air were plentiful. The necessity of light for young children is not half appreciated. Many of the affections of children and nearly all the cadaverous looks of those brought up in great cities, are ascribable to this deficiency of light and air. When we see the glass-rooms of the photographers in every street, high up on the top-most story, we grudge them their application to a mere personal vanity. Why should not our nurseries be constructed in the same manner ? If mothers knew the value of light to the skin in childhood, especially to children of a scrofulous tendency, we should have plenty of these glass-house nurseries, where children may run about in a proper temperature, free of much of that clothing which at present seals up the skin —that great supplementary lung—to sunlight and oxygen."

10. " It is a well established fact that, as the effect of isolation from the stimulus of light, the fibrine, albumen and red blood-cells become diminished in quantity, and the serum, or watery portion of the vital fluid, augmented in volume, thus inducing a disease known to physicians and pathologists by the name of *lukæmia,* an affection in which white instead of red blood-cells are developed. This exclusion from the sun produces the sickly, flabby, pale, anæmic condition of the face, or ex-sanguined, ghostlike forms so often seen amongst those not freely exposed to air and light. The absence of these essential elements of health deteriorates by materially altering the physical composition of

the blood, thus seriously prostrating the vital strength, enfeebling the nervous energy, and ultimately inducing organic changes in the structure of the heart, brain and muscular tissue." *Dr. Forbes Winslow.*

XXI. WHEN SUNLIGHT IS INJURIOUS.

1. Very bright and hot sunlight is injurious and sometimes dangerous when allowed to fall directly on a sensitive or over-heated brain, on inflamed, or over-sensitive eyes, etc. It is more especially apt to be dangerous to those who indulge in alcohol, opium and other cerebral stimulants, or to those who have large active brains and full flow of blood, especially of the red arterial kind. In such cases the tendency is to *sun-stroke,** and the blue or violet principle is needed as counterbalancing agents.

2. The *symptoms of sun-stroke* are usually head-ache, vertigo, dimness of vision, nausea, often developing into coma, or even delirium and convulsions, ending in many cases in insanity, softening of the brain, or death.

3. For the *Prevention of Sun-stroke,* the following are hints. especially when there is tendency to a hot brain :—

Wear a light-colored, well-ventilated hat with blue lining.

Avoid meats and other heating foods. Eat a plenty of fruit.

Wet the hair on the temples and top of the head often, but not behind.

Ladies should avoid the use of large masses of hair.

If the hot brain pressure is felt coming on, dash cold water on the face and temples, or in the absence of that, clasp and squeeze both temples with the fingers to crowd the blood back, and rub the back-neck powerfully to draw the blood from the cerebrum.

Where especial danger is apprehended, wear a cool, wet bandage around the forehead and head.

4. For the *Cure of Sunstroke* the great object should be to cool off and draw away the mass of congested blood from the front brain. I will detail the process which I adopted in a some-

---

* The use of the term *Coup de Soleil,* so difficult to pronounce by English speaking tongues, or of any other foreign words unless a more exact meaning is to be conveyed thereby, smacks of pedantry. If we cannot manifest our learning otherwise than by employing useless words, we are weaklings, sure enough.

what remarkable case on Fourth Avenue, New York, a report of
which was given in the N. Y. Daily Graphic, and I believe that
most cases, not only of sun-stroke, but of apoplexy, if taken in
time, could be cured in the same way, especially as I know of
many other cases which have been treated on a similar plan.

This man was supposed to be dead or dying, by his distressed
wife, when I was called in, and according to her account he had
already lain nearly three hours in a state of coma, brought on by
the intense heat.   To make matters worse his friends had
drawn him off into the darkest corner of the room, where was
the least air, and they lacked even the discretion to loosen his
shirt collar or any part of his clothing.   Hastily loosening his
clothing, I called for ice-water, meantime pounding him briskly
over his back, legs, and feet, and making downward passes from
his head.   When the ice water came, I put a quantity of it over
his face, forehead, temples, and top-head, but was especially careful not to put any on the cerebellum and back-neck, after the plan
which is frequently adopted, as this, by its contracting character,
would tend to deaden a great vitalizing center, and also to close
the channels of egress for the blood in its movement from the
front brain.   The ice-water caused him to start slightly and
show signs of life. But the great agency upon which I depended
was a pail of as hot water as could be endured, which I poured
from a dipper on the back of his neck and lower occiput, as he
was turned on his stomach and held out from the lounge, being
careful not to reach as high as the upper back-head.   This soon
started him into new life, he showed some slight convulsions,
vomited, and then rose up, exclaiming, " all right ! " and declaring that he was well.   I told him that he had better avoid business for a day or two, but he chose not to, and from that time
onward did not lose an hour.   The same hot water treatment is
also admirable for paralysis, apoplexy, brain-pressure, vertigo, etc.

XXII.   Sleep–Producing Elements.

1. There is great danger of making a mistake, in the processes for inducing sleep from the fact that the philosophy of
sleep is not generally understood.   This will be found explained
to some extent in chapter Tenth, VII, 1.   Intense action of the
vital ethers of the front brain causes mental activity and conse-

quently wakefulness. When these ethers are drawn off to other portions of the body, the front brain becomes quiescent and sleep is produced. The best condition for intellectual action and wakefulness is when there is a free and uninterrupted flow of pure and well oxydized blood, for such flow stimulates the activity of the mental ethers as they flow through the contiguous nerves, while the ethers that flow through the blood are also active. Such blood is also favorable to sleep in the time of sleep, as it causes a brisk action of forces in other parts of the body, which relieves the head. When, however, through impoverished or imperfect blood, or when from over-excitement of the cerebrum the front and upper brain become congested so as to blockade the free channels of these mental ethers, consciousness dies out, and what is called sleep (sometimes coma) ensues, but a very imperfect style of sleep it is, which serves but a poor purpose in building up the system. This condition is induced by opium and some other narcotics. From the following synopsis of the opinion of the London Lancet, it will be seen that even the old school of practice is beginning to repent of the use of one of their most common remedies :—

" Sleep produced by narcotics or so-called sedatives, is poisoned. Their use gives the persons employing them an attack of cerebral congestion, only differing in amount, not in kind, from the condition which naturally issues in death. There is grave reason to fear that the real nature of the operation by which these deleterious drugs, one and all, bring about the unconsciousness that burlesques natural sleep, is lost sight of, or wholly misunderstood, by those who have free recourse to poisons on the most frivolous pretences, or with none save the exigency of morbid habit. Great responsibility rests on medical practitioners, and nothing can atone for the neglect of obvious duty."

2. From the above it may be seen why opium, which has a considerable of the exciting principle of yellow and red, may induce sleep. Having a strong affinity for the brain, it at first excites that organ and gives animation of thought and feeling; when so much blood has been drawn there as to produce congestion, the sleepy feeling approaches. The reason why it tends to prevent diarrhœa, is that the heat of the bowels is drawn towards the brain.

3. While the blue, indigo and violet are naturally cooling and soothing to an excited brain and nervous system, and especially promotive of sleep, yet in cases of costiveness, the yellow light over the bowels, or substances charged with light through yellow chromo lenses (See IX of this chapter), often cause such action of the bowels as to call the excitement from the brain and produce sleep. In most cases, however, the violet and blue are the natural sleep-producing principles for an excitable or feverish brain. I would advise persons who are costive, and yet nervously excitable, to take yellow-charged water during the daytime and blue charged water on retiring. A warm hand on the back neck or lower spine, or a hot foot bath will assist in inducing sleep.

XXIII. PRACTICAL INSTRUMENTS FOR COLOR-HEALING.

1. Thus far we háve seen an overwhelming array of facts to show the marvelous healing power of light and color as a new and blessed reality which is just dawning upon mankind, and it will now be well to consider briefly some of the instruments by means of which this power can best be utilized. Having endeavored thus to crystallize the different color potencies into a therapeutical *science*, it is now important also to gain some hints on chromo-therapeutical or chromopathic *art*.

2. *The Material through which Colors are transmitted*, is a matter of great importance. There have been so many thoughtless directions with reference to this subject, so many mere assertions without proof, and entirely contrary to established laws, that it is high time some definite standard was reached. General Pleasanton recommends the mazarine glass, and this is colored with cobalt. Dr. Pancoast, in his *Blue and Red Light*, says : " 1. There is no special virtue in one blue pane of glass over any other of the same shade ; cobalt blue is the best, and glass colored in the process of manufacture, is better than painted glass, because the pigment applied externally imparts more or less opacity to the glass. 2. There is no special advantage in any particular method of arranging the glass in any particular sort of frame ; an ordinary sash placed upright in the window frame, is as good as any other frame in any other position. 3. The blue ray cannot be focalized—it refuses to be modified, or

changed, or concentrated by the most powerful lens," etc. Admiring these gentlemen for the interest they have taken in this admirable cause of light and color, I am sorry to have to differ totally from the above conclusions excepting in the matter of painted glass. *What is the use of colored glass excepting its power to transmit certain colors*, and why have not these gentlemen inquired into the colors which different kinds of glass transmit ?

3. *Cobalt blue Glass*, is brilliant to look at, and multitudes have purchased foreign *Mazarine Blue* glass at high prices in order to gain what was supposed to be some mysterious potencies, although American manufacturers are now making it equally well. But this same cobalt glass through which people fondly suppose that they are gaining the cooling, soothing principle of blue almost solely, transmits nearly every color in the spectrum both visible and invisible, hot and cold. " The spectrum obtained under this glass," says Prof. Robt. Hunt, was perfect from the extreme limits of the most refrangible rays down to the yellow which was wanting. The green ray was diminished, forming merely a well defined line between the blue and the yellow rays. The orange and red rays were partially interrupted." " The extreme red (thermel) forms a well defined circular image." (Researches on Light.) Sir John Herschel also has shown how finely the very hottest invisible rays below the red, the thermel, are passed through cobalt glass. The real character of the cobalt color-transmissions, then, is as follows : while it transmits the blue, indigo and violet, and the fine rays far into the invisible trans-violet, it also transmits something in the hottest portion of the prismatic scale, including thermel, and part of the red and orange. It is quite unfit then for a hot, excitable brain, or for a very sensitive and over-nervous person, and is by no means the best for inflammatory conditions, although it would be excellent for persons with some degree of nervousness from its predominance of electrical colors, and also with some dormant conditions of bodily function, especially if still farther aided by white or orange light. Thus far I have never had a single patient who could endure the mazarine colors long upon the head, and one lady, the wife of General P., who let them fall upon an inflamed stomach, complained of their heating qualities.

Contrary to Dr. Pancoast's assertion, too, I find by experiment, that the blue light can be brought to a focus just as readily as red or yellow light, although of course it does not form so brilliant a focus as the more luminous colors, and moreover as to "the special advantage of any particular method of arranging the glass in any particular sort of frame," the testimony of Mrs. Proessel, already given, shows that special methods have special advantages, and I shall soon attempt to show just how these colors should be arranged in order to the finest physiological effect in describing the *Chromolume*, the *Chromo-Disc*, etc. But first of all it is important to know the exact chemical properties which are transmitted through different kinds of glass.

3. *Deep Blue Glass*, colored by *Cupro-diammonium-sulphate*, or, in the old nomenclature, the *cupro-sulphate of ammonia*, ($N_2 H_6 Cu$) SO_4, has a rich deep color, and is the true vehicle of the color electricities almost entirely unadulterated by the thermal rays, consequently it should stand at the head of all the colors for the general calming and cooling of the brain, nerves, or inflammatory sections. It "obliterates all the rays below the green ray, those above it permeating it freely." "The most refrangible or chemical rays well insulated." (Hunt.) So far as I know there is no glass in the market of exactly these ingredients, although I have been able to get my blue chromo-lens made with nearly these materials.

5. *Deep Iron Green*. The description of this and other styles of glass is condensed mainly from Hunt's "Researches on Light." Glass colored green with iron oxide admits the violet, blue, green and orange freely, and some yellow and red. Is scarcely surpassed for its cooling electric effects.

6. *Very brilliant Copper Green*. Admits violet, blue, a small amount of orange, a fair amount of yellow, and a full amount of green.

7. *Violet Glass* (Manganese). The yellow rays nearly wanting ; red shortened ; green fades into black shadow, and all the other rays blended in an intense oval patch of blue. The chemical action extends into the trans-violet.

8. *Red or Pink Glass* (Gold). Very beautiful. The spectrum becomes an oval spot of intense redness covering the visible thermal rays, embracing thermel, and extending to blue.

9. *Red-Orange* (Silver). All the more refrangible rays decidedly obliterated, and even the green somewhat shortened ; but in the place of the blue and violet rays there is some red. The yellow and orange are considerably reduced, the red standing out in great brilliancy, giving the glass the general character of red-orange.

10. *Pure Yellow* (Coloring matter Carbon). Is lacking in the violet and indigo rays ; strong orange and yellow-green reduced—a weak blue—acts far up in the fine trans-violet rays.

11. *Yellow by Iron.* Transmits thermel, some red, considerable orange, strong yellow, small amount of decided green rays, some indigo. Gives the fine tonic effect of *refined iron.* I have given the colors as they are usually named. What is commonly called yellow is really nearer a yellow-orange in many cases. Numerous other kinds of colored glass are used, but space is wanting here, and these are the leading qualities.

COLORED SOLUTIONS.

12. *Thermel and red. Solution of Carmine in supersulphate of Ammonia.* Transmits thermel, red and lower half of orange.

13. *Yellow. A saturated solution of Bichromate of Potash.* Beautifully transparent ; red and yellow.

14. *Green. Chlorate of Iron and Copper.* Highly transparent, transmitting blue, green, yellow and orange.

15. *Fluorescence. One part of the Sulphate of Quinine to* 200 *parts of water* on a plate glass trough transmits the whole of the visible spectrum, and develops a " celestial blue " in the invisible trans-violet portion over a space about equal to the visible spectrum. When the solution is made stronger the violet is more or less cut off. Other fluorescent materials have been spoken of elsewhere.

16. *Blue. Cupro-Sulphate of Ammonia,* described in No. 4.

17. *Other solutions* can be made of material much the same as those given in the different colored glass, with a spectrum which must be similar. Very many other combinations, both in glass and in solutions, are practicable.

XXIV. HEAT TRANSMITTED BY COLORED SUBSTANCES.

1. The following table, prepared by Robt. Hunt, shows that the greatest heat is transmitted not by red or ruby glass, as might be supposed from the well known heat of red, but by the orange glass which transmits not only the red and thermel, but something of the electrical blue, thus adding another fact in proof of the principle which General Pleasanton's discovery seemed to verify, namely, that a small amount of electrical rays added to a mass of warm rays, causes a greater heat that the warm rays alone.   Next to the orange glass, a transparent substance trans-mitting all the rays gives the most warmth, then the yellow glass, then the red, while the green and some grades of blue glass are coldest in their transmissions, though cobalt blue is warmer than " *brown-red,*"—or more properly speaking very red brown.

COLORS.	COLORS TRANSMITTED.	HEAT.
Ruby (gold).	Red and thermel.	87°F.
Brown-Red.	Red, orange and portion of thermel.	83°.
Yellow. .	Red, orange, yellow, green and blue.	88°.
Cobalt Blue.	Violet, indigo, blue, some green, and some orange, red and thermel	84°.
Orange. .	Little blue, green, yellow, orange, red and thermel	104°
Deep Green.	Orange, yellow, green and blue .	74°
Clear glass (with a little water), all the rays . .		89°

2. Without the water in the last case, the heat would have been somewhat greater, though still less than that transmitted by the orange glass.   Other grades of glass, to be hereafter ex-perimented upon, will probably modify this table somewhat.   The foregoing facts show that a substance may appear to transmit yellow, orange, etc., and nothing else, judging by its main effect when the light shines through it, whereas the spectrum will reveal several other colors which are also transmitted.   Such facts do not signify that the pure red and thermel rays of light are not the warmest, nor that the blue, indigo and violet are not in themselves the coldest.   It is true, however, that any careful

observer can see, in what is usually called yellow glass, tints of orange ; in other words, its real color as it appears even to the unaided eye is yellow-orange. The coldest rays transmitted, as given in this table, are in connection with deep green, although of course a blue or violet equally deep must be still colder.

XXV. The Chromolume.

1. Having ascertained the color potencies which are transmitted through various hues of glass, as well as of fluids, we are now prepared to inquire how they should be combined in order best to harmonize with physiological law in the cure of human ailments.

2. *The Head and Brain.* In the first place the head being the positive battery of the whole system, and the brain having seven or eight times the amount of blood in proportion to its size that is averaged in other parts of the body, together with a great mass of nerve matter, its general tendency is to be especially warm and sensitive, consequently we need for its purpose the nerve-and-blood soothing colors, such as blue, indigo and violet, and the absence of the warm colors. For this reason panes of glass colored by the cupro-sulphate of ammonia already described (XXII, 4), would be most admirable for this purpose, especially as it gives free passage to the violet, indigo and blue rays, and almost entirely excludes the thermel, red, orange and yellow. The Mazarine blue glass, although handsome, is more heating as we have seen than other grades of blue, and therefore poorly adapted to the brain. Theoretically, the violet ray being the most refined and cooling, would naturally be the best for the head, but there is no violet glass known that can give us the pure violet without a goodly share of red, and this interferes with the best effect for most brains, for which reason the blue and indigo shades are on the whole the best. We will need, then, 12 or 15 inches in depth of the cooling style of blue glass to cover the head well, while its horizontal width may be about 15 inches. This we will form into a graceful ogee curve at the top, and for the sake of developing its power best will place a border of red orange, 2 or 3 inches in width, over its top and sides, to arouse its best affinitive action and give beauty of effect.

3. *The Neck and Thorax.* Joining immediately on to the

last named glass, we shall need another piece for the neck and upper thorax, reaching considerably over the lungs and heart. This like the other should be cooling in its nature, being over a somewhat excitable region, and yet can well tolerate a certain amount of heat, so under ordinary circumstances the mazarine blue glass, colored with cobalt, will probably be the very best which could be employed for that region. We will need about six inches of this and will border it with red, colored with gold.

4. *The Hypochondrium.* We come now to the upper bowels, including the liver, stomach, spleen, duodenum, etc., and constituting the central region of *digestion*. What color is most needed for good digestion? Two important substances are used in digesting food, gastric juice and saliva. The gastric juice being an acid, and consequently electrical, would have its action increased by the thermal colors, such as red and yellow, and the same colors would also stimulate the blood, muscles and nerves of the stomach, while the saliva, having the alkaline or thermal principle predominant, would have its chemical action increased by the blue or violet, which would also tend to counteract too much of the inflammatory action of the red. A medium purple glass transmits these principles and thus becomes par excellence the color for regulating digestion. Six inches of this will answer, and a border of yellow or greenish yellow, especially the canary yellow of uranium, will form its chemical affinity.

5. *The Umbilical Region.* The bowels are aroused into animation by the yellow color more especially, as has been abundantly shown, and a small strip of yellow glass three inches in depth, bordered by its affinitive violet, will be sufficient.

6. *The Hypogastrium and Loins.* For the loins and lower viscera, a green glass will have a fine tonic effect, and will be very soothing to any inflammatory conditions, such as cystitis, uterine or ovarian irritation, etc. Nearly every variety of green glass transmits the orange, yellow, green and blue rays. The yellow and orange will animate the nerves, while the blue will have a cooling effect and tend to constrict and draw up relaxed muscles. If the parts are dormant, yellow-green would be preferable—if inflamed and over-active, blue-green. A border glass of dark red will be nearly a chemical affinity.

7. *Lower Limbs.* For the rest of the way covering the limbs

and lower extremities, the warmest colors are most desirable, especially as these parts are farthest from the vital centres. Having ascertained that the warmest effect comes through the orange or red-orange glass, this will be the most proper material, while the mazarine blue and the cooler blue will be excellent affinitive colors for the border on each side. About 15 inches of this will be sufficient, as the patient should sit or recline while receiving the colors.

8. The whole of this combination enclosed in a walnut frame with metallic frame work inside for the different colors, I have termed the CHROMOLUME,* which means literally *color-light*. Its colors being arranged very much on the law of harmonic contrast, as well as according to the principles of chemical affinity, it constitutes one of the most beautiful ornaments imaginable for a drawing-room, or bed-room window, and certainly one of the best of all instruments for vitalizing, healing and toning up the human system.

XXVI. THE USE OF THE CHROMOLUME IN HEALING.

1. *Position of the Instrument.* The lower end may rest upon the lower ledge of a window, while a cord is attached to the upper end, and being passed through an improvised loop at the top of the window may come down and be held by the hand, or wound around some hook or nail at the side of the window. In this way the upper end of the chromolume may be allowed to hang some distance from the window or parallel to the window to make the light strike in the right place, or the whole instrument may be drawn up further towards the top as circumstances may require. An invalid chair in which a person may be placed at different angles would be desirable, but an ordinary lounge or rocking chair will answer.

2. *Treatment of Head.* A majority of persons who are in feeble health, or who use the brain too intensely, have the head too warm, and the liver, stomach, and bowels too dormant, and the

---

* From χρῶμα *color*, and *lumen*, light. Some may object to the union of a Greek and Latin root in the same word, but as we may thus gain so euphonious and expressive a term by the means, it seems quite whimsical to raise this objection. What are these two old dead languages good for except to be resurrected for use in the living present, in all kinds of combinations which are most concise and musical?

arrangement of the colored glass in the chromolume as already described, is just suited to such conditions. In case the brain

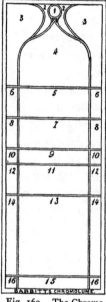

Fig. 169.   The Chromo-
lume.*

1. Light Yellow colored with silver for the disc, 3 inches in diameter.

2,2. Light colored violet, (Manganese.)

3,3. Red-Orange (Silver), 17 in. long.

4. The cool grade of blue 14 in. deep by 16 broad, colored by cupro-sulphate of ammonia, or similar materials.

5. Mazarine Blue, 6 × 16 in., colored with cobalt.

6,6.   Ruby red on the left and gold-red on the right, $2\frac{1}{2}$ × 6 in.

7. Purple, 6 × 16 in., Manganese and gold.

8,8. Light Greenish Yellow, $2\frac{1}{2}$ × 6 in., colored with uranium oxide.

9. Yellow, 3 × 16 in., colored with iron or other metal.

10,10. Deep Violet, $2\frac{1}{2}$ × 3 in., manganese.

11. Green, 6 × 16 in.

12,12. Dark Red, $2\frac{1}{2}$ × 6 in.

13. Orange, $16\frac{1}{2}$ × 16 in.

14,14. Light Violet, $2\frac{1}{2}$ × 16 in., manganese, etc.

15. Red-Orange, $2\frac{1}{2}$ × 16 in., silver.

16,16. Blue, $2\frac{1}{2}$ × $2\frac{1}{2}$ in.

* I have designed two sizes of the Chromolume, both prepared after the above design, the glass part of the larger being 57 by 21 inches, the inside column being 16 inches, and the borders $2\frac{1}{2}$ inches each in width, while the smaller is 53 by 18 inches, the central column being 14 inches, and the borders 2 inches in width. The larger can be furnished at $10, the smaller at $9, and an extra charge of $1 for boxing when they are to be shipped. What is called the crystalline style of glass, consisting of foliations over the whole surface, and being more beautiful and somewhat more effective than the glass in common use, will cost one quarter more when the border alone is supplied with it, and one half more when the whole frame is supplied with it. Those wishing a chromolume can address: BABBITT & CO., *Science Hall*, 141 *8th St.* (Near Broadway), *New York*. In very special cases of disease, by giving a brief and clear explanation of the symptoms to be treated, the glass in the instrument will be changed to suit conditions as far as possible. The glass for a chromolume may not always be found of exactly the grade or character of what is named above, but some of the choicest and richest grades that can be found will be provided. These instruments will be furnished only to order.

The CHROMO-DISC can be furnished, including five colors of crystalline glass, a lens 2 inches in diameter to concentrate the rays, for $5. The price of the crystalline glass is $1 per square foot.

and nerves, however, are in the negative condition which induces facial neuralgia and general coldness, the instrument should be raised a little, so that the face and ears at least should come in the range of the mazarine glass.

3. *Treatment on the Skin.* Decided benefit can be received from sitting in the light of the chromolume with the ordinary clothes on, much more benefit by sitting in a white garment or covered by a sheet, and still more benefit by allowing the rays to fall directly upon the skin. In this last case a person takes a full air bath as well as a color bath. With dark clothes on, the light is degraded into mere heat, although of a fine quality.

4. *Treatment of the Back.* After using the light in front for some time, the patient should turn over and let it strike on the back in much the same manner as on the front. If the back of the neck and lower spine and hips are especially cold, the patient should slip down farther into the warm rays, the upper spine and occiput coming under the mazarine glass, and the lower spine coming under the orange and green glass combined. By animating the occiput, and the cervical and brachial plexuses of nerves, reaching as low as the shoulders, a life-giving power is communicated to the arms, lungs, motor nerves, etc., which will prevent, or tend to cure, rheumatic, paralytic, or inflammatory conditions of those parts, while by thoroughly animating the lumbar and sacral plexuses of the lower spine, the lower viscera and limbs will receive a new life, and sciatica, lumbago, rheumatism, gout, paralysis, etc., be relieved. In female or other difficulties which cause the small of the back to be hot and weak, that portion should be under the green glass, and the hips, which are apt to be cold, under the orange. The green, which is one of the most cooling of all glasses will thus tone up the back, while the orange glass, by its great heat, will call away the warmth from above, and animate those nerves that give warmth to limbs and feet, which in such cases are generally too cold.

5. *White Light with the Colored.* In most baths of the chromolume light, it would be well for a part of the time *to have a portion of the body under the direct sunlight,* keeping the head in most cases in the blue light, or if even that is too strong for

a very sensitive brain, the light can be shut off altogether from the head, by hanging cloth or paper over the upper part of the instrument. If a correct anti-thermal blue glass can be found, such a precaution will not be necessary.

6. *If the bowels are habitually too free or inflamed,* the narrow strip of yellow glass can be covered up, and the body slipped down farther under the green, the tendency of which is cooling, anti-inflammatory, and constricting.

7. *For sluggish action of the kidneys,* tendency to dropsical affections, Bright's disease, etc., it would be well to have the junction of the yellow and purple glass come just above the small of the back, remembering also to have the white light fall on that portion for a time each day, especially the white and colored light combined.

8. *For Feverish and Irregular Condition of the Sexual System,* the green glass light should come over the small of the back and lower spine, the orange commencing at the lower part of the hips. This rule is of great importance, and will tend to save the patient from the fearful wreck that overtakes vast multitudes of mankind, and from a condition which, if not arrested in time, will baffle the power of all drugs to heal. It should be pursued perseveringly, days, weeks and months if necessary, for there is a quiet, deep-reaching and marvelous power in well regulated light to heal all such difficulties, as well as to build up exhausted nervous systems generally.

9. *Artificial light* may be used to fine advantage with the chromolume, especially if the lamp or gas-burner is directly behind the blue or green shades of glass. Such lights having a larger relative amount of carbon than sun-light, the yellow and orange principles are more active, which fact explains the cause of their being more exciting to the eyes and nervous system than the light of day, causing inflammation of the eyes (ophthalmia), dimness of vision (amaurosis), etc. Blue and violet light constitutes a beautiful balancing power for such conditions. (See Chapter on Vision.) The great advantage of being able to use artificial light, especially in a country like England, in which direct sunlight in winter is very scarce, and also during the darker portions of our own year, must be apparent to all. Artificial light has much the same character as sunlight, with the excep-

tion that it is feebler, less white, and more irritating, but when it is purified by being strained through glass, and its yellowish and reddish character offset by a certain amount of the blue and violet element, it can be made very valuable. The electric light has great power and purity. Although the light for general purposes may well be placed directly back of the blue glass, yet for special conditions it must be changed ; thus, for head-ache, sleeplessness, etc., place it back of the upper blue; for sore throat, and most lung difficulties, place it back of the mazarine blue ; for indigestion, back of the purple ; for costiveness, back of the yellow; for uterine or ovarian inflammation, back of the green, etc.

10. *A convex Lens for concentrating the rays*, hung behind any particular kind of glass, according to the part of the body which needs most power, greatly intensifies and hastens the action of the light, but this should not generally be done over the brain, or over the heart in case it is subject to palpitation.

XXVII. THE CHROMO-DISC.

1. Another instrument which I have devised, and which I call the Chromo-Disc, although not possessing the resplendent array of colors of the chromolume, and not, like that instrument, having the power to cover the whole system at a time, has some advantages as follows :

It concentrates the light at any portion of the body with several times its ordinary intensity.

It can be moved about with the greatest ease to any desired position.

It is admirably adapted to artificial lights, as it can be placed on a table, bureau or chair, and turned to any point of the body. It works equally well with sunlight.

It is supplied with the blue, the yellow, the red, the purple, and the opalescent white glass, which last admits all the rays in a softened refined form. The different styles of colored glass are all of the beautiful kind with foliated work, called crystalline glass.

It is supplied with a small lens two inches in diameter, so that in the case of tumors, mother's marks, or very dormant conditions, it may concentrate the rays with still greater power, or the

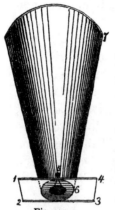

Fig. 170.
The Chromo-Disc.

lens may be used separately at times. Fig. 170 represents the Chromo-Disc. Diameter at the smaller end about 5 inches, at the larger end 15 inches, length 19 or 20 inches from 6 to 7 ; material, tin with a Japan varnish on the outside; 1, 2, 3, 4, is a frame about 5 by 12 inches, in which the glass is inserted so as to cover the small end of the disc, and will hold a white and colored pane simultaneously when desired ; 5, is an aperture through which the lens can be inserted when needed. It concentrates the light with about 4 or more times the ordinary intensity if kept bright. The portion of the body upon which the light falls should be as near the small end as possible to get the greatest power. The instrument complete with the five kinds of crystalline and opalescent glass and the lens can be furnished at $5. It can be held in the hands with the large end as perpendicularly as possible to the sunlight, or can be laid on a table and its ends raised by means of books or other objects so as to get it in exact range with the sun's rays or with artificial light. Under the hot rays of summer, shining directly into the disc without the intervening of windows, the skin can be rubricated in from 30 to 100 seconds on some tender portions of the body, while in a still longer time blisters can be drawn, although the latter style of violence should not be practiced on ordinary occasions. If, however, it should be deemed necessary to vesicate the skin in severe cases, the vesication caused by sunlight is much less injurious than that caused by the ruder drug escharotics. Vesication can be caused the most readily through the yellow or red glass, or without any glass at all. The chromo lens, however, is superior to the disc for purposes of vesication or for concentration of power.

XXVIII. General Healing with the Chromo-Disc.

1. *For Nervous Excitability, hot or Inflammatory Conditions, Fevers, Acute pains,* etc., the BLUE is the proper glass to use, as this admits the violet, indigo and blue, and a portion of the fine

trans-violet. Where the condition is somewhat dormant, and yet nervous, slip the blue glass along and let in some of the white light, at least a part of the time.

2. *For arousing the arterial blood, warming cold extremities,* etc., the RED glass is excellent, but should also have more or less of the YELLOW glass which really transmits a greater variety of warm rays than the red, as we have seen.

3. *For arousing nervous action, warming up and thawing out,* so to speak, *hard negative inflammations, and vitalizing a cold, chronic condition,* the YELLOW glass is best.

4. *For animating the venous blood, stimulating the stomach, liver, spleen,* etc., the PURPLE glass is best, although the yellow is very fine for the liver also.

5. In many of the above cases, the glass may be moved along a part or the whole of the time, so that the white rays may combine more or less with the colored ray, and thus add power and variety of effect. In case the direct white light is too strong, and especially in case of gas-light or candle light where there is no glass to strain the light of its coarser elements, the white glass can be inserted by the side of the colored glass.

6. For very sensitive places like the brain, the blue should be used, and the disc should be held six inches or more from the head so as to give a soft diffused light.

XXIX. Hints for Treating Special Diseases with the Chromo-Disc.

1. *Diseases of the Brain and Nervous System.**

For a *Very Hot Brain,* blue glass only. A wet bandage over front and side brain in emergencies.

Congestion of the Brain. Blue over the front brain, blue and white or purple and white, over the occiput (back-head) and

---

* In presenting this list I do not, by any means, give the only method that is useful, but the one that is the most directly indicated on general principles. Much must be determined from the patient's feelings and symptoms. It should always be remembered, however, that in dormant or chronic conditions, the thorough rousing treatment, which is required under any true method of treatment, must often bring up old symptoms, and in some cases cause uneasiness for days or even weeks before relief may come. In my explanations I shall aim to avoid technical terms and use as simple language as possible to be brief. By the term white, I mean white glass.

and cervix (back-neck).   (Feet in hot water.)   If the cervix is cold, use the yellow awhile.

Softening of the Brain.—Blue and white over the front brain, and at times blue and white or even yellow over the occiput.

Hydrocephalus (*Water on the Brain*).—Yellow and white over the occiput, also blue and white in front.

Facial Neuralgia.—Blue over temples, ears and face.

Heat of Spinal Column.—Blue, or blue and a little white.

Apoplexy.—Blue on front brain ; (hot water over the lower occiput and cervix, as in sunstroke, XXI, 4.)

Paralysis.—Yellow and white over lower occiput, also over upper and lower spine, purple over pit of stomach ; yellow over bowels.   When the spine is warm use blue.

Convulsions.—Blue over pit of stomach, as well as over the occiput, spine, etc.

Hysteria.—Blue over the head ; also blue, or blue and white over the womb, small of back and pit of stomach.

Sciatica.—Blue and white over lower spine.

2. *Diseases of the Respiratory Organs.*

Pneumonia.—Blue over the lungs, blue and white over the cervix * and lower occiput.

Pleurisy.—Blue and white where the pain is acute.

Hemorrhage of lungs.—Blue.   (Feet in hot water.)

Consumption— Tubercular and Chronic.—Yellow and white over the lungs, also over the cervix.   Occasionally use purple and white, or blue and white when too much heat exists, and when sleeplessness and hot brain occurs use blue on the head.

Bronchitis.—Blue and white over upper lungs, alternating at times with yellow and white ; the same over the cervix.

Aphonia (*loss of Voice*).—Yellow and white over the throat and cervix.

Croup.—Yellow and white alternating with blue and white over throat and cervix.

Sore Throat.—Blue in front, yellow on the cervix.

3. *Affections of the Organs of Circulation.*

Palpitation of the Heart.—Blue over the heart, several

---

* It should be remembered that some nerves of the cervix connect directly with the lungs.

inches off ; also purple over the digestive organs and yellow over bowels.

Fatty Degeneration of the Heart, or other dormant conditions ; red and white, or yellow and white. If the excitement becomes too great, use the blue.

Goitres and other *dormant Tumors* should have a lens and strong sunlight, or the red or yellow glass. Positive or hot inflammations should have the blue. Great cures can be thus wrought.

4. *Diseases of the Skin.*

Purpura (purple spots).—Yellow—sometimes the purple.

Nævus (mother-mark).—Has often been scattered by Mr. Augustus Barnes by sunlight focalized on the spot by a lens. I would recommend also some use of the blue glass to counterbalance the red principle, and at times the use of the red or yellow to scatter the same.

Erysipelas Red Pimples, Rash, and hot conditions of the skin generally indicate the counterbalancing blue principle, excepting probably such diseases as the *Small Pox* and other *Exanthemata*, which may be treated as in the next paragraph. Scabies (Itch) and other diseases in which parasites occur, need the blue, which, as will be seen in the next chapter, often destroys animalcules.*

Pustules, White or *Watery Pimples*, etc., should be treated, I think, with an alternation of yellow and blue glass, the former to animate and scatter the dead conditions, the latter to cool off the heated parts.

In diseases of the skin it is very important, of course, to attend to diet and have the liver, blood, bowels, etc., in good working order.

5. *Zymotic Diseases (Epidemic, Contagious, Endemic).*

Eruptive Fevers, or *Exanthems*, such as *Small Pox, Scarlet*

---

* In such diseases as well as Erysipelas and overheated conditions, I have often afforded the patient a remarkable relief by having him bathe with carbolic acid, a tea-spoonful of the acid being used to a quart or more of water. The carbolic acid seems to destroy the parasites developed by over-heat and excess of the alkaline principle, while pearlash, occasionally used, will destroy the excess of animalcules developed by too much acidity. A teaspoonful of pearlash can be used with a quart or three pints of water. All systems abound in animalcules, but when any part becomes excessive in its action, or out of balance, it is liable to have an excess of them.

Fever, Measles, etc., should, I think, have the virus well brought outward by the stimulating character of red or yellow. After this is well developed, the cooler principle of purple, then blue and white, and then blue alone can be applied to reduce the fever.

Whooping Cough.—Yellow and white, also blue and white at times upon the throat.

Diphtheria.—Blue over the throat and pit of stomach, and yellow and white at times on the cervix. Start the bowels into action in this and the other zymotic diseases by the yellow glass over them. At times rouse the throat with yellow.

Intermittent Fever, or Ague and Fever.—In this disease the negative condition of the system seems first to draw the heat from the skin to the internal organs, leaving the surface where sensation is most acute, in a chilled condition, after which the interior organs, becoming surcharged with heat, react and send a thermal wave to the skin, thus giving the burning effect of fever. Thus while the patient feels cold he is internally hot, and *vice versa.* Now as the *solar plexus,* stomach, etc., which are central portions of the visceral system, must be overheated during the chill, my plan would be to concentrate the blue light directly on that point, especially the pit of the stomach, where it can penetrate very deeply and establish an equilibrium, while on the other hand, during the fever, the same portion being too cold could be animated by the yellow glass, which should also extend somewhat over the bowels, as they are known to be torpid during the hot stage. On the same plan the drinking of very hot water during the fever, and of cold water (say lemonade) during the chill, would hasten the winding up of the disease very materially. When the head aches use blue glass over it, especially during the fever, as it will both soothe the head-ache and check the fever.

In *Atonic Fevers* in which the forces are negative, flowing inward too much, such as *Typhoid, Ship, Jail, Camp and Yellow Fevers,* the blue glass is most important for the head, perhaps the blue and white for the cervix, the purple somewhat over the stomach and liver, but the blue over the bowels if the diarrhœa is bad.

In *Entonic Fevers,* in which the forces are positive and inflammatory, flowing outward, exemplified by *Bilious Fever, Typhus Fever,* etc., bring the blue to bear strongly upon the head, especially the temporal and frontal region, the yellow upon the bowels, etc., as symptoms may indicate.

6. *Diatheses.*

Inflammatory Rheumatism, needs of course the blue glass over the inflamed parts, but especially on the upper and lower spine, the upper spine including the lower occiput, the cervix and the brachial plexus having a direct power over the whole system, and especially over the arms and hands, while the lower spine including the lumbar and sacral plexuses, rules the legs and feet.   Open the bowels with the yellow, tone up the stomach and liver with the purple, use blue sometimes over the heart, etc.

Chronic Rheumatism, in which the parts have become dormant and hard, and crooked by long standing, need the yellow over the upper and lower spine, as well as over the parts directly affected ; sometimes the red may be used, and if the excitement becomes too great, the blue and white may be used, or blue alone.

Gout should be treated on the same general principles as rheumatism, somewhat more attention being given to the kidneys, which may be quickened with yellow, while a nauseated or agitated stomach should be soothed with the blue, and hot painful toes with the same.

Scrofula, as we have already seen, is caused or promoted greatly by a want of light, as well as of pure air, to vitalize the lungs.   The stomach should be well toned up by purple, the liver by purple, and sometimes yellow, the bowels by the yellow unless they are irritated and too free, the lungs perhaps by blue and white and a careful diet used, consisting much of vegetables, cereals and fruits, rather than fatty and heating substances.   By all these instrumentalities the blood is gradually made pure and the system enabled to eject its morbid matter.

Goitres, and other hard negative conditions especially require the yellow, the red being sometimes substituted, while a lens to concentrate the rays intensely will make still quicker work with it.

Nasal Catarrh, having such close connection with the brain, would perhaps be more safely treated with blue and white than with yellow light, and a sensitive brain cannot endure even this more than five or ten minutes at a time when the catarrh is bad.

7. *Diseases of Stomach, Liver, Bowels, Kidneys, Uterus, etc.*

Gastritis, Nausea, and other *irritated* or *inflamed conditions of the stomach*, indicate the use of blue ; very dormant conditions can have the yellow, but purple is best in most cases for stomach and liver.

Constipation : yellow over the whole bowels, especially the left and lower portion and briefly over the liver and stomach. Ten to twenty minutes will suffice with the disc.

Diarrhœa: Blue over the bowels, and briefly over the liver and pit of stomach.

Worms : purple over the stomach, also yellow over the stomach and bowels.

Cholera Infantum, or *Summer Complaint :* blue over the bowels and spine, and sometimes over the head and stomach. This will be found very effective. Even sunlight on the whole body would be excellent.

For the Liver in the case of a dormant or sluggish action, use the purple and yellow alternately just over and below the ribs.

For Inflammation of the liver (*Hepatitis*), use the blue.

For *Dormant Kidneys*, as in *Bright's Disease*, etc., use the yellow and red alternately, sometimes inserting the white, just above the small of the back, but if the small of the back itself is hot, use the blue. When the kidneys are irritated or evidently inflamed, use the blue, or blue and white. Treat other parts of the system as symptoms indicate.

Diabetes : I would recommend yellow, or yellow and white over the kidneys, liver and lungs, blue and white for the lower bowels, while the brain, bowels, etc., are to be regulated according to the symptoms. When the region of the kidneys seems over-excited or warm, use the blue. This disease is considered incurable by drugs, but occasionally full baths of sunlight over the whole body, with bathing, manipulation, etc., to start the skin, correct diet, together with the above treatment, will be powerful to heal even this disease, from what I have learned.

Inflammation of the Bladder (*Cystitis*). Blue over the hypogastrium, yellow over the lower spine, etc. In Chronic Cystitis, however, yellow in front may sometimes be used.

Uteri Lapsus (*Falling of the Womb*). Blue and white over the hypogastrium, also over the small of the back. Make upward passes over the lower bowels.

Inflammation of the Ovaries : blue.

Deficient Menstruation: alternation of yellow and red over the hypogastrium, breast, and lower spine.

Excessive Menstruation: blue over the hypogastrium and small of back. Tone up the liver and digestion.

Hemorrhages, Burns, Wounds, etc.: blue.

8. General Suggestions in Healing.

While treating local diseases, the whole system should be toned up and perfected so that a disease may remain cured. Among the leading things to be done is to see that the bowels move freely and properly, to have the blood well vitalized by purple over the liver, stomach, and lungs, or when especially inactive, by yellow over the same, and to have a due amount of the out-of-door sunlight, pure air, and nourishing but simple food. Wonderful as are the healing properties of light and color, so gentle, so penetrating, so enduring in their effects, and often so potent when coarser agencies are worthless, we must not be so narrow-minded as to consider it a panacea for all ills, and when we commence using it deem it unnecessary to attend to bathing, manipulation, friction, open air exercise, food which is heating or cooling, or demulcent, or laxative, according to conditions, proper sleep or other important considerations. While I have endeavored to make the general principles of chromatic healing so simple that private individuals may accomplish wonders by themselves, yet such is the complicated nature of disease, that a physician will be necessary to direct the use of the different kinds of glass in many cases, but this physician, however, should be familiar with the foregoing principles of Chromo-Chemistry and Chromo Therapeutics, either from his own investigations or from the study of this work. It is the intention of the Author to write a work on " Human Development, Including the Philosophy of Cure and the Upbuilding of Man by Nature's Diviner Methods," in which the aim shall be to present many new, practical and simple plans for developing both the mind and body as concomitants to light and color, and also to crystallize into a science, as far as may be, the subjects of therapeutics and psychophysics.

The use of colored glass by itself can be used on the same principles as the foregoing which are pointed out for the chromo-disc, only of course it will require a longer time.

XXX. The Chromo Lens.

1. Taken all in all, however, there is an instrument which is cheaper, more convenient to handle, and exerts greater power in a short time than perhaps any other style of healing instrument which has thus far been invented, and that is the Chromo-Lens,

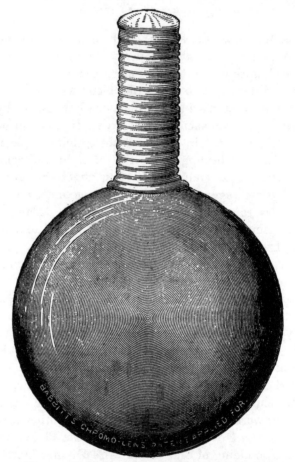

Fig. 171. The Chromo-Lens, one fourth of the actual size.

fig. 171. This I have had made of a pure crystal grade of glass, of three different colors, namely: the blue, of a character greatly superior to the mazarine blue in its exclusively soothing and electrical effects; the yellow-orange or amber-colored; and the transparent.

2. A remarkable fact with reference to these double convex

lenses is that they are hollow, the whole lens being five and a half inches in diameter, and one and a half inches through at the thickest point in the middle. Their capacity is about eight ounces, or half a pint.

3. Another remarkable thing about these lenses is that they are generally intended to be used only when filled with a liquid. This liquid may be water, and when thus filled, the more transparent lenses will sometimes ignite paper when placed in the direct light of the sun, 7 to 11 inches from the object, and of course would rubricate the skin in a few seconds if thus held, or vesicate it in a few seconds more.

4. The third remarkable thing about them is, that the substances placed within the colored lenses, and charged by the sunlight become medicated with an exquisite principle which is more gentle, enduring and far reaching in its effect than ordinary drugs. The simplest substance to charge thus is water, a dose of which may consist of from one or two teaspoonfuls to as many tablespoonfuls.

5. Two very distinct styles of power are developed by the aid of the lenses, 1st, by concentrating a certain color upon any desired portion of the body by holding the lens of that color in the sunlight ; and 2dly, by charging the water with a therapeutical quality in harmony with that of the colored light itself for taking internally.

6. The water will become more or less charged in a few minutes of good sunlight, but I usually hang my lens in the window and let the sun constantly rest upon it, although in quite hot summer weather, the water should be changed for fresh water every two to four days, especially that in the yellow-orange lens. The handle, of course, should be kept on, as it consists of a stopper as well as a handle, and protects from the full sunlight as well as from impurities. This handle is composed of a handsóme nickel-plated material which when screwed on brings the glass against a layer of cork so that the metal itself does not come in contact with the enclosed liquid.

7. Some *solutions* for the *Transparent Lens* are as follows, which I give without trying to astonish the reader with Latin terms or mysterious hieroglyphics difficult to be written, feeling confident that *pure water* would be just as effective if called by

its English name as if called *aqua pura*, that one drop would be just as much if written 1 *drop*, as if written 1 *gutta*, or 1 *minimum*, and that it would be just as accurately prepared if I should say *mix*, as if I should say *misce, misce cum aqua*, etc:

Solution for RED or slightly RED ORANGE :—

Sodium Salicylate. . . . . 2 grains
Tincture of iron. . . . . 4 drops.
Mix and fill the lens with water.

This is admirable for all cold and dormant conditions, being warming to the blood and animating to the nerves. It would be excellent for deficient menstruation if held over the lower viscera, more or less rousing to the bowels, and suited to dormant kidneys when held just above small of back.

Solution for BLUE :—

Cupro-diammonium sulphate. . . 20 to 40 grains.
Tartaric acid. . . . . 5 grains.
Mix and fill the lens with water.

If it is desired that a few of the warming rays should be transmitted through the lens, 20 drops of the sulphate would suffice, but 40 drops would make it more suitable for use over the brain or for an excitable nervous system. 25 or more drops of Ammonia would add depth to the blue. Another solution for the blue which will admit more red rays than the above is as follows :—

Solution of INDIGO. . . . . . . 25 drops.
Fill lens with water and filter if necessary.

A FLUORESCENT MIXTURE.

The following mixture which is more or less transparent to all the rays, being fluorescent, is remarkably attractive of the exquisite trans-violet forces :

Quinine Sulphate. . . . . 20 grains.
Dilute Sulphuric acid to dissolve it. . 20 drops.

For nervous persons soften with 10 grains Cupro-Sulphate of Ammonia, to give blue effect.

As the sunlight partakes more or less of the nature of that which it passes through, it must carry the effects of the quinine and sulphur of this mixture into the system receiving it, and thus have a refined tonic character, just as the first solution named above carries the effect of iron, sodium, carbon, hydrogen and oxygen, and is exceedingly animating.

Solution for YELLOW-ORANGE :—

Potassium bichromate. . . . . 20 to 30 grains.

Mix with the 8 oz. of water and filter.

Laxative, and animating to bowels and nerves generally.

8. The *Colored Lenses*, however, have a special value over the transparent ones, inasmuch as they are always *charged* with a beautiful, deep color and require only water within, which of itself becomes exquisitely medicated for taking internally when desired. Although the solutions which are yellow-orange and red may be used with much effect in connection with artificial light, the others need the more electrical light of the sun, which is proportionally less potent in the thermal colors, for which reason on cloudy days, or at night, they cannot so well be used. If we put water, however, in the real chromo-lenses, it becomes charged while the sun is shining, so as to retain much of its power for days or even weeks, and can be used at any time internally. This is a great advantage.

9. *Sugar of Milk*, of the granulated kind which will *flow* easily in and out of the lenses, is an admirable neutral substance, which when put into these lenses will store up an immense amount of medicinal power, enough in fact to make hundreds of doses at a time. These may be kept strongly charged by letting them hang up against a window, or even by letting them occasionally come into the sun. The only trouble with sugar of milk is, that the lens containing it cannot be used for bringing the light to a focus on the external system, and the sugar should not be removed from it unless it can be placed in some entirely opaque substance, or in a bottle having the same color as the lens. For this reason water is better, if a person is not going to travel and is willing to take a little more trouble in charging it every few days. To have the advantage of both, two sets of lenses would be necessary. When sugar of milk is charged it would be well not to have the lens full, as an occasional shake will bring the more interior portions outward the better to receive the light, although the light would permeate the whole by turning both sides towards it. I would recommend an amount as large as two or three peas for a dose. I caused a lady who had

been so agitated by a fever that she could not sleep, to sink into a very comfortable slumber by as much of the blue-charged sugar as would lie on the point of my knife, but the sleep became still deeper the next night by doubling the dose. She was delighted with it from the fact that it left no bad influence behind, as opium or chloral had done.

10. The *Blue Chromo-Lens.* After much trouble I have succeeded in getting a very perfect and beautiful blue, or rather what might be called an indigo-blue, very much in resemblance to *ultramarine,* for my lens. Nearly all blue bottles and vials, and most of the blue sheet glass of the day, are colored with cobalt of the mazarine hue, which, as we have seen, transmits a large amount of the hot and exciting rays, quite unfit for the best cooling and soothing purposes. To test blue glass, hold a burning match behind it, or any other artificial light and a strong reddish cast will be perceptible in mazarine panes, or a yellowish cast in some other styles, but the blue lens seems almost absolutely impervious to the red or yellow or other thermal colors, admitting only the blue, indigo-blue, violet and blue green, or the electrical hues. Portions of the lens as seen by sunlight have a violet cast, and I at first feared it might be caused by admitting the red with the blue rays, but on testing it I have not been able to force the least particle of red light through it, and even the violet light of an ordinary lamp is too coarse, or at least too feeble to pass through to much extent. It thus gives great purity of effect which is most desirable in therapeutics. The many cases which I have already enumerated of healing by means of blue light, or by blue and white light, or by objects charged with blue and violet light, show the remarkable value of being able to control this color especially in such cases as the following :—

All nervous and excitable conditions ;
Fevers, inflammations and hemorrhages ;
All conditions with a surplus of the red element ;
Diarrhœa and visceral excitement ;
Nausea, pleurisy, palpitation ;
Menorrhagia, or excessive menstruation ;
Points of acute pain, or too great heat ;
Neuralgia, headache, spinal irritation, etc.

In treating the head, especially on the front and upper part, or the temples, the blue only is a sufficiently soft and soothing color as a general thing, although in the case of some persons who have cold foreheads and dormant conditions from nasal catarrh, the purple or even the yellow may be ventured upon for a short time. In treating the body with the blue, the white light may be allowed to come upon the skin around on the outside of the lens, excepting in the case of erysipelas or extreme irritation of the skin, when blue alone is allowable. In *small pox, scarletina* and other eruptive fevers, it would be desirable to use the yellow-orange lens and a warm sunlight also, at first for a day or two, until the virus is brought outward, if the room is sufficiently warm to prevent catching cold ; then the purple may be used for a day or two, and then the blue to cool the fever. The general principles of treatment as explained under the caption of *Chromo-Disc* will apply here. The blue lens must not be deemed weak, because it does not burn like the others. It works with a quiet power. I may not always succeed in getting them made so free from thermal colors as the present stock.

11. The *Yellow-Orange,* or *Amber Colored Lens,* is rather darker than yellow-orange, and while admitting yellow as the leading color, admits also some orange and red and yellow-green, which last, being thermal, works in harmony with the rest. This lens will perhaps be deemed the most valuable of all by a majority of persons, having a vitalizing and warming power, and being especially adapted to such cases as the following :—

All cold, dormant and chronic conditions ;

All anæmic or impoverished states of the blood ;

All pale, sallow complexions with poor arterial blood

Constipation of the bowels ;

Amenorrhœa, or suppressed menstruation ;

Dormant liver, kidneys and lower spine ;

All hard, chronic tumors and negative inflammations ;

Bronchitis, ulceration of lungs, cold cervix ;

Paralysis, chronic rheumatism, chills ;

Despondency, stupid brain, dropsy, exhaustion, etc.

The white sunlight may also come in to advantage all around the lens on the person. There are very many cases in which the following condition occurs which may nonplus some persons : The stomach and epigastrium may be hot and irritated, thus calling for the blue principle, while the bowels are constipated, thus requiring the yellow-orange ; what shall be done? The blue lens could be held over the pit of the stomach, and the amber colored one over the bowels simultaneously, or at least during the same sitting ; or the yellow charged water may be sipped before each meal in the day-time, and the blue charged water on retiring, to soothe the stomach and bring sleep. This last plan is especially desirable with nervous persons who are costive and wakeful.

12. The *Purple Lens*, which we sometimes have made, is useful—

> For animating the venous blood which is purple ;
> For use over the stomach, spleen, kidneys, etc. ;
> For animating the blood without being too exciting.

13. The greatest heat will probably be produced by the transparent lens, as the other lenses have been made with too deep a color to transmit all of the rays which they are naturally fitted to receive. While this depth of color makes the lenses somewhat less powerful in concentrating the rays to a focus by refraction, it makes them all the better for charging the water or other substance which may be placed within. They generally prove as powerful as any one will wish to endure, if placed in a hot sun, and brought very near to a focus, especially when window panes do not intervene. The blue lens must be excepted from this remark, as the stock which I have thus far received may be focused upon the hand for many seconds without giving the least perceptible heat, even under the sun's most powerful rays. I have set paper on fire in two seconds with the transparent lens, and this without being able to bring it to a perfect focus. This will show its power as compared with the ordinary small solid lenses, such as will cost from $2 to $4, as they must be brought to several times as fine a point of light and heat before they can ignite paper. Under a moderate sunlight, however, it will not always ignite paper.

14. *Food* or *Drink* can be charged in a few moments by means of the chromo lenses, so as to have it produce different medical effects, according to the color used. I have known a single teaspoonful of yellow charged water to act as a laxative to the bowels, and if a person is constipated he could charge his bread or his beverage through the amber-colored lens for one, two or three minutes, or through the blue lens if the bowels are too free, or when nervousness or sleeplessness occurs.

15. The rock against which some skeptical or rash persons split when dealing with these fine forces, is the desire to have them act with a rude power similar to that of coarse drugs and to have an immediate effect. This will sometimes happen, and the patient occasionally becomes more than satisfied of it, wishing he had taken a little smaller dose of sunlight, but in many cases it works so gently as to be almost imperceptible,—2 hours, 6 hours, 12 hours or 24 hours after it is taken, but its effect is much more lasting than those of ordinary drugs, as it deals more directly with the fine nervous forces. Some are cured of costiveness gradually and effectively by the *yellow water*, and yet cannot tell just when or how it was done. Persons who have an active condition of the bowels, sometimes fail to perceive any effect from the charged water, at least in an ordinary dose, as positive forces seem to be met with·positive forces, and one gentleman, after having become cured of habitual constipation and made strong by its means, says it no longer has the same effect upon him. That is all right, for the affinitive conditions which once attracted it are gone and no longer need it.

16. Because the blue light or blue-charged elements tend to soothe and bring sleep, it must not be considered the only thing which can do this. The yellow-charged elements often give a very exuberant feeling, animating the brain, but in many cases they in a short time so animate dormant bowels without causing pain, as to draw the forces from the brain and thus induce sleep.

17. A small assortment of these lenses will constitute a little *drug store in minature*, a veritable *home doctor*, capable of drawing down from the skies those fine celestial medicines which penetrate softly and deeply into the human system, which work radically upon both mind and body, and which must save great suffering and many doctor's bills.*

18. Examples of the great healing power of the different colors of sunlight, or of substances charged by these colors, are given on page 290 onward and page 322 onward, etc.

---

* The lenses have burnished nickel plated handles which screw on or off at pleasure, and hold a piece of cork air-tight upon a glass screw that projects from the lens itself. The price of each lens, put up in a paper box, carefully wrapped, and supplied with a pamphlet to explain the method of use in different diseases, is $1. A solid lens of the same size would cost $6 to $8. The least outfit should have two

XXXI. The Solarium.

The ancients had small terraces built on the tops of their houses which they called Solaria, and in which they took their sun baths. Something similar but modified to suit modern wants would be admirable. A solarium could be built entirely above the body of a house on the roof, or could be arranged just under the roof in the garret where there is room. The glass in either case should be overhead in order to be exposed to the sun all day, and should run north and south or northeast and southwest, so that when a person lies under it, the head could be to the north or northeast. The glass could be arranged somewhat as in the Chromolume, only having the red-orange longer to cover limbs and feet, or it can be arranged as follows to good advantage, making up the main center of colored glass 15 inches wide, the first color at the north for the head being of cupro-sulphate of ammonia blue glass 12 inches deep, or at least deep blue glass which excludes red and yellow rays, then the mazarine blue 12 more inches, then 4 inches of yellow, then 8 inches of green, then 8 inches of red purple, and then 28 inches of red-orange for legs and feet. For the sake of a fine chemical action, place on each side of the blue panes a strip of red or red-orange glass 2 or 3 inches wide, on each side of the yellow, a strip of violet, on each side of the green, red or dark red, on each side of the red-purple, yellow-green or yellow, and on each side of the red-orange, the blue or indigo-blue (sulphate) glass. Beyond all of this on each side, the clear glass may extend all the way to a

lenses if possible, the amber colored and the blue. A much better outfit would be the amber colored, the blue, and the transparent, which if taken at one time will be put at $2.50, thus saving half a dollar. A still better outfit would be the two colored lenses and three more transparent ones, which latter could have three of the leading solutions made up ready for use at any time, and would be superior to the former where greater heat is desired. The price for these five would be $4. By a very oppressive and entirely unnecessary regulation of the United States Post Office department, no glass of any kind, however free from fluids, or carefully packed in boxes, can be sent by mail, and consequently must be sent by Express or otherwise. When ordered it would be well to send the money in a registered letter, or by a Post Office order, in which last case the Post Master should be requested to make the order payable at station D, New York. By thus paying in advance it saves the expense of the return charges, which would be necessary if sent C. O. D. Lenses having some slight indenture or other flaw, and having a cork instead of a handle, are furnished at 25 cents. Address, or apply to, Babbitt & Co., *Science Hall*, 141 *Eighth St. (near Broadway), New York.*

width of from 12 inches upward. A lounge can be placed directly under the colored glass lengthwise, or with the foot moved around one side a part of the time, so that much of the body can have the white light as well as the colored light. The children of a household should be sent up into the solarium for a play spell each day, and a plenty of pure air should always be allowed to come in when the weather is not too cold. The power, purity of blood and activity of the skin which children would thus gain, would be quite beyond most people's expectation.

XXXII. THE HYGIENE OF COLOR IN DRESS.

1. *White or light colored clothes transmit more light to the body than those of any other color, while black or dark colored clothes absorb the light and degrade it into the coarser principle of ordinary heat.* But the reader may say, Is not an object white from the fact of its reflecting all the colors? How, then, can it transmit them? The white reflects a large amount of all the rays, but all those rays which penetrate the interstices of a white garment sufficiently far, pass on as white ones beyond it from the repulsive nature of all the thread , while a black garment from its great affinitive attraction for all the rays greedily absorbs them and prevents their escape on the other side. A sufficient proof of this is the fact that a black or blue curtain will darken a room far more than a white or buff-colored one. But the dark colored curtain of itself will be warmer than the white one. The experiments of Dr. Franklin, in which he put various colored cloths on the snow, are well known. The darker the color of the cloth, the more deeply did the snow melt beneath it under the solar rays. But this did not signify that the black transmitted the heat most, but absorbed it, and the garment thus warmed melted the snow because of contact with it. If the cloths had been placed some distance above the snow, the light colors, *transmitting* the heat most rapidly, would have melted the snow the most, just as we have seen that yellow and orange and red glass transmit more heat than the blue (XXII.). The rule is that if radiant heat " be entirely transmitted, no elevation of temperature is produced in the body through which it passes," and the very fact that a body grows warm under the heat rays shows that

the rays are not transmitted, but absorbed. For this reason
black clothing is much more endurable in winter than in summer, as it absorbs and will not transmit the heat away from the
body, being in contact with it, while it also absorbs the sun's
rays and converts them more or less into heat. The fact that
black is a good radiator of heat does not change the principle,
for it radiates toward the body as well as away from it.

2. *As a tonic for the cuticle the full white light is doubtless unsurpassed*, for which reason light-colored clothing has
a more animating effect than the dark. A lady physician, who
for years superintended the ladies' department of a Turkish
Bath establishment, informs me that she can generally tell what
ladies have been in the habit of wearing black from the withered
appearance of their skin. A certain physiologist has declared
that he can cure any person of a cold by causing him to wear
white clothing for two days. The skin and its contiguous nerves
being thus made active by the light, the lungs, liver and kidneys
are far less burdened, and the external system becomes positive
and able to resist noxious influences. Of course bathing, friction
and pure air greatly add to this power. This animating principle
of light comes from the thermal rays, especially the yellow assisted by the red.

3. In a condition of fine health, white *underclothes* next to the
skin are doubtless best, as they transmit more or less of all the
rays. When a person, however, is very cold, pale and bloodless,
red drawers and stockings are admirable, and even red under-
vests, in case the system is not too excitable. Red stockings
are excellent, but if others are worn, red tissue paper can be
wrapped around the feet and the stockings pulled over them. I
have sometimes intensified the natural vitalizing power of red
tissue paper by passing my warm magnetic hand over it several
times, after which it has been able to warm the coldest feet, making some so hot in fact that the paper has had to be removed. The
same paper charged with white, and especially with red or yellow
light, just before putting it on, would warm the feet in a more
natural and penetrating way than the coarser heat of hot bottles
or flat-irons. For hot pit of the stomach, bowels or spine, blue
paper next to the skin and pinned to the underclothes would be
admirable, and this could be made still more soothing as a seda-

tive and nervine by charging it with light under blue glass. For an over-heated and excited system, however, blue or lilac under-vests of rather thin material are desirable, for although the blue will absorb the heat rays more than yellow or red, yet it reflects the cool electrical principle and has a quieting effect.

XXXIII.—THE GENERAL VAGUENESS OF IDEA CONCERNING COLORS.

1. The darkness which surrounds the subject of light is so great as to be easily *visible* to any thoughtful mind. In fact scientists of high standing, physicians, editors, professors, and men of general erudition in other matters, seem to be in dim eclipse as to the potencies of color and light as well as to their law of action. In this department they see men as trees walk-ing, and one color is about the same as any other, or as all others combined. For these thousands of years has the sun been send-ing its resplendent power upon the world, and painting its lessons upon all things, and yet men's eyes have not been opened to see them. They stand in the midst of an infinite temple whose pil-lars and domes link the heavens and earth together, and yet they treat the matter almost as indifferently as they would a dark cavern, and are ready to cast stones at those who, seeing more than themselves, attempt to lead others to witness the same. But as soon as men learn the great fact that the positive side of all force lies in *the fine* rather than *the coarse*, they will gradually cease their cry of " delusion," " fanaticism," etc., and finally be thankful that others have been able to lead them into nature's diviner pathways. Men must first be taken up with the crude and the tangible, and with the more material side of things which is all right, as this must never be ignored, but now, after all these ages of failure in reaching interior principles, it is high time that they should attempt something in advance. I will mention a few examples of popular opinion, admitting also admiringly the great achievements of our scientists in the external phases of this very department of late years.

2. *General Pleasanton*, of Philadelphia, himself not a scientist, but a gentleman of much practical common sense, has laid the world under a debt of gratitude for his very useful experiments with blue and white light, in the development of vegetable, animal

and human life, and for his success in awaking public attention
to so important a subject. To be sure this is only one small
side of the question, a kind of a one-idea presentation of the subject of light, but I am free to admit that if we were to be limited
to one simple combination of colors, it is as good as any other,
especially for our nervous and over-active Americans who get
thereby the soothing blue, and the diversified power of white light,
both of which become chemically intensified by being massed
side by side. He has shown by actual experiments, too, how
decidedly vegetation can be forwarded in its growth by a small
amount of blue, combined with a large amount of sunlight, for
which we must thank him. Having helped our common humanity
by means of experiments of so much value, we may easily for-
give the utterly amorphous arrangement of matter in his book,
and the many theories therein advocated which will scarcely
stand a crucial test. The danger consists in putting so much stress
upon blue as the pivotal color, and leading people to adopt in all
cases merely a single combination, which in some conditions of
disease must be attended with danger just as in opposite conditions it might be most helpful.

3. *Dr. S. Pancoast*, also of Philadelphia, has gone "one
better" than Gen. Pleasanton, inasmuch as he has ascertained
that there are two colors which have special potencies. " Red
and blue," he says, "are the only absolutely independent colors."
In his work just issued, called " Blue and Red Light," he has a
chapter of great value in which he gives ten remarkable cures
made under his own direction by means of blue and red light,
the most of which I have quoted in this chapter. In this color-
healing, being a physican, he has shown more discrimination
than General Pleasanton, and his results are perhaps more striking. The rest of his work will be considered of but little
value by most readers, being founded upon the old Kabbalistic
mysteries which, having pursued " for over thirty years," in connection with experiments of his own, have seemingly blinded
him to the far grander discoveries of the present. As a specimen
of his style, notice the following remarks : " All nature owes its
every form and feature of physical life to Light, the mighty unit,
not to seven rays. The ancients fully understood this, and they
never thought of light as seven rays riding through space on

seven broomsticks, or waving on seven distinct sets of waves ; they knew accurately and perfectly all that man can know of the secrets and mysteries of nature—of the essence and nature of light. * * *   The ancients knew vastly more of the causal world than all the scientists from Galileo or Newton to the present day have ever learned—incalculably more than the Tyndalls, Schellens, and other wave philosophers will learn for centuries to come, unless they go to these old sages and learn of them " (p. 68). Such infatuation of our author may be accounted for by his having turned square around from the on-marching hosts of the present, and setting his face towards the presumed gods of the past, has marched steadily towards them. Turning briefly to look upon the scientists of to-day, they seem to be far behind himself and the ancients whom he follows, whereas the probable truth is, he and the ancients are far behind them. Too many men are looking worshipfully to the past, and making progress, if at all, backward. The progressive nature of man must, on the average, make the present better than the past, the future better than the present. The ancients had many grand minds in their midst but they lacked instruments, such as telescopes, microscopes, spectroscopes, and a hundred other things which are absolutely necessary to exact knowledge. The printing press alone, to say nothing of the steam engine, the use of gunpowder which is the great peacemaker, the sewing machine and multitudes of other things, would overbalance in importance all of the inventions of the ancient world. But what has this profound wisdom of the past taught our author, as manifested by his writings? One thing which he asserts repeatedly is that *the whole physical universe has light for its source*, it being the universal motor, the one prime source and cause of every motion of the universe," etc. Men are ever prone to ride off on one wheel of the universe and forget all the rest. Thales declared that *water* was the principle of all things, Anaximenes traced all things to *air*, Heraclitus, to *fire*, others to *electricity*, etc. A knowledge of atomic law and chemical action will show that all of these elements and forces are merely sub-agents or wheels in the great machinery of nature, none of which have any creative action. Such reasoning reminds one of a musician who should seize upon a single string of his harp and declare that all the music is to be found in that, the others being merely inferior members, dependent upon the one. But I have not space here to refer to his many theories, and will simply notice an expression with reference to his favorite two colors :—" Two rays produce the two opposite forces, or principles of light —the red, the positive, polarizing, integrating force or principle ; the blue, the negative, depolarizing, disintegrating force or principle " (p. 267). That the truth is exactly the opposite of what he states here must be quite evident from his own admissions in other places, in which he shows that the red is the heating, and the blue the cooling ray. But as heat is the melting, burning, disintegrating, and depolarizing principle, then must the heat ray, which is red, be the same ; and as cold is the crystallizing, polarizing and organizing principle, so must the cold blue ray have the same effect. The Doctor's medical practice seems to be more correct than his theories, and I would have been thankful for more cases of his color-healing. Before leaving this book I would remark that I know of no ancient who had any but the crudest ideas of color. Aristotle called *yellow, white* and *black* the three primary colors ; Pythagoras had *yellow, red, white* and *black* as the primaries ; Plato supposed that an inward fire in the organ of the eye caused the effect of light, just as Pythagoras recognized a hot vapor emanation as causing the same. Such ideas would not indicate that even these greatest of the ancients " knew accurately and perfectly all that men can know of the secrets and mysteries of nature—of the essence and nature of light." It is folly to let " distance lend enchantment to the view," to such an extent that mankind are to be considered as moving on a *down hill grade ;* for if all the great men belonged to the past, the present must be imbecile in comparison, while the future must sink into idiocy and ruin.

4 The *Scientific American,* a paper with a deserved reputation in the philosophy of mechanics, but evidently quite uninformed with reference to the finer forces, has published a series of articles on the " Blue Glass Deception," as it terms it, which I answered at the time in the *N. Y. Evening Mail.* In these articles that paper presented an array of learned authorities, which, failing to designate the distinctive features of the different colors, and tearing down rather than building up ideas that are well

known and established, their general effect must have been to have deceived the public to a far greater extent than did General Pleasanton, whom they charged with the "Blue Glass Deception." I will quote simply one point as a specimen of its assumptions :—" In some instances where it is desirable to diminish the intensity of light, blue glass may be used; but any mode of shading the light, as by ground glass, thin curtains, would without doubt serve equally as well." In other words, according to this paper, blue has no particular potency, and acts simply as a principle of shadow, thus being a kind of superfluity in nature whose place is better supplied with black. It is high time that the *Scientific American* had learned 1st, that the blue has a great and special chemical power quite different from the solar rays as a whole, and quite different from other simple colors ; 2dly, that the blue developes phosphorescence, while shadow will not, the red will not, the yellow will not ; 3dly, the blue will develope germination while the yellow and red tend to destroy germination ; 4thly, blue light will dash a bottle of hydrochloric acid into atoms, while red, or orange, or yellow light, or shadow will do nothing of the kind ; 5thly, blue light will darken the salts of sensitive metals, as in the case of photography, whereas the thermal rays cannot; 6thly, blue is caused by fine vibrations which are cooling in their nature, as shown by the thermometer as well as by sensation, while the red and yellow are caused by coarser vibrations of a warming character. It is sad, then, that the public should be so misled by an influential paper whose words are quoted far and wide and whose authority gives weight to its utterances. The blue also destroys animalcules as will be seen.

5. The *Liberal Club* of New York, which meets at Science Hall, and embraces some gentlemen of fine attainments and real acumen, had a lecture and discussion on the Blue Glass Cure, some time since. The lecturer, though presenting many points of historical interest on the subject, made it his main business to criticize the positions of General Pleasanton. He, like some other members of the Liberal Club, had been misled by the sophistical arguments of the *Scientific American*, and on the whole, although many good things were said, the audience must have left with their ideas more mixed than when they came. The lecturer evidently could not see that one color had any special advantage

over another or over all of the colors combined, as signified in
the following language, when speaking of the healing power of
light :—"We do not believe that this is increased by any electro-
magnetism developed by the interposition of colored glass, for
the unmodified sun-light is capable of producing all the beneficial
effects which are now erroneously attributed to some added influence of blue glass." This is an assertion unsustained by facts,
and contrary to any correct deduction, as according to his own
experiments the full white rays of the sun coming through clear
glass were far hotter than those which came through blue glass,
or through blue and clear glass in equal proportions. Even if
we wholly omit the wonderful chemical powers of the blue, is it
not plain that its coolness alone would render it more suitable
for inflammatory or feverish conditions than the full power of
the sun ? The remark is often made that "we should use the
pure light of the sun as God and nature have given it to us."
This is very plausible and very delusive, for, as we have already
seen, although the pure white light is best for ordinary use, and
especially for well persons, yet in certain conditions of disease
the blue is best, in other conditions the yellow, in other conditions still the red or orange. On the same plan we may take
water as nature has furnished it, but is it not often best to take
hot water, or cold water, or filtered water ? It is well to take
pure air as nature provides it, but suppose the blood is badly
deoxidized and dormant, would it not be useful to take a little
oxygen alone at times to bring about harmony, or to have the
air changed to greater heat or cold according to conditions ? But
man is ever modifying nature in his food, sleep, clothing, medicines, and it would be the merest empiricism to attempt to restore
the sick by giving vegetables, meat, etc., in their ordinary unchanged condition. So in sunlight, one of the mightiest of all
agencies, we shall be empirical if we do not in one case administer the electrical rays, in another the thermal or luminous, in
another the concentrated rays, etc., according to conditions. At
the same meeting of the Liberal Club, a learned doctor arose
and advised the people to " cover the whole windows with blue
glass if they chose as a process of shading their rooms, but to
avoid the checker-board process advocated by General Pleasanton." Thus the people were counselled to adopt a plan which

would be positively dangerous in many cases, especially if it is to be occupied constantly. Seeing the blind thus ever leading the blind, until people fall into the ditch, and seeing a divine cause thus imperilled, by those who should understand the methods of human upbuilding, is my excuse for dwelling thus long on the subject, and for aiming to establish a definite system of rules founded on Nature, whose paths are ever those of peace and harmony.

A Word to Physicians.

While physicians are doubtless as noble as any class of professional people in the world, and perform many self-sacrificing deeds for the good of the suffering, for some of which they never expect any remuneration, yet like all other people, some of them have their selfish side and their *hard* side. While some grand natures among the medical fraternity are rejoicing in the newly discovered power of light, yet it is very common for practitioners to turn from the matter almost without examination and exclaim "fanaticism," "humbuggery!" Two things lead them to this course, 1st, if the people can thus heal themselves with light it will tend to destroy the physician's practice ; and 2dly, it seems impossible that so soft, intangible and noiseless a thing as light can have any special power to heal, and having been educated in the old medical rut, few have the force of character to enable them to get out of it sufficiently to examine an entirely new thing. As to the first point I would say, Fellow Physicians, dare we look into our mirrors and ask the person therein revealed, if he is so base a creature as to let the sick and suffering and discouraged humanity around him moan and die rather than have his income diminished ? If so, he is unworthy of the grand title of physician or philanthropist, and the world at large who are quick readers of human motives will gradually dismiss him and press onward to these "waters of life" without his aid. If, however, he can learn to put his whole soul into the upbuilding of his patients with a feeling that he *must* cure them, by whatever agencies of earth or heaven, he will not be allowed to suffer greatly even in his earthly ledger, while his celestial balance account will be triumphantly in his favor. The truth is that the

physician will often be needed for the scientific administering of
light, and this though unequaled in some things must also be
supplemented by other agencies and by the utmost skill that can
be brought into action. Even then he must find himself duly
humbled at times by cases which will conquer him. CHROMOP-
ATHY is based on eternal truth, and the sooner any great truth
is adopted,·the better it is for all concerned. As to the second
point, it should be remembered that the mightiest worlds are
wafted on the breath of gravitation which is incomparably more
intangible and subtile than light, and hence the exquisite and soft
character of a force should always be construed in its favor as
an element of power instead of weakness. It should be remembered that man occupies the highest scale of refinement in the
realms of visible being, consequently the elements which best
administer to him must be refined. One great advantage in the
finer forces, is that they animate not merely the physical nature,
but enkindle the mental and moral faculties into greater activity,
whereas grosser elements frequently quicken only the lower
animal nature. I appeal, then, to physicians in behalf of humanity, in behalf of their own ultimate success and their own
full-orbed development as men of power and skill, and truth, to
give loving audience to the great achievements of light and its
sublime source in the sky, whose chariot wheel is hinged upon
the heavens and must continue to roll on with its almost omnific power, however much puny man shall oppose. Mount the
great wheel-work of nature and it will bear you onward triumphantly : oppose it and it will crush you.

XXXIV. SUMMATION OF POINTS IN CHROMO-THERAPEUTICS.

1. *Chromo-Chemistry gives us the basis for the first time of an exact
and exquisite Materia Medica.*

2. *Chromopathy deals with more refined and penetrating elements than
Allopathy, Hydropathy, or Electropathy.*

3. *The power of Red to stimulate the arterial blood and arouse the
system is shown not only in drugs but in cases of healing by red light.*

4. *The red is injurious in over-excited conditions.*

5. *The yellow aided by some orange and red, is the central principle of
Nervous Excitement as shown 1st, on principles of Chromo-Chemistry;*

2dly, *by the potencies of drugs in which the yellow, etc., predominate, and* 3dly, *by the action of yellow light in disease.   Yellow is especially predominant in laxatives and purgatives, and combined with a fair amount of red or orange, forms the leading element in Cerebral Stimulants, Emetics, Diuretics, Diaphoretics, Tonics, Rubefacients, Emmenagogues, etc., the red being especially decided in the latter two.*

6. *The yellow is injurious in all over-active, nervous conditions, such as Delirium, Diarrhœa, Sleeplessness, etc., and is the most decided principle in poisons.*

7. *The Violet, Indigo and Blue are Refrigerant, Astringent, Nervine, Soothing, Anti-Inflammatory, etc., the violet being more directly soothing to excited nerves and the blue to excited blood.   This is proved not only by principles of Chromo-Chemistry, but by a large number of well known drug potencies in which these colors rule, as well as by these colors in light as attested by the treatment of many diseases.*

8. *Blue and Violet are contra-indicated in dormant, cold conditions, such as paralysis and many chronic diseases.*

9. *Substances charged with the different colors of light possess the same kind of potency as the direct rays themselves, as attested by various cases of disease treated therewith.*

10. *Pure Sunlight is the best for the general use of man and nature, is vitalizing to the general system, especially to the skin, and in warm seasons is particularly stimulating and healing.   Tumors, Colds and many other diseases have been cured powerfully by it.*

11. *The Lack of Sunlight induces a long catalogue of diseases, such as scrofula, impoverished blood, consumption, paleness, mental imbecility, etc., etc.*

12. *Strong and hot Sunlight is injurious to hot brains (as in sunstroke), weak and over-sensitive Eyes, etc.*

13. *We have seen that the color potency which each kind of glass transmits is not to be determined entirely by its appearance; thus cobalt (mazarine) blue glass presents a very deep and fine blue with an almost imperceptible amount of red to the eye, and yet as tested by the prism it admits blue, indigo, violet, green, orange, red and thermel, and is thus imperfect as a glass for the cool principle, while blue glass colored with the cuprosulphate of Ammonia would be far superior.   We have seen that although*

the red is the hottest visible color, yet that red glass does not transmit as much heat as the orange or even yellow glass; hence glass must be used according to the power it transmits, and not entirely according to what it appears to the eye.

14. *Blue and violet light are best for inducing sleep in nervous conditions, but narcotics have both thermal and electrical colors which first excite and then depress the system.*

15. *The Chromolume is a beautiful instrument, combining a series of various colored pieces of glass arranged on chemical and physiological laws, and adapted to the various organs of human beings, all of which are covered simultaneously.*

16. *The Chromo-Disc is an instrument which concentrates the rays mainly by reflection, and the Chromo-Lens another instrument which concentrates them by refraction, and both are intended to throw great power on any part of the body which may be the most affected, and thus develop a rapid action.*

17. *The general philosophy of Chromopathy will lead us to apply the electrical rays through blue or indigo glass for all inflammatory, feverish, relaxed, nervous and over-excitable conditions, to apply the red rays through ruby glass, to arouse the arterial blood, the purple rays through purple glass to animate the venous blood and the digestive system, the yellow and orange and red rays through yellow or orange glass to awaken the nervous system and kindle new action in dormant bowels, kidneys, lungs or in cold and paralyzed parts. The cupro-sulphate blue glass already described is the coolest of all; when combined with an equal amount of white light through white or clear glass it is warmer, but less warm than white light alone; the orange, especially the red-orange, is the warmest of all, and when combined with an equal amount of white light the effect is made more cooling. Of course solutions of different colors, or even thin colored drapery can be used in the place of glass. The same general principles as the above, applied differently, should rule in Dress.*

18. *We see, then, that every color has its own peculiar power, different from all the colors as combined in white, or from each of the other colors when taken singly. To say that each or all of the colors have pretty much the same character, and that none of them have any very special potency, as is too generally done, is to assert that the universe has been filled with a*

meaningless array of hues which are quite worthless except as they gratify human fancy.

19. *If these principles of Chromopathy are founded on immutable truth, physicians who oppose them are projecting boomerangs which shall rebound directly into their own faces and into the faces of the suffering community who are confiding their lives into their hands.*

We have thus in light, color and other fine forces, the basis of a nobler philosophy of cure which must rule in the future, from the fact that refined elements alone can be adapted to the higher nature of man, who is himself the most refined portion of the known universe.   The coarser elements of his nature can be built up with food or with what may be called *food medicines.*

If drugs are to be taken, only the purer and finer kinds should be administered, and these should be kept in bottles whose color is consistent with the nature of the medicine itself.   As this is a department of science in which our druggists and chemists themselves are very deficient, a hint will be in place here.   Alkalies, cathartics, emetics, diaphoretics, diuretics, and stimulating substances should be kept in orange or amber colored bottles, while acids, astringents, sedatives, refrigerants and soporific elements should be kept in blue bottles.   Even diffused light would have some influence in refining and increasing the properties of the enclosed drugs; but if the full sunlight, or even gaslight, could fall upon them for a time each day, their effect when taken would become more penetrating, refined and enduring.

In the chapter on Chromo Culture of Vegetable Life, it will be shown that the red is most active in developing the reproductive principle in plants.   From its power over nervous action, the yellow may be supposed to be most active in animal life, aided also by the red.   In proof of this, Dr. Downes and Mr. Blunt, in a paper read before the Royal Society, showed that yellow generates animalcules most rapidly, and red next,—that blue light destroyed animalcules, and even white light would prevent their forming.   We know the warm light of summer will generate insect life, while blue light will destroy it, from its axial principle.   In yellow fever and other malarial conditions of the system in which animalcules are abundant and produce putridity, blue glass must be invaluable.   See next chapter, VIII.

CHAPTER SEVENTH.

CHROMO–CULTURE OF VEGETABLE LIFE.

I. Review of Ground already Covered.

In Chapter Fifth on Chromo-Chemistry, the following departments of this subject, have already been considered :—

1. The law of Chemical Repulsion, by means of which certain color-potencies in the sun-light and atmosphere stimulate the same color in plants (XIX, 1).

2. The brilliancy of plants, and other substances, depends upon the amount of sunlight which they receive (XIX, 12).

3. The germination of Plants is brought about by the electrical colors through chemical affinity (XX, 9).

4. Chlorophyl, the green coloring matter of plants, is formed by chemical affinity (XX, 10).

5. The formation of the bark of trees (XX, 11).

6. The green coloring matter of leaves may be formed under the light of a lamp, but not under a Drummond light (XX, 12).

7. The development of flowers, and the perfecting of their reproductive principle, require both thermal and electrical rays (XX. 13).

8. Why flowers incline to the sun (XX, 14).

9. How the harmonic contrasts of flowers are developed by chemical affinity (XX, 15).

II. Germination.

1. *The Electrical Rays penetrate more deeply into the soil and cause more rapid germination, as well as more rapid sub-soil growth than the thermal rays, or than both thermal and electrical combined as in white light, or than shadow.* The reason of this rapid growth as explained under the law of Chromo repulsion (Chap. Fifth, XIX), is, that the blue principle of light

must stimulate into greater action, the same principle of plants, which is so abundant in their green parts, and it may also awaken their chemical activity, in connection with the soil which abounds in thermal elements. We have already seen that the electrical rays penetrate the soil more deeply than the thermal, because the affinitive thermal elements of the soil draw them on, and probably, too, because they are more fine and penetrating than the others. Robt. Hunt, after trying a great number of experiments with different colors, says :—"In every instance, germination was set up by the agency of the radiations, which had permeated the blue glasses in a less time, and at a greater depth in the soil, than in comparative experiments in which the seed was exposed to the full influence of light, and its associated radiations, as combined in the ordinary solar beam," and declares that "*the germination of seed is more rapid under the influence of the actinic (electrical) rays, separated from the luminous ones, than it is under the influence of the combined radiations, or in the dark.*" (*Researches on Light, p.* 224.) We have already seen that the thermal rays tend to impede or destroy germination, and most plants cannot germinate at all under the influence of the full white light, for which reason seeds and sprouts must be shut out from the light by being buried in the soil.

2. Mr. Charles Lawson of Edinburgh, wrote a letter to Professor Robert Hunt concerning the germination of seeds, which strikingly illustrates this subject. I quote the following from it :—

"It is our practice to test the germinating powers of all seeds which come into our warehouses before we send them out for sale. Our usual plan formerly was, to sow the seeds to be tested in a hot-bed or frame, and then watch the progress and note the results. It was usually from 8 to 14 days before we were in a condition to decide on the commercial value of the seed under trial. My attention was, however, directed to your excellent work 'On the Physical Phenomena of Nature,' about five years ago, and I resolved to put your theory to a practical test. I accordingly had a case made, the sides of which were formed of glass, colored blue or indigo, which case I attached to a small gas stove for engendering heat ; in the case shelves were fixed in the inside, on which were placed small pots, wherein the seeds to be tested were sown. The results were all that could be looked for : the seeds freely germinated in from 2 to 5 days only, instead of from 8 to 14 days as before. I have made some trials with the yellow ray in preventing the germination of seeds which have been successful ; and I have always found the violet ray prejudicial to the growth of the plant after germination."

The last remark should not be construed as meaning that the violet in combination with thermal rays, was prejudicial to the growth of a plant, but rather the violet alone. The violet or blue, may be made a means of intensifying the thermal rays when properly combined with them.

3. "The effect of red or calorific rays," says Prof. Hunt, "is to produce rapid evaporation from the soil, and the surface of the plants; even when this evaporation is met by an increased supply of moisture, germination is much retarded, and the young plant grows slowly, its leaves assuming a brown or red tint, showing that the chlorophyl—the coloring matter of healthy leaves—is prevented from forming" (p. 378). For fuller account of this process of germination, see Chapter Fifth, XX, 9.

III. Healthy Growth above Ground

Requires the thermal as well as the electrical rays, for with the electrical rays alone or in darkness, plants become tender and watery. Woody tissue consists of lignin and other of the harder parts of plants in which carbon, being a very prominent element, the yellow rays are of the first importance, being those which propel the atmospheric carbon into the plant, as was seen in chromo-chemistry, the yellow propelling the yellow. Experiments show that as soon as the first plumules (leaf buds) appear above the soil, it is necessary to have a plenty of luminous and heating as well as electrical rays. Professor Hunt's experiments show that the woody substance was formed most rapidly under a medium in which the yellow (luminous) rays were most abundant, next to which in power came a white medium admitting all the rays in abundance, then a red medium in which the heat rays were most active, and least of all a blue medium with the electrical rays in greatest abundance. "If the young plant," he says, "continues to grow under the influence of the rays which have permeated the blue, it will for some time grow with great rapidity, producing, however, succulent stalks which soon perish. Even in the earliest stages of growth it will be found that the plants grown in the full sunshine, or under the influence of yellow or red media, representing the luminous and calorific principles, give a larger quantity of woody fibre and less water than those grown under actinic influence." In Prof. Hunt's experiments through the blue medium, many thermal rays were admitted, according to his own estimate, or the plants could not have had the very rapid growth which he speaks of. It is not probable that plants could grow at all under mere thermal or mere electrical rays. Dr. Edward Newberry, of New York, has shown me plants grown under blue glass in which only a comparatively small amount of the thermal rays were admitted, whose growth had been greatly more rapid than those under white light, but their substance was very feeble and imperfect. In his experiments, however, with red-leaved plants, the blue retarded their growth, there evidently being too little of the blue element in them for the blue rays to act upon as a stimulus.

IV. FLORESCENCE AND THE REPRODUCTIVE FUNCTION OF PLANTS,

Require especially the calorific rays on the thermal side of the question, and an abundance of oxygen on the electrical. " I have rarely succeeded," says Prof. Hunt, "in getting plants to flower under the influence of any of the media which cut off those rays usually termed the calorific rays. For instance, under intense yellow, deep blue, or very dark green glasses, however carefully the plants may have been attended to, there was seldom any evidence of the exertion of their reproductive functions. * * By removing plants when in a healthy condition from the influence of isolated light or actinism, to a situation where they may be exposed to the effects of those heat radiations which are of the least refrangible class, flowers and seed are rapidly produced." (p. 237.)

We have already seen in Chapter Fifth, XX. 13, from the experiments and opinions of Priestly, Scheele, Ingenhousz, and Saus-

sure, that *flowers require more oxygen than any other portion of
the plant, and will not be developed without it.*   For this reason
they should not be shut up too much in close air, and must also
have heat and moisture for their finest unfoldment.   But mere
heat in its coarser forms will not answer, the grade of heat which
is manifested in the red color being necessary, as has been
shown by experiment.   "*If the red rays are obstructed, flowers
will not form.*"   The thermel also combines with the red in the
process of florescence.

V.   Blue and Transparent Glass for Hot Houses, etc.

1. While blue glass by the side of an equal quantity of clear
glass does not increase the heat within an enclosure, a large
proportion of clear glass, with a small proportion of blue combined, must add considerably to the heat, according to the experiments of General Pleasanton of Philadelphia, and according to a principle which we have seen to be true, namely, that
the greatest possible heat is developed by combining a certain
amount of electricity with thermism.   General Pleasanton con-
veys the impression, however, that an equal amount of blue and
clear glass causes a greater heat than clear glass alone, but
this is disproved by all experiments that I have ever known on
the subject.   We have seen that orange colored glass transmits a
greater heat than red glass itself, or even than transparent glass.
Why is its heat greater than that of the red glass as long as the
latter transmits red and thermel, the very hottest of all the
rays ?   Evidently because the orange glass transmits not only
these hot rays but a small portion of blue and green as an intensifying principle.   In the same way when General Pleasanton
arranges his Grapery with only one-eighth of his lines of glass
blue, and the rest transparent, the electrical rays transmitted by
the blue, seizing the contiguous and affinitive portion of the white
rays, create such a chemical activity as to increase not only the
heat, but the potency of all the rays, as both theory and practice
show.   It occurs to me that if a strip of red glass three or more
inches wide on one side of the blue, and of orange on the other
side, and then a half a dozen lines of clear glass would create a
still greater chemical power as there would then be masses of af-

finitive rays thrown side by side. If the red should be considered rather exciting, a yellow glass would perhaps be almost, if not quite equally good, especially to place on one side of mazarine blue glass, while the orange or red-orange is on the other side. Such an arrangement would seem especially desirable for conservatories in which the leading object is to develop flowers, as we have seen that the red principle which passes freely through both orange and yellow glass, is a necessity in floriculture. Where flowers are the leading object, another combination would probably be still better, namely, a half a dozen lines of clear glass, and then a line of red or red-orange glass, with a strip of blue on each side.

2. The *Heat* caused by having every eighth row of glass of mazarine blue, and then seven rows of ordinary transparent glass in the grapery of General Pleasanton, is described as follows in " Blue and Sun-Lights " :—" On the 31st day of March, 1872, I visited my farm to give directions to apply heat to start the growth of the vines in my grapery at the commencement of the season. The weather was very cold, patches of ice and snow lay in places on the fields, which the sun shining with great brilliancy was unable to soften or melt. In the open air, protected from sunlight, the thermometer (F) marked 34°, 2° above the freezing point of water. On entering the grapery in which there had been no artificial heat from fuel of any kind for the space of nearly a year, my son and myself were astonished at the great heat that there was within it. On examining the thermometer which hung on one of the middle posts of the grapery, completely sheltered from the sunlight, about 4 feet from the floor, we were amazed to find that it marked 110° F. Here was an increase of 76° of temperature over that of the outside air, and produced by a film of glass not exceeding one sixteenth of an inch in thickness, but associated as blue and plain glass. * * I have had occasion to observe since that date, that during the passage of strong sunlight through the blue and plain glass of the grapery, the temperature through the day within the grapery varied from 100° to 115° (F.), while that without, at the same times of the day would range from 32° upward to 60° or 65° " (p. 46).

VI. THE MARVELOUS VEGETABLE GROWTH

1. Caused by this arrangement of blue and clear glass is thus detailed by General Pleasanton, the account of which has already attracted attention on both sides of the ocean :—" On a venture I adopted (caused) every eighth row of glass on the roof to be violet colored,* alternating the rows on opposite sides of the roof so that the sun in its daily course should cast a beam of violet light on every leaf in the grapery. Cuttings of vines of some twenty varieties of grapes, each one year old, of the thickness of a pipe-stem, and cut close to the pots containing them, were planted in the borders inside and outside of the grapery, in the early part of April, 1861. Soon after being planted the growth of the vines began. Those on the outside were trained through earthen pipes in the walls to the inside, and as they grew they were tied up to the wires like those which had been planted within. Very soon the vines began to attract great notice of all who saw them from the rapid growth they were making. Every day disclosed some new extension and the gardener was kept busy in tying up the new wood which the day before he had not observed. In a few weeks after the vines had been planted, the walls and inside of the roof were closely covered with the most luxuriant and healthy development of foliage and wood."

"In the early part of September, 1861, Mr. Robt. Buist, Sr., a noted seedsman and distinguished horticulturist, from whom I had procured the vines, having heard of their wonderful growth, visited the grapery. On entering it he seemed to be lost in amazement at what he saw ; after examining it very carefully, turning to me, he said, ' General ! I have been cultivating plants and vines of various kinds for the last 40 years ; I have seen some of the best vineries and conservatories in England and

* To call Mazarine blue glass "violet colored," is a misnomer, and an error which is quite too commonly adopted by the public in general. The use of this word was corrected by the General in another place. I once inquired of a dealer in New York if he kept violet colored glass. He said he did and forthwith showed me some mazarine blue glass. I informed him that it was not violet. "It isn't, hey?" said he triumphantly, and forthwith lighted a match and held it behind it, as dealers are apt to do, thus giving it a reddish appearance near the light. I informed him that the redness came from the red light of the match, and that sunlight was the true test of color, holding it up to which only the sharpest perception could see any red at all. It is really nearer an indigo than a violet.

Scotland, but I have never seen anything like this growth.' He then measured some of the vines and found them 45 feet in length and an inch in diameter at the distance of one foot above the ground ; and these dimensions were the growth of only five months ! He then remarked. ' I visited last week a new grapery near Darby, the vines in which I furnished at the same time I did yours ; they were of the same varieties, of like age and size when they were planted as yours ; they were planted at the same time with yours. When I saw them last week they were puny, spindling plants not more than five feet long, and scarcely increased in diameter since they were planted—and yet they have had the best possible care and attendance ! ' The vines continued healthy and to grow, making an abundance of young wood during the remainder of the season of 1861."

2. "In March, 1862, they were started to grow, having been pruned and cleaned in January of that year. The growth in this second season, was, if anything, more remarkable than it had been in the previous year. Besides the formation of new wood and the display of the most luxuriant foliage, there was a wonderful number of bunches of grapes, which soon assumed the most remarkable proportions—the bunches being of extraordinary magnitude and the grapes of unusual size and development."

3. "In September, of 1862, the same gentleman, Mr. Robert Buist, Sr., who had visited the grapery the year before, came again—this time accompanied by his foreman. The grapes were then beginning to color and to ripen rapidly. On entering the grapery, astonished at the wonderful display of foliage and fruit which it presented, he stood for awhile in silent amazement ; he then slowly walked around the grapery several times, critically examining its wonders ; when taking from his pocket paper and pencil, he noted on the paper each bunch of grapes, and estimated its weight, after which, aggregating the whole, he came to me and said, ' General ! do you know that you have 1200 pounds of grapes in this grapery ? ' On my saying that I had no idea of the quantity it contained, he continued, 'you have indeed that weight of fruit, but I would not dare to publish it for no one would believe me.' We may well conceive of his astonishment at this product when we are reminded that in grape growing

countries, where grapes have been grown for centuries, a period of time of from five to six years will elapse before a single bunch of grapes can be produced from a young vine, while before him in the second year of the growth of vines which he himself had furnished only 17 months before, he saw this remarkable yield of the finest and choicest varieties of grapes."

4. "During the next season (1863) the vines again fruited and matured a crop of grapes estimated by comparison with the yield of the previous year to weigh about two tons (4000 pounds !) ; the vines were perfectly healthy and free from the usual maladies which affect the grape. By this time the grapery and its products had become partially known among cultivators, who said that such excessive crops would exhaust the vines, and that the following year there would be no fruit, as it was well known that all plants required rest after yielding large crops ; notwithstanding new wood was formed this year for the next year's growth, which turned out to be quite as large as it had been in the season of 1863, and so on year by year the vines have continued to bear large crops of fine fruit without intermission for the last nine years. They are now healthy and strong, and as yet show no signs of decrepitude or exhaustion."

5. The following is quoted from a letter of Commodore Goldsborough of the U. S. Navy, to Gen. A. J. Pleasanton, with reference to plants grown under alternate blue and clear glass : " In a very short time the plants began to manifest the effects of the remarkable influences to which they had been subjected. Their growth was rapid and extraordinary, indicating unusual vigor, and increasing in the length of their branches from an inch and a half to three inches, according to their species, every 24 hours, as by measurement."

In the above experiment there was evidently too much blue to develope hard and healthy conditions of the plants.

VII. PLANTS WHICH BECOME WITHERED AND PARCHED

By too much of the thermal rays, are properly revivified by the affinitive blue and violet rays.

1. Gen. Pleasanton gives an account of an experiment which Mr. Buist made with a number of geraniums, many of which

became sickly, some died, some lost their leaves, and others the brilliancy of their colors. "It occurred to Mr. Buist that if he should paint with a light blue color the inner surface of each pane of glass in one of his houses, having a margin of an inch and a quarter in width of the glass in its uncolored condition all around the painted surface on each of the panes of glass, and then place his sickly geranium plants in the house under this glass so painted, the vigor of his plants might be restored. The experiment was made and was successful. The plants began to revive soon after they had been placed in this house. In two days thereafter, they began to put forth new leaves, and at the end of ten days their vigor was not merely restored, but were more healthy and vigorous than he had ever seen similar plants of the same varieties to have been. Their colors were not only restored, but their tints were intensified."

2. "A lady of my acquaintance," says Gen. Pleasanton, "residing in this city, informed me that having some very choice and rare flowering plants in pots in her sitting room, which were drooping and manifesting signs of disease, she threw over them a blue gauze veil, such as ladies wear, and exposed them to the sun-light, when she was highly gratified to discover that in a very short time they were fully restored to health and vigor."

VIII. Insect Life as Influenced by Colors.

1. As the thermal light is a principle of reproduction in vegetable life (See IV.), it is doubtless the same in animal life, especially as it is well known that an increase of heat up to a certain point developes countless animalcules throughout the air and water, as well as in animal and vegetable life. This being the case, the contrasting *principle of blue must have the opposite effect and tend to destroy all insects which are the result of heat.**

2. This, and the following paragraph, I extract from General Pleasanton's work:—"A professional gardener in Massachusetts, near Boston, had been trying for several years to protect his young plants, as they were germinating, from various minute insects which fed upon them sometimes as soon as they were formed. For this purpose he adopted nearly every expedient of which he had any knowledge, and even used the primary rays of

* Since writing the above, Dr. Downes and Mr. Burns have confirmed it by showing that the yellow then the red develop animalcules most rapidly.

sunlight separately.   Nothing succeeded, however, in these experiments but the blue ray, which proved itself to be a perfect
protection against the attacks of these insects.   He made a
small triangular frame, similar in form to a soldier's tent, covered
it with blue gauze, such as ladies use for their veils.   Having
prepared a piece of ground, he sowed his seed in it, and covering
a portion of the ground thus prepared with his little blue frame
and gauze, he left the other parts exposed to the attacks of the
insects.   His plants outside of this frame were all eaten by
insects as soon as they germinated, while those under it escaped
entirely from their depredations.   This experiment was tried
many times and always with similar results."

3. "Having introduced blue glass into the windows of the
sleeping apartments of my servants in one of my country houses,
it was observed that large numbers of flies that had previously
infested them, were dead soon after its introduction, on the inside sills of the windows" (p. 3).

4. In the foregoing cases the "primary rays of the sunlight"
had no power to destroy the insect life, but the blue did have the
power.   This is still another fact which overthrows the assertion
of those uninformed people who declare that neither blue nor
any other color has any power which is not possessed by ordinary
white light.   In fact the ordinary white light of summer greatly
increases the amount of insect life.

IX.   Effects of Light and Shadow on Plants.

1. Many sensitive flowers and plants close up at the approach of darkness as if in sleep, and are awakened in the morning by the stimulating power of light.   DeCandolle showed that
artificial light will awaken them.   Constant shadow would soon
destroy the life of plants entirely.

2. Although color is much more negative at night than in the
day-time, other laws of force reign in full power during the darkness.   "When obscurity overspreads the earth," says Pouchet,
"all at once, every flower of the *cactus* displays its innumerable
long yellow and white petals, and its corona of 500 stamens
waves and trembles around the pistil, then its vast calix exhales
the odor of vanilla which perfumes the whole green house."

The *cacalia ficoides*, cited by Liebig, assimilates oxygen during the night, and by morning becomes as acid to the taste as sorrel. By the influence of the sun's thermal rays it loses this taste by noon, and becomes bitter by evening. Prof. Robt. Hunt and others have shown that even in the night plants do not wholly cease to emit oxygen. The upward radiations of the earth may assist in this.

X. Light of Plants.

Mademoiselle Linnæus first discovered that the flowers of the monkshood sent out passing gleams of light, which were generally attributed to electricity. This seems to be a kind of phosphoresence developed in connection with the vital electricity of the plant.

XI. Affinities and Repulsions of Plants.

Mathiolus spoke of the "friendship of plants." "Indeed," an old botanist says, "that there is so much affection between the reed and the asparagus, that if we plant them together both will prosper marvelously." "A kind of sympathy between certain plants has long been observed to exist, as if one loved to be under the shade of the other. Thus on the banks of our rivulets the amaranth colored flowers (inclining to violet) of the purple *loosestrife* (Lythrum salicaria), constantly adorn the vicinity of the willow. Other plants, on the contrary, seem to experience an aversion, one for the other, and if man inconsiderately compels them to approach each other, they languish, or die. The *flax* plant, for instance, seems to have an antipathy for the *scabiosa arvensis*" (*Pouchet's Universe, p.* 462). This seeming friendship among plants is doubtless owing to their chemical affinity, and their repulsions, to there being too much sameness of elements. Thus the loosestrife, spoken of above, in which violet is a strong principle, harmonizes with the willow in which yellow is a strong principle, just as we have seen that yellow and violet always form a chemical attraction for each other.

XII. Color as Related to Fragrance.

Alfred Russel Wallace of England has shown in Macmillan's

Magazine, that the flowers having the most showy colors are less fragrant than those which are white or pale or possessed of modest colors. This seems to have a kind of a parallelism to the fact that most birds having a gorgeous plumage are poor singers. "The sweet odors of flowers, like their colors," says Wallace, "seem often to have been developed as an attraction or guide to insect fertilizers, and the two phenomena are often complementary to each other. Thus many inconspicuous flowers—like the mignonette and the sweet violet—can be distinguished by their odors before they attract the eye, and this may often prevent their being passed unnoticed; while very showy flowers, and especially those with variegated or spotted petals, are seldom sweet. White or very pale flowers, on the other hand, are often excessively sweet, as exemplified by the jasmine and clematis ; and many of these are only scented at night, as is strikingly the case with the night smelling stock, our butterly orchis, the greenish yellow *Daphne pontica* and many others." He then refers to Mongredien's work which gives a list of sixty species of fragrant flowers of which more than forty are white and a number of others have greenish, yellowish or dusky inconspicuous flowers.

XIII. Adaptation of the Seasons to Vegetable Growth.

Prof. Pynchon in his " Chemical Forces," thus sums up what scientists have discovered with reference to the influence of the seasons on plants :—" There seems to be a nice adaptation of sunlight to the varying condition of vegetation, at the different seasons. In the spring, when the process of germination is going on, there is a large excess of chemical (electrical) rays, which, as we have seen, tend powerfully to hasten the process. The excess of the chemical rays at this season of the year, is proved by the greater facility with which photographic operations may be carried on. As summer advances, and the influence of the illuminating rays is required to promote the decomposition of carbonic acid by the leaves, and the consequent growth of vegetation, the quantity of the illuminating and heating rays both increase in a very great degree relatively to the chemical rays. In the autumn as plants approach maturity, and as seeds are to be formed and fruit ripened, the illuminating and chemical rays both diminish, and the heating rays are increased. This furnishes a very extraordinary and curious instance of design in nature. Advantage is often taken of these principles by the horticulturist in the cultivation of plants. When the seeds are to be forced, they are covered with dark blue glass, because this absorbs all the illuminating and calorific rays, and allows only the chemical rays to reach the plant. As the plant advances toward maturity, light is needed, and yellow glass is substituted in place of blue. When the period of maturity arrives, heat has become more essential, and red glass is employed in place of the yellow. In this manner the gardener closely imitates the changes in the composition of sunlight which are made in nature " (p. 264).

XIV. Summation of Points concerning Vegetable Life.

1. *For many things concerning the germination, growth, and chemical principles concerned in the development of plants and flowers, see Chapter Fifth.*

2. *The electrical rays penetrate the soil and cause germination; the thermal rays, or the solar rays as a whole, in most cases prevent or destroy germination.*

3. *The healthy growth of plants above ground require both the thermal and electrical rays, the solid and woody fibre being unable to form without the luminous rays, especially the yellow, to deposit carbon from the atmosphere.*

4. *The flowering, seeding and fruitage of plants are accomplished more by the red and thermel than by the other rays.*

5. *The heat of hot houses and the progress of healthy vegetable growth, is increased to a remarkable degree by a small amount of blue combined with a larger amount of clear glass.*

6. *Withered plants are often revived by blue rays.*

7. *The electrical colors which are transmitted by blue glass often destroy the insects which feed upon plants.*

8. *Light animates and quickens the action of most plants: shadow renders them more negative and is favorable to oxydation.*

9. *Plants are affected by the chemical affinities and repulsions of other plants near them.*

10. *Brilliantly colored flowers are less apt to be fragrant than those which are white or inconspicuous.*

11. *The spring time of the year is cooler, and consequently more electrical and better adapted to germination than the summer, while the summer and early autumn are better adapted to fruit and seed than the spring, from the force of the thermal rays.*

CHAPTER EIGHTH.

CHROMO–PHILOSOPHY.

I. THE PLAN OF THIS CHAPTER

Will be to present a few leading ideas concerning Refraction, Reflection, Absorption, Transparency, Polarization and some other points which, under the ordinary theories, are but dimly apprehended, while the general points of optical mathematics will be almost wholly omitted. These are already ably presented in various works, and it is important that I dwell somewhat upon points which should be cleared if possible of their confusion. The ordinary dynamic theory of force being only one side of truth, renders it about as difficult to get a clear perception of optical and many other facts, as it is to drive a carriage with one wheel, whereas a mere child can comprehend the leading ideas of the subject if presented in harmony with nature. Suppose we try to make a child understand the *reflection of light* by telling him that light consists of waves of some fixed ether which sometimes sweep obliquely against an object and then roll off just as obliquely away from it. He naturally thinks of waves of water, which will often roll up against an object and then break into all kinds of confused shapes, and of course scarcely gets the least correct idea of the movement of light. Tell him, however, that light consists of ether made up of countless little fire-balls which strike against an object, and bound off just as any other wonderfully elastic balls will do, and he has some conception of the matter immediately. Seeing a red object he asks what makes it look so red? The answer will be, because it reflects red waves of light and absorbs all the rest. But why does it reflect the red waves, and why absorb the others? The teacher now is nonplussed, for being unable to understand the matter for himself, much less can he explain it to another. The child, however, can

get some idea of the matter when he is told that all red bodies
have a little spring-work in each of its atoms which vibrates with
lightning speed and is of just the right size and style to dash the
fire balls of the red light in all directions, some of which coming
to the eye give the effect of red, while the other parts of the
atoms act as little suction springs to draw in the other colors
and hide them. The explanation of refraction, transparency,
absorption, etc., becomes very simple when explained on this
more natural plan which is in harmony with all things around
us.

II. REFRACTION.

1. The learned Dr. Eugene Lommel, Professor of Physics in
the University of Erlangen, presumes to put a final extinguisher
upon the theory which considers light as a material or fluidic
element, as follows :—" On this (material) view, refraction is
explained by supposing that the particles of a refracting medium
exert an attraction or influence upon the supposed luminous
substance, and the conclusion is arrived at that light propagates
itself more rapidly in the strongly refracting medium than in
the feebler one. The direct contradiction which is presented
by these opposite conclusions affords an opportunity of finally
settling the long contest between the material and undulatory
theories of light. Foucault has shown by means of very ingenious experiments that light does travel more slowly in water than
in air. If, therefore, the reasons formerly adduced should still
be considered to leave any doubt in regard to the nature of light,
there can now be no question that the undulatory theory must
be regarded as the only true theory of light." (*Light and Color,*
p. 237.)

2. The above man of straw, which the Professor has been
demolishing, has no real bearing upon the case, as refraction
has nothing to do with the slowness or swiftness of the propagation of light either in or out of the refracting medium. It seems
to me that the mists which have so long surrounded this subject
may be cleared away by the following explanation which would
appear to be a triumphant proof of the correctness of the etherio-
atomic law. A few words with reference to the nature of re-

fraction will be appropriate. In fig. 172, *si* represents a ray of light passing through a line of polarized atmospheric atoms to a piece of glass. At *i* the atmospheric atoms do not, of course, enter the glass, but their spirals striking it obliquely, find a harder and more resisting medium which gives a jolt to the ethers that flow through them, *bending* or *refracting* them farther towards a perpendicular line in the direction *ir*.

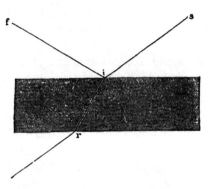

Fig. 172. Refraction and Reflection.

Having reached *r*, the atoms of glass pass the luminous ethers on into the less resisting medium of the air again, whose lines of atoms being more yielding than those of the glass are swung around a little at *r*, so that the pathway of the light is afterward exactly parallel to the general direction which it pursued from *s* to *i*, in case the outlines of the refracting medium are parallel.

3. But the refraction of the individual colors is seen in fig. 173, in which 1 is an aperture to let in a solar beam, 2 is the prism by which it is refracted, while the separated colors from the visible solar spectrum from red to violet, above and below, which

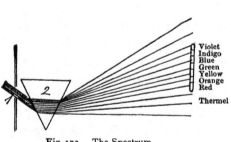

Fig. 173. The Spectrum.

Violet
Indigo
Blue
Green
Yellow
Orange
Red

Thermel

TRANS-VIOLET RAYS. Professor Stokes has traced these to a distance ten times as great as the length of the visible Spectrum.

THE SOLAR SPECTRUM, or range of the visible rays.

TRANS-RED RAYS. These have been traced more than twice the length of the visible Spectrum by Müller.

are the invisible trans-violet and trans-red rays that are many times more than the visible. How is it that all the colors are thus shaken apart, the red being refracted the least, and the violet the most of the visible rays? This is very easily understood if we remember that the color spirals of the atmospheric atoms through which the rays of light pass, become more and more fine and consequently elastic as they go from the red up to the violet, thus :

The extreme red vibrates 458,000,000,000,000 times per second.

„	Red	„	471,000,000,000,000	„	„	„
„	Orange	„	506,000,000,000,000	„	„	„
„	Yellow	„	535,000,000,000,000	„	„	„
„	Green	„	577,000,000,000,000	„	„	„
„	Blue	„	622,000,000,000,000	„	„	„
„	Indigo	„	658,000,000,000,000	„	„	„
„	Violet	„	699,000,000,000,000	„	„	„
„	H. grade of Violet		727,000,000,000,000	„	„	„
„	Extreme Violet		789,000,000,000,000	„	„	„

4. If the number of vibrations to produce an average thermel should be put at 425,000,000,000,000, then the upper thermel must have twice as many, or 850 trillions, as each octave of colors, like the octaves in music, must be made with double the number of vibrations of the one below it. This is in accordance with the supreme system and harmony which reigns everywhere in nature.

5. The waves of the solar ethers caused by these vibrations are so small that, in the case of the red, it would require about 39,000 of them to extend one inch, while the violet gives about 60,000 waves to the inch. Now suppose a fasciculus, or beam of light, to strike a glass prism diagonally, the orange spiral of the atmospheric atoms through which it comes, being finer than the red spiral, must jolt its luminous contents further one side than the red can do, while for the same reason the yellow spiral must jolt or refract its contents farther than the orange, the violet farther than the yellow, and the trans-violet still farther. Is not the separation and refraction of all the rays then beautifully accounted for in this way? And is not the whole process an almost irresistible argument, to show that the luminous ethers must come through elastic atomic channels in harmony with the foregoing atomic law?

6. Fig. 174 shows how the different rays of light are drawn to a focus, or rather to different foci by this same power of refraction. 1, 2, 3, 4, 5, are different rays of light falling upon a double convex lens; 3 is not refracted as it strikes the glass

perpendicularly; the electrical rays which are the most refrangible come to a focus sooner than the others at or near
the point E ; the luminous rays near L, and the heat rays near
H.   If, therefore, in using a lens, the greatest heat be required,

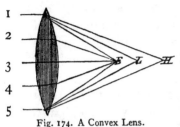

we must not expect it exactly
where the light comes to the most
intense and dazzling point, but a
little beyond; if we wish the
largest quantity of the yellow principle without the electrical rays we
must bring the rays to a luminous point on the object ; if we

Fig. 174. A Convex Lens.

wish the electrical rays also, we must bring the lens a little
nearer to the object, while for the trans-violet rays it must be
still nearer.   The more convex the surfaces of the lens are, the
shorter will be the foci.   Objects seen through a convex lens
are magnified ; those seen through a concave lens are diminished, exactly contrary to what is the case with objects seen in
convex and concave mirrors.

III.   THE REFLECTION OF LIGHT.

1. This will be treated of here in only its salient points, and
with a desire to correct some misconceptions that scientists have
fallen into on the subject.   *All reflection of light is caused by
chemical repulsion.*   But here the critic may meet me with such
words as these :—" Have you not said that the reflection of light
is simply the rebound of incandescent particles of matter, in
other words, of immensely elastic and minute fireballs ?   Would
you assert that the bounding of a ball is an act of chemical repulsion ? "   The bounding of a mass of matter called an India rub-
ber ball would not be chemical repulsion, in its ordinary sense,
because chemical forces deal with atoms and molecules, not with
masses as such.   In these phenomena of light we deal with
atoms and consequently with chemical laws.   But we may take
a reddish metal like copper, and when it becomes oxydized its
surface is dim because its atoms are but feebly active so that its
forces are influx and absorptive rather than repellant.   Let its
surface be burnished, however, and all its external atoms will be

thrown into the greatest activity, its animated spirillæ repelling the rays of light, especially those which are red-orange, into our eyes, and thus giving a flashing appearance. Again submit the same metal to a red, and especially a white heat, and the repulsion is much greater still, dashing the rays back into the eyes until they become almost dazzled. Exactly the same principle of repulsion or reflection of light exists when the copper is made to burn with a flame, for then not only the incandescent metal repels the light, but the incandescent contiguous gas which constitutes flame also. If we ignite strontium its flame repels red light, while ignited sodium repels a yellow-orange, ignited mercury a pale blue, ignited arsenic a beautiful lilac, and so on with all other substances which, when excited, repel certain colors in all directions according to which of the color spirals may have the most repellant activity.

2. The mistake of the scientists of the day seems to be that of supposing all self-luminous bodies to have the power of absorbing the very same colors which they emit, not realizing that a yellow flame is repulsive of the yellow principle just as much as is a yellow object which is cold, and even much more intensely so, while the same is equally true of all other colors. They admit the principle that *similars repel*, but here all at once they make similars attract and absorb each other quite contrary to all principles of chemical affinity. In making these remarks I am not denying that a certain fine element of each color may be, and probably is, received into the spirillæ of each atom similar to the coarser element that is reflected from these same spirillæ, but whenever a flame looks red it must be because the red spirillæ of ignited gaseous atoms repel the red ethers to our eyes, rather than transmit them through their interior channels, heat being especially repulsive. A knowledge of atomic action makes this subject doubly clear. That which has led to this error seemingly is the effort to account for the dark Fraunhofer lines in the solar spectrum. The luminous vapor or flames of different substances gives bright lines in the spectrum. Why, then, does the sun give a spectrum with dark lines perhaps in the very same places? They account for this by asserting that the luminous atmosphere of the sun *absorbs* the similar elements that are thrown out from the intensely incandescent surface of the

sun, the luminous sodium of the photosphere, for instance, absorbing the rays that are sent out by the still brighter luminous sodium of the sun's body, and so with iron, magnesium and other substances. To prove this they throw a sodium flame into the spectroscope, and it casts the double bright band of yellow-orange at D, but when they place a much brighter light beyond that so that the sodium flame comes between the bright light and the spectroscope, a comparatively dark line appears in the very same place, thus showing, as they say, that the sodium light has *absorbed* the sodium rays from the brighter light, and left a dark line where before was a brighter one. Had they but put the word *reflected* or *repelled* in the place of *absorbed*, how completely it would have harmonized with the principles of all known science, besides explaining the phenomenon in question on the most simple plan. Notice a little more minutely how this principle must act in the propulsion of solar light earthward. The sodium of the sun's surface, wrought up to an intense brightness by the immense heat and chemical action, propels in all directions with tremendous force the sodium ethers which are of the right grade of fineness to constitute the D grade of color in the spectrum. Sodium must repel or reflect sodium, iron must repel iron, etc. Nothing else in the known universe can systematically do this, otherwise the spectroscope cannot be trusted. As the fiery emanations of the sodium move outward from the sun's surface they encounter the luminous sodium of the photosphere, which at once repels at least its coarser particles towards the sun, being deprived of which the sodium line in the spectrum is shorn of its brightness sufficiently to be called dark. That grade of ether, however, which is fine enough to enter the sodium spirillæ must pass on to the earth and be represented among the luminous portions of the Solar Spectrum.

3. To show how eminent men are settling down upon this great error as an established fact just as they are becoming more and more persuaded that a mere dynamic theory of force is a scientific truth, I will quote the following from Schellen's excellent work on Spectrum Analysis:—"Ångström gave expression as early as 1853 to the general law that the rays which a substance absorbs, are precisely those which it emits when it becomes self-luminous. In the year 1860, Kirchhoff published his

memoir on the relation between the emissive and absorptive powers of bodies for heat as well as for light, in which occurs the celebrated sentence : ' The relation between the power of emission and the power of absorption of one and the same class of rays, is the same for all bodies at the same temperature,' which will ever be distinguished as announcing one of the most important laws of nature, and which on account of its extensive influence and universal application will render immortal the name of its illustrious discoverer." Tyndall also states that " a body absorbs with especial energy the rays which it can itself emit " (*Notes on* Light and Electricity), and scientists generally have adopted this form of expression, the tendency of which is constantly to mislead the mind with regard to the philosophy of luminous action. How important it is that our scientific men, to whom the intelligent world looks for guidance, should build upon correct basic principles.

4. All tangible substances reflect more or less of the rays of light ; thus, mercury reflects two-thirds of all the rays which strike it perpendicularly, while even water reflects 18, and glass 25, out of every 1000 under the same circumstances. This shows that even the so-called transparent substances do not transmit all of the rays. When the light strikes obliquely on a substance, the reflection is far greater. Thus, at an incidence of 40° from the zenith water reflects slightly more than a fiftieth of all its rays ; at an angle of 60°, one fifteenth ; at an angle of 80°, one-third ; and at an angle of $89\frac{1}{2}$°, which is nearly in a horizontal direction, nearly three-fourths. In fig. 172, most of the rays are received and refracted in the direction of *ir;* but a few will always be *reflected* in the direction of *if,* which forms the same angle with the glass as does the incident ray *si.*

IV. Absorption.

1. The absorption of light or color takes place in all substances which have a special *chemical affinity* for this light or color. This affinity attracts the rays into the substance itself so as to hide their color and yet not so strongly as to send them entirely through and beyond it as in transparent substances. One cause which prevents the rays from being transmitted entirely through a substance, is doubtless, in many cases, the presence of

transverse polarizations of the atoms, which establish counter and impeding currents, just as transverse and amorphous conditions in electricity prevent good conduction. Some examples will illustrate this point: thus a substance like soot has an affinity for all colors sufficient to draw them within the surface and present a black appearance ; snow has a repulsion for all of the colors and reflecting them all into our eyes gives the effect of white; blood has a repulsion for red, an especial affinity for blue, and a sufficient attraction for the other colors to draw them in out of sight, thus leaving only the red visible ; an orange repels the orange color and attracts all the rest, especially the indigo ; gold repels the yellow and attracts all the other colors, especially the violet, and all opaque substances attract and absorb all the colors excepting that which appears or is reflected to the eye, having necessarily the greatest attraction for the color which forms the chemical affinity of the one which is visible. In substances like colored glass it is the transmitted colors which are visible, while the rest are either absorbed or reflected ; thus in red glass the red color is much of it transmitted, while the other colors are either absorbed or reflected.

2. In substances which are gray, like the ordinary granite, a part of all the rays are absorbed and a part of all reflected, thus forming a compromise between white and black ; in *red-gray*, a part of all the colors are absorbed, and a part of all, especially the red, are reflected, the red being in predominance. This is less properly called *russet*. The same principle rules in *blue-gray*, which is another and more correct name for *olive*, the blue being reflected more emphatically ; also in *yellow-gray*, sometimes called *citrine*, in which the yellow is reflected more than the rest, etc. When the rays are all reflected rather feebly the effect must be a *dim-white*, or a very *light gray*, or *grayish white*.

3. It should be remembered that what seems to be a *violet* is not always formed by a single violet ray, but is very often in practice simply the union of blue with a smaller amount of red, just as a medium purple is the mixture of equal quantities of red and blue ; in other words the blue and red are reflected and the other colors absorbed.* A violet-colored glass, if it transmitted

* It should be remembered that no red and blue pigments on earth can ever be

only pure violet rays, would be the coolest and most nerve-soothing medium that could be procured, but it always transmits many red and blue and sometimes violet rays. Manganese violet glass transmits almost entirely blue with less red.   Orange very often is formed by the red and yellow combined, not by the simple orange ray, and green by blue and yellow instead of the single green ray as in the spectrum, for Helmholtz has shown that such colors in the spectrum are not formed by the over-lapping of two colors.

4. We thus see that while the *absorption* of colors is caused by chemical affinity, *reflection* is caused by chemical repulsion, or possibly, at times, by what might be called *mechanical repulsion*, or mere elasticity of atomic spring-work.

V.   TRANSPARENCY.

When a substance has such a strong chemical affinity for all the color-ethers as to be polarized and traversed in various directions by them, it may be said to be transparent.

If the colors are partly absorbed and partly transmitted, so that objects appear only dimly and imperfectly on the other side, it is translucent.   It is settled beyond question by scientific experiments, that we cannot get the effect of light through our atmosphere without the incandescence of the countless particles or luminelles which float everywhere around us.   The solar ethers and mere illuminated gases cannot give us the effect of light suited to our ordinary vision without the ignition of some solid particles.   How, then, can glass transmit light to us as long as these luminelles must be partially prevented from passing through it in connection with the solar ethers ? Perhaps by having an incandescence of its own atoms caused by the passage of these ethers.   The polarized atoms of glass must take the place of the polarized atoms of the air in conveying the luminous ethers and transmitting them beyond.

found which will produce, when combined, an absolute violet like that of the sunlight, or even an indigo, as the violet combines a fine grade of blue with a red of the next upper scale, which is too fine to be visible if taken alone, and the indigo consists of blue modified slightly by a red tinge, which belongs also to the upper invisible scale rather than to the lower red.

The oxygen and nitrogen gases, as existing in their expanded condition in the air, cannot give us any proper amount of light even when ignited by the solar ethers, but it is necessary to have molecules or minute masses of chemically combined or solid matter to give us this effect, or in the absence of that to have matter like glass, crystal, etc., which, possessing a powerful affinity for the luminous ethers, can be permeated and to some extent perhaps ignited by them. If the atoms of glass thus assume a kind of an incandescent condition, the reader may ask why do they not burn the fingers when touching it ? The careful reader of the foregoing has seen before now repeated examples of grades of heat which do not possess the burning character of the coarser style of incandescence produced by ordinary fire, as in the case of moonlight, or phosphorus, by means of which luminelles are ignited without appreciable heat. When the sun shines the luminous ethers extend in direct lines all the way to the sun that we may the better see it.

2. Prof. Tyndall says : " When a ray of light passes through a body without loss ; in other words, when the waves are transmitted through the ether which surrounds the atoms of the body without sensibly imparting motion to the atoms themselves, the body is transparent. If motion is in any degree transferred from the ether to the atoms, in that degree is the body opaque." (*Notes on Light and Electricity, p. 76.*) As our scientific men have a conception of only this one ether, and that a stationary one, they must necessarily make it a pack-horse for a great many theories which would at least be considered very strange if applied to anything else. Thus light must move with all its trillions of waves a second, sweeping through the ether, without awaking any action of the atoms over which and around which it moves. Are atoms so stupidly inert as this and yet the home of all the amazing chemical forces ? If hot light is thrown upon still water for many days we know a great change is taking place among the atoms, countless microzoa are generated, and putrefaction takes place, and yet its transparency continues through the whole. It is only the violent agitation which prevents the light from polarizing the atoms, such as in the twisted sweep of a vortex of water, or the effervescence of chemical action which at times interferes, at least in part with their trans-

parency.   But the opticians and scientists, having only this one
ether system to work with, must do the best they can, and, being
desirous of explaining all things in some way, have bestowed
upon it many shapes, many styles of power, many grades of fineness and coarseness of action, many thousands of colors, each of
which must have its own special size of undulation without any
known cause therefor, many degrees of swiftness and slowness
of movement, being the universal steed for carrying not only
light, but electricity, magnetism, gravitation, etc., as well as
having many grades of elasticity, so that they may get some
clue to the mysteries of refraction.   Tyndall, in common with
others, in his efforts to explain double refraction, says:—" The
arrangement of the molecules of a substance carries with it an
arrangement of the surrounding ether, which causes it to possess
different degrees of elasticity in different directions" (p. 102).
What should we think if any one should say that water when
saturating certain bodies, such as a sponge for instance, is
caused by the molecules of those bodies to have *different degrees
of elasticity in different directions*, or that the air, when permeating a bundle of straw for instance, is liable to become more
elastic horizontally than perpendicularly or obliquely?   When
the laws of force have been developed on a true basis, men of
masterly abilities, like Tyndall, Faraday and others, will not be
led into weak theories to explain the mysteries of things, and
will be able to penetrate still more profoundly into the arcana
of nature.

VI.   POLARIZED LIGHT.

1. I can only dwell briefly here on this intricate subject, the
phenomena of which must be studied in works on optics.   The
principal trouble in studying these works, however, is that attempting to square everything with the mere undulatory theory,
it is scarcely possible to get at the real philosophy of the matter,
and it becomes a difficult thing to understand.

2. Light, when passing through certain substances such as
tourmaline, or undergoing the ordinary simple refraction in certain
substances, or of double refraction in others, or reflection at some
one special angle, passes through a certain change in its character which is usually termed *polarization*, a term which is not very

appropriate, as all light must be propagated through polarized lines. In fact what is called polarized light, or heat, more commonly takes place in substances, the atoms of which resist in certain directions, the polarizing influence of light. The great Newton perceiving that such a substance as Iceland spar, from its double refracting powers, had two sides, considered that it must be polarized, something like a magnet which has its duplex poles, hence the name. I will mention briefly two or three varieties of polarization.

3. *Tourmaline.*—If thin plates of the crystal called tourmaline should be cut parallel to what is called the optic axis and placed side by side in the same direction, a ray of light striking them perpendicularly is able to pass through them both ; but when one is placed at right angles with the other, the light after passing through the first plate has become so shorn of its usual power, that it is unable to penetrate and polarize the second plate in which the atomic lines move differently. This is illustrated by figs. 175 and 176. This seems to come from the fact that light cannot polarize and penetrate the atoms of either plate with the same freedom which it could those of ordinary glass, on account of the rigidity of their atomic lines in certain directions.

Fig. 175.   Fig. 176.

4. Polarization of light by both *Single Refraction* and *Reflection* is illustrated by fig. 172, in which is a bundle of plates of glass that should have 16 or more laminæ. *si* is the unpolarized ray of incidence, falling on the glass at *i* at an angle of 56° 45' ; *if* is the reflected portion of the ray, and *ir* the refracted ; *ir* being at right angles with *if*, and both having that changed character which is called *polarized*. In fact all reflected light includes a portion of polarized rays which vanish from view if we attempt to transmit them at certain angles through an object. Light from incandescent bodies, such as hot iron, etc., is polarized under a certain angle, but flame lights are unpolarized, and as the sunlight is unpolarized, Arago concluded that the rays which we receive must emanate principally from the luminous or flame-like gases of the solar atmosphere which hide the still brighter incandescent surface of the sun. All rays reflected at an angle of 53° (53° 11')

from water, or 56¾° from glass, or 57° from rock crystal, or 68° from diamond, are polarized.

5. *Double Refraction.* Light passing through certain substances forms a double image, or is refracted in two quite different directions, and in different planes. Thus, fig. 177 represents a rhombohedric crystal of Iceland spar, upon which the light falls obliquely, making a double image of objects seen through it. The two lines of light constituting these two images

Fig. 177.   Crystal of Iceland Spar.

are sometimes said to be *oppositely polarized*, but they are doubtless swept off into the diverging lines of atoms, a part of the rays going into one line which they are able to bend according to the usual laws of refraction, while the other atomic lines are rigid and cause the light to bend in their own direction. This point may be rendered more clear perhaps by means of fig. 178, which consists of lines of atoms whose spirillæ pass around

Fig. 178.

them very diagonally. We will suppose that, by means of light, electricity, or some other force sweeping in the direction of 1, 2, the spirillæ of the layers of atoms in that direction should become so excited and potent as to draw the neighboring lines of atoms around in the direction of their own forces, or from 4 to 3. Such lines constitute *transverse diagonals*, as has been explained in Chapter Third, and doubtless have converse lines contiguous to them so that all the rays of light can be combined in the same direction. Suppose now, streams of solar ether should strike at 1 and 3, it is obvious that they would be refracted in different directions, the one not far from 2, and the other not far from 4, unless the atomic lines were so under the control of light as to yield entirely to its direction, which is evidently not the case with tourmaline, Iceland spar, and various other crystals. If we should suppose a beam of solar ethers to approach at right angles to the line 3, 4, and strike at the points 1, 3, is it not evident that it would deflect the line 3, 4, much more than it would the line 1, 2, from striking the former *squarely*, and the latter only obliquely? In other words, may not the line 2, 4, be thrown so far around as to cause what is called an *extraordinary refraction*, while 1, 2, is thrown into merely an *ordinary refraction?* Fig. 179, which I take from Guillemin's Forces of Nature, will

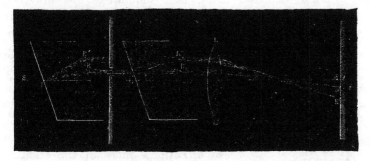

Fig. 179. The Polarizer and Analyzer.

illustrate this subject of double refraction and polarization. Light that has been doubly refracted by passing through one of these crystals, becomes so modified or shorn of some of its elements of power that it is said to be *polarized*. In the diagram, SI is a line of light which falls upon a crystal of Iceland Spar at I. It is there refracted into what is called the ordinary ray IR, and the extraordinary ray IR'. If we intercept one of the rays by a screen and pass the other through another crystal of Iceland Spar, it will be again divided into an ordinary ray I'R, and an extraordinary one I'R'. The lens LL' is used to concentrate the light upon a screen, while the second crystal is made to revolve and show the variety of intensity and color which its different positions produce. The first crystal is called the *polarizer*, the second, the *analyzer*, from the fact that it analyzes the light, and shows what modifications have been produced by the polarizing influence of the first.

Jonathan Pereira, M.D , F.R.S., author of a work on Polarized Light, seemed to have hit very nearly upon a true conception of the way the light is conducted through crystals in connection with atomic lines. I will quote his description of the refracting processes in connection with *selenite*, a crystallized hydrated sulphate of lime: "The optical structure of films or thin plates of selenite, having a thickness of from $\frac{1}{20}$ to $\frac{1}{60}$ of an inch, is very curious. In two rectangular directions they allow perpendicular rays of polarized light to traverse them unchanged: these directions are called the *neutral axes*. In two other directions, however, which form respectively angles of 45° with the neutral axes, these films have the property of double refraction. These directions are usually denominated *depolarizing axes;* but they might be more correctly termed *doubly refracting axes*. In order to render these properties more intelligible, suppose the structure of the film to be that represented by fig.

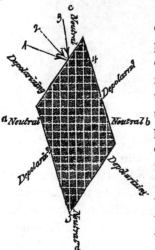

Fig. 180. Imaginary Structure of a Plate of Selenite.

180, in which the film is seen to be crossed by two series of light lines or passages, the one perpendicular to the other. These are to represent the neutral axes. We may imagine that in these directions only can the ethereal molecules vibrate. A ray of incident polarized light, whose vibrations coincide with either of these lines, is transmitted through the film unchanged. But a ray of incident polarized light, whose vibrations form an angle of 45° with these lines, or, in other words, which coincide with the diagonals of the square spaces, suffers double refraction; that is, it is resolved into two vibrations, one parallel with *ab*, the other parallel with *cd*, and therefore the directions of the diagonals of the squares are called the *doubly refracting* or *depolarizing axes*. But the two resulting vibrations are not propagated, in these two rectangular directions, with equal velocity, the one suffering greater retardation than the other; so that the waves at their emergence are in different phases of vibration." The foregoing will be understood much more clearly by those who have become acquainted with the working of atoms in Chapter Third.

There it may be seen just how atoms may combine into various rectangular, rhomboidal and other shapes with converse, transverse and paraverse lines of polarity, and that the transverse lines occur in one layer of atoms running parallel to each other, crossed at right angles by a similar layer of other atoms. It is then apparent just how rays of light, striking in the direction of arrow No. 2, fig. 180, would be about equally divided in the two atomic channels running towards 4 and 5, with the exception that refraction must somewhat modify these lines in direction. It is evident, too, that rays in the direction of arrow 1 must be projected in greater abundance towards 4 than 5, and thus make the former more luminous, while those in harmony with arrow 3 would pass more largely towards 5 than 4, thus making the latter more luminous and the former more feeble. It can easily be seen, then, just why such a crystal gradually rotated must constantly be changing its intensity of light until one dies out altogether. The unreasonable idea that a stationary ether retards the progress of light in one direction more than in the other, and this from its greater elasticity in different parts of the crystal or in different directions, should not be held for a moment, as long as double refraction can so easily be accounted for on principles in harmony with nature. Fig. 178 will also illustrate this point.

6. Polarized rays are the means of developing many beautiful combinations of color by means of refraction.

VII. The Undulatory Theory.

1. We have already seen in Chapter Second and elsewhere how utterly incompetent is the undulatory theory of light to account for many of the phenomena of light and color. That the light sweeps through cosmic ether and the earth's atmosphere is quite evident, and that both the ether and atmosphere must be subject to many undulations from the passing of comets, worlds, nebulous matter, and meteorological conditions, just as water is subject to waves when a vessel sweeps through it, is also evident; but what has that to do with the question of whether light is a substance or not a substance? The phenomena of interference, as well as other phenomena, may take place

from these atmospheric waves, and also, possibly, from the spiral waves of fluid ether as they emerge from a line of atoms. If the different colors are caused simply by waves of different size and frequency, as our theorists suppose, how is it that some waves are warm and exciting and expanding like the red, while others are cool and contracting like the blue? What power in heaven or earth can formulate waves of the exact size and rapidity to constitute red, and what to constitute violet, or the countless other tints and shades which must have their exact processes

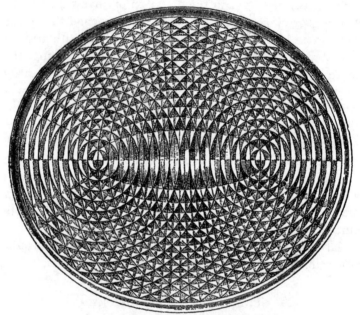

Fig. 181. Propagation and Reflection of Liquid Waves.

and their exact sizes kept up through all the millions of miles which constitute their path-way in space? By the etherio-atomic law we may see how the definite size of the spiral color-channels regulates the color, with just such a number of vibrations which can be continued from the distant stars to our earth. If the polarized lines become broken by means of atmospheric waves, they are formed again with lightning-speed, and so the light is uninterrupted.

2. Every boy knows that when different stones are thrown into the water near each other, the waves thus aroused more or

less impede or obliterate each other. He knows, too, that winds
and counter currents will soon entirely destroy the forms of any
waves which may be started, so far as any perceptible effect is
concerned. If light and color depend upon such wave conditions
which have to pass through the tempests of the upper sky, and
the countless eddies which may be supposed to exist in the cosmic ether, the chance for illumination in this world would be
rather uncertain. And yet scientists have striven to believe
that because counterwaves of a gentle character can pass each
other, and retain to a considerable extent their identity for a
little while, so can luminous waves of ether start from the sun's
surface, and, passing unimpaired through the boiling maëlstroms
and tempests of the solar atmosphere, which are a thousand
times more fierce than the maddest billows of the ocean, finally
break in undisturbed peace on our earthly shores with every color
effect occupying its exact proportions in the solar spectrum!
The dynamic theorists seem to find comfort in the pretty experiment of the physicist, M. Weber,
represented by fig. 181, which represents an elliptical dish of mercury.
In one focus of its ellipse, a drop
of the fluid is allowed to fall which,
spreading over its calm surface in con-
centric waves, is reflected from the
other end in a series of waves which
encircle the other focus much as
though a drop of the liquid had been

Fig. 182. Billows.

allowed to fall there also. This wave movement in a quiet enclosed dish is quite a different thing from the stormy undulations
which take place in the fields of space. Take even a tempest
on the ocean, which is as nothing in comparison with what is
constantly occurring in the sun's atmosphere, and what becomes
of any regular system of undulations. Fig. 182 correctly represents a storm at sea. Fig. 183 gives a feeble representation
of a solar cyclone, as observed by Secchi.

    3. Those who insist that colors are formed by different
sized waves of ether, exactly as sound is, should tell just how
it is that 39,000 waves to an inch are formulated by the sun
to produce the effect of red, or 44,000 to produce yellow, or

51,000 to produce blue, or 60,000 to produce dark violet.   In
music, the pitch of high or low tones depends upon short or
long waves, and these depend upon a small or large tube in such
instruments as flutes, whistles, etc., or upon small or large chords
or other vibratory arrangements by which an exact size of undulations are produced.   Per-
haps our dynamists will yet
decide that there is an infinite
number of invisible whistles
distributed all around the sun,
or around all gas lights, or can-
dles, to formulate waves of the
right size for violet, and whistles of a still larger size for
yellow, and so on.   At any rate
there is a wonderful precision
and beauty of effect brought

Fig. 183.   A Solar Cyclone. May 5,
1857 (Secchi).

about by some process, and we ought to know how this can be
done before being too positive in our theories.

4. "Do not several sorts of rays," says Newton, "make vibrations of several bignesses which, according to their bignesses,
excite sensations of several colors, much after the manner that
the vibrations of the air, according to their bignesses, excite sensations of several sounds?" ("Optics, by Sir Isaac Newton,
Kn't, 3d Edition, p. 320.")   This remark by the great Newton has
been re-echoed all along down through the two centuries since
his day, and has a side of truth in it.   But it should be understood that it is not entirely the wave action, or the up and down
movement even in sounds, that makes its impression upon the
mind as sound, but rather the rhythmic flow of electricities which
become intensified at regular intervals by the condensation of
air, as in fig. 184, which I copy from Guillemin's Forces of

Fig. 184. Undulations.

able to pass on through hundreds of miles of wire, unattended by its aerial body until it reaches its destination, when it again assumes its atmospheric clothing as a help-meet for reaching the ear so strongly as to affect human consciousness. Light also uses the air, not in the masses of atoms, which constitute waves, but in lines of single atoms, the different sized spirillæ of which constitute their distinctive *principles* of power as colors, When the sound-waves reach the ear, the air stops mainly at the tympanum, but the interior electrical ethers pass on to the membranous labyrinth and scala media, and there give the impression of sound. When light passes on to the eye, its conducting air lines stop at the cornea, but the luminous ether within passes on to the retina, and there impresses the pictures of the outward world.

5. Suppose, for the sake of argument, I should admit that light, heat, etc., are simply conditions of matter, mere non-entities, that result from the vibration of atoms or undulations of ethers: will my dynamic friend please inform me, what starts these vibrations, these undulations, into action? Everything must have a cause. Will he answer, that the sun's projectile power, brought about by chemical repulsion, gives the starting impulse? Truly, but we have seen in Chapter Fifth that all chemical repulsions as well as attractions are brought about by the flow of ethers in connection with atoms, or rather by the sweep of the finer through the coarser atoms, and we have seen in Chapter Second, that all power in the known material universe must be exerted in connection with fluidic forces, so that if we admit the undulatory theory, we must combine with it some winds of force which glide over or through the atmospheres and produce these undulations, thus forcing us at last to admit that in all electricities, colors, and other forces, there is a tangible something which constitutes the life of these forces.

6. The above remark makes it evident that what is called the dynamic (spirit-like) theory is really a grosser and more material conception of force than what is called the material theory, especially than the etherio-atomic law advocated in this work, which combines the truth of both sides of the question,—for what are waves themselves but matter, and what are the forces that project these waves but matter, acting in a much more crude

way than those amazingly fine ethers which, as we have seen by
multitudinous facts, dash with lightning-speed through the spiral
frame-work of atoms, so skillfully arranged as to be almost self-
acting and spirit-like, the atoms drawing on and quickening the
ethers, and the ethers firing up the atoms.

VIII. Summation of Points in Chromo–Philosophy.

*1. The knowledge of atoms and of the true principles of force greatly
simplifies the explanation of optical phenomena, some of which can never be
understood under the old theories.*

*2. Refraction consists in the jolting of the color ethers, which constitute
light, out of their direct course by the striking of the spirillæ which convey
them against a medium of different density. The fine, elastic spirillæ
which carries the violet must necsssarily jolt its ether farther one side than
the coarser spirilla which carries the red.*

*3. The Reflection of Light results from chemical repulsion. The
Fraunhofer lines are the result of reflection, not of absorption, as usually
supposed. Wrong theories prevent correct knowledge of the real potencies
of color.*

*4. Absorption results from the chemical affinity of a substance for the
colors which fall upon it, attended also with a sufficient amount of friction
or of transverse atomic lines to prevent these colors from passing entirely
through the substance.*

*5. Transparency comes from the fact that certain substances have such
a chemical affinity for all the ignited color-ethers, as to draw them on with
great power and transmit them beyond. Those substances whose atoms
cannot be polarized by light are not transparent.*

*6. Polarization is a modification which light undergoes by certain angles
of reflection and refraction. The word tends to mislead.*

*7. The theory of undulations is true so far as it concerns some of the
phenomena of light, but it has nothing whatever to do with the formation
of light, or with light as a substance.*

CHAPTER NINTH.

CHROMO–DYNAMICS, OR THE HIGHER GRADE LIGHTS AND FORCES.

I. INTRODUCTORY POINTS.

1. At last we come to a triumphant series of facts in proof of the fine fluidic forces which constitute the inner *soul of things*, and also in corroboration of the etherio-atomic law. By their aid we may ascend toward the key-stone of the great archway of power, and deal with those more subtile laws and potencies of vegetable, animal, human, and even world-life which are revealed by the higher grades of light and color.

2. We have seen in Chapter Fifth, XXIII, that there are strong proofs of new and beautiful grades of light and color above that which impresses the outward vision. The following semi-prophetic and semi-philosophic passage from Professor Tyndall, hinting at the fact that man has powers which may yet be developed to see these higher colors, is already being verified by actual facts :—" If we allowed ourselves to accept for a moment that notion of gradual growth, amelioration and ascension implied by the term evolution, we might fairly conclude that there are stores of visual impressions awaiting man far greater than those of which he is now in possession. For example, Ritter discovered in 1801, that beyond the extreme violet of the spectrum, there is a vast efflux of rays which are totally useless as regards our present powers of vision." That many persons are able to see these colors, and that many more can be developed into this power, will be shown more fully in the next chapter, in which also rules will be laid down for attaining it. This chapter will be devoted principally to the explanation of Odic light and color, together with some of the marvelous forces connected with man and nature which are revealed thereby, while the next chapter will deal more especially with man.

II. ODIC LIGHT.

Baron Reichenbach, one of the most eminent scientists of Austria, made the discovery that a fine force issues from all known elements and substances, and appears in beautiful lights and colors which can be both seen and felt by persons whom he called *sensitives*. Having a spacious castle near Vienna, admirably adapted to his investigations, with an abundance of philosophical and chemical apparatus, and a private cabinet containing minerals and substances of every kind, he instituted thousands of experiments which extended over years of time and were conducted with a skill, a patience and a severe love of truth, which must make his name immortal, especially as connected with the great force of nature whose laws and phenomena he thus discovered. This subtile power he named OD, or ODIC FORCE, or ODYLIC FORCE. As these fine invisible emanations constitute the basic principles of all other forces, and are forever working through all things, it is of vast moment to understand them, and it would seem almost criminal for our medical and other scientists to be so indifferent with reference to them, so long as human happiness and upbuilding are so greatly promoted by a knowledge of their laws. " Nature is eternal," says Reichenbach. " After a thousand million years will the odic light flow and shine as it does to-day, but the endeavors to overcome such a truth when it has once happily been found and disclosed, are paltry and poor." While such men as Berzelius, the great chemist of Stockholm, and Dr. Gregory of the Edinburgh University, and Dr. Elliotson, President of the Royal Chirurgical Society of London, and various other eminent thinkers and scientists, have freely admitted the greatness of the discovery of Reichenbach, too many even to this day *ignore*, or rather keep themselves ignorant of the whole matter. Even so well known a physician as Dr. Brown-Séquard sneers at the odic and other fine forces, and hosts follow in his track, thus riveting the shackles of prejudice more and more tightly about the people by their example. A body of rather superficial physicians of Vienna, anxious seemingly to combat Baron Reichenbach, rather than ascertain the exact truth, met together and had Miss Reichel, one of the sensitives whom Reichenbach had experimented with, attempt to describe the odic lights. They surrounded her, held each of her hands, overpowered her by their own hostile atmosphere, mocked her and jeered at her, till the poor sensitive girl, in her anger and excitement, could do little or nothing to illustrate a great principle and then condemned her and the cause. It is well on the whole, perhaps, that they took such a course, otherwise we should not have had such a scathing and crushing exposure of their folly by Reichenbach as a warning to all similar cases of folly and ignorance. Dr. William B. Carpenter, the well known physiologist, considers Baron Reichenbach's experiments unreliable because he employed so many women in testing them. To this I would answer, 1st, that his experiments would more likely have been unreliable if he had *not* employed ladies freely in the matter, for woman's perception of the fine forces is as much superior to man's as man's ratiocinative talent is generally superior to woman's, and it is singular that so able an observer has overlooked this fact; 2dly, the Baron *did* employ numerous men who could see the Odic lights, including Prof. Endlicher, member of the Vienna Academy; Baron August von Oberlaender, Dr. Ragsky, Imperial Professor of Chemistry, Vienna; M. Karl Schuh, Natural Philosopher, Berlin; Dr. Huss, Physician in ordinary to the king of Sweden, and other gentlemen of scientific attainment. In all he experimented with about 60 persons, including many who were in sound health as well as many who were sick, having a greater number of ladies than gentlemen, as it should be in this class of researches, as the former were able to see longer flames and generally describe them more definitely than the latter. Some of the ladies, including the Baroness Natorp, Baroness von Augustine, and others, were persons of culture.

2. Aided by the knowledge of atoms, chromo-chemistry and chromo-Therapeutics, I think we may easily see the inner meaning and potencies of the odic colors, and ascertain their scientific bearing in a way which Reichenbach himself was unable to do without these aids. We should remember that every color has a certain exact style of power, no matter what the grade of fineness or coarseness may be; the odic blue and violet, like the visible blue and violet, being electrical, penetrating and cool in their nature, while the red either in a drug, or in the visible sunlight, or in the finer invisible odic rays, is a warming and exciting

principle ; in short, that every color must ever work after the
same law, the only difference being that a color of a finer grade
has a softer and more penetrating power than the same color of
a coarser grade, and has also a greater influence on the finer
mental forces, though not so direct an influence on the physical
system.   It is proper now to inquire into the nature of Odic
light, as viewed by Reichenbach's sensitives.   In some cases I
shall condense his points, in others quote his exact language.

III.   NATURE OF ODIC LIGHT AND COLOR.

1. *Odic Light exhibits exactly the same laws and phenomena
as the ordinary visible light.*   " The odic light appears in five
forms, producing different sensuous impressions, namely, in the
condition of 1, incandescence ; 2, flame ; 3, threads, streaks
and nebulæ ; 4, smoke ; 5, sparks."   Prof. Endlicher and others,
when the flame at the end of magnets was blown upon, saw it
flicker about and grow larger just as ordinary flames do before
the wind.   Madame Kienesberger woke up in the night and
seeing the iron window frame on fire with odic light, became
alarmed, supposing it to be real fire.   When she went to put it
out it vanished, then reappeared when she lay down.   In other
words, when she was perfectly quiet and impressible, she saw
the lights, but when moving around, her finer vision was interrupted.   When a magnet became very weak there was " incandescence with no flame, only a little smoke," just as is the case
with a smouldering fire.   " Od shares with heat the peculiar-
ity of two different conditions, one inert, slowly making its way
through matter, a radiation.   The od from magnets, crystals,
human bodies, is felt instantaneously through a long suite of
rooms."   Odic light follows the same laws of refraction as common light, as it may be condensed and brought to a focus by a
lens, and also the same laws of reflection, although the same
substances that reflect ordinary light, are not always of the
right grade to reflect odic light, as the latter is often able to
pass through opaque bodies and make them transparent.

2. *An Odic Atmosphere or static ether must exist and bear
the same relation to odic light as the ordinary atmosphere does to
the ordinary light.*   As the odic light is twice as fine in its vibrations as ordinary light, the odic atmosphere must also be

twice as fine, and its luminelles on the average, about twice as small as the ordinary luminelles.   This is a deduction from the analogies of nature, and also from the fact ascertained by math-ematicians, that the vibrations, which are twice as fine and rapid as those in the thermel, occur a little above the violet just about at the place where the odic thermel in the new color-octave would be expected to commence.   In this finer atmosphere odic electricity, odic magnetism, odic thermism, as well as odic light and color exist with all their activities, as we shall see hereafter. To show that the odic light is not dependent upon our atmos-phere, being in reality partially smothered by it, and that it must have its own peculiar atmospheric medium, I will quote an ac-count which Reichenbach gives of his experiments with a mag-net as viewed in the dark while the air is being withdrawn by an air pump:—" M. Firka, Johann Klaiber, and Mme. Kienesberger, also saw nothing at first : but when the air was half removed, they saw the contents of the bell jar become luminous, the mag-net in the odylic glow.   On further exhaustion, Klaiber saw the flame appear on both poles, first dull, then brighter as the air was removed more completely, increasing in vividness at every stroke of the piston, so that at last very bright flames flowed about under the bell jar.   When the air was admitted, all light suddenly disappeared to the three observers, and it returned as soon as the pump had again been worked for a time."   Mlle. Zinkell saw the flames beautifully brilliant, especially after the exhaustion of the air, one pole being blue, the other red, with a mixture of rainbow hues.   Several others, including a blind man by the name of BOLLMAN, saw the same variations.   These facts seem to indicate that there is a finer grade of oxygen and hydro-gen and carbon, or some similar elements, to feed these flames, and a finer grade of gaseous or rather of ethereal matter as their basis, for those essences which are finer than the gases may be termed *ethers*.

3. *The Odic Light may appear in connection with all known objects, but more especially when these objects are under the action of the fine forces, such as electricity, magnetism, heat, light, etc.*   I will quote the summing up of results obtained by a vast number of experiments, from Dr. Wm. Gregory's translation of Reichen-bach's " Researches (Dynamics) on Magnetism, Electricity, etc.,

in their Relations to the Vital Force." (London Edition) :
"The time-honored observation that the magnet has a sensible
action on the human organism is neither a lie, nor an imposture,
nor a superstition, as many philosophers now-a-days erroneously
suppose and declare it to be, but a well-founded fact, a physico-
physiological law of nature which loudly calls on our attention.
It is a tolerably easy thing and everywhere practical, to convince
ourselves of the accuracy of this statement ; for everywhere
people may be found whose sleep is more or less disturbed by
the moon, or who suffer from nervous disorders. Almost all of
these perceive very distinctly the peculiar action of a magnet,
when a pass is made with it from the head downwards. Even
more numerous are the healthy and active persons who feel the
magnet very vividly ; many others feel it less distinctly ; many
hardly perceive it ; and finally the majority do not perceive it at
all. All those who perceive this effect, and who seem to amount
to a fourth or a third of the people in this part of Europe,
(Vienna), are here included under the general term 'Sensitives.'
The perceptions of this action group themselves about the senses
of touch and of sight ; of touch, in the form of sensations of
apparent coolness and warmth ; of sight, in the form of luminous
emanations, visible after remaining long in the dark, and flowing
from the poles and sides of magnets. The power of exerting
this action not only belongs to steel magnets as produced by
art, or to the loadstone, but nature presents it in an infinite
variety of cases. We have first the earth itself, the magnetism
of which acts more or less strongly on sensitives. There is
next the moon which acts by virtue of the same force on the
earth, and of course, on sensitives. We have further all crystals,
natural and artificial, which act in the line of their axes : also
heat, friction, electricity, light, the solar and stellar rays, chemical action especially, organic vital activity, both that of plants
and that of animals, especially that of man ; finally the whole
material universe. The cause of these phenomena is a peculiar
force, existing in nature and embracing the universe, distinct
from all known forces and here called ODYL " (p. 209).

5. *Length of Odic Flames.* These appeared of various sizes
according to the intensity of the force by which they were
produced and the clearness of vision possessed by the sensitive.

" Prof. Endlicher saw, on the poles of an electro-magnet, flames 40 inches high, unsteady, exhibiting a rich play of colors and ending above in a luminous smoke which rose to the ceiling and illuminated it. M. Delhez saw the flames of the same size, but did not distinguish the colors. The flames appeared to him darker below (red), brightest in the middle (yellow), and darker again above (blue). Mlle. Glaser saw, over the poles of the same electro-magnet, flames five feet high and smoke rising from them to the ceiling. The flames exhibited the most beautiful and varied play of colors, blue predominating over the northward, reddish yellow over the southward pole. Mlle. Zinkel saw the flame of the northward pole 40 inches high, that of the southward pole upwards of one foot in height. Both were colored, blue predominating in the former, red in the latter" (p. 342). An odic flame which appeared 16 inches long to Miss Glaser when issuing from a nine-bar horse-shoe magnet, was lengthened to 64 inches when a current from the electrical machine was applied to it. Miss Sturman while in a dark room perceived a " flame-like light" over a large rock crystal, " half the size of a hand, blue, passing into white above, remarkably different from the magnetic light," which had more of the yellow and red in it. She also said that " isolated filaments of a reddish color ran up in the upper part of the white." Streams of light several inches long would often be seen issuing from human fingers, and also from different parts of the body, from plants, and various other substances.

5. *Odic Polarization. As the solar ethers polarize the atoms of substances through which they pass, or follow the laws of substances already polarized as in many crystals, so do the odic forces either polarize bodies or sweep through atomic channels already polarized.* " It was discovered that every crystal presented two such points in which the force peculiarly resided. And these points lay diametrically opposite to each other in every crystal ; *they were the poles of a primary axis of the crystal.* Both acted in the same way, but one much more strongly than the other, and with the distinction that from one appeared to issue a cool, from the other a softer, gently warm (seeming) current of air." (*Dr. Ashburner's Translation of Reichenbach*, p. 56.) Reichenbach uses the word *seeming* in this and other cases, not being sure that

when the sensitives so constantly told him that the fine influences were *warm* or *cold*, it could be anything but an apparent effect, as it would not move a thermometer. This comes from his being unaware of the fact, 1st, that there are different grades of heat and cold, the finer of which cannot be measured by coarse instruments, any more than meal can be measured in a coal seive; 2dly, the cold end of crystals and other polarized objects always emitted a *blue flame*, which as we have seen is constantly the effect of the cold and electrical current; 3dly, it always produced the cooling and contracting effect on the sensitive which comes from cold, while the other pole would produce the warming and exciting effect of heat and have red for its predominant color. These phenomena show the truth of many points already laid down in the previous part of this work. Reichenbach admits that the scientists of his day were unsettled as to which should be called the positive or negative end of a magnet, or a crystal, and being in doubt himself finally concluded to call the north end from which the blue rays emanate the *negative*, and the south or red end the *positive* pole, which is exactly wrong, as the more powerful external force, like the north pole, must be positive, and the weaker south pole negative. He finds the whole right side of the human body emitting the cold blue rays in predominance, and the left side the warm red rays, and so calls the former negative, the latter positive, which would seem still more improper than the terms as applied to a magnet. The power of a magnet comes especially from its *electrical currents* arranged in curves, and the positive principle of electricity is in the blue; if we are speaking of an object in which thermism rules, then the red constitutes the positive principle of power. It would be better to designate the different ends of a polarized substance as *electrical* and *thermal*, as these terms afford an exact meaning. The reader who has become familiar with the atomic theory will see just why a polarized substance must be warm at one end when it is cold at the other, as cold and heat move in exactly contrary directions. Reichenbach's sensitives found the small end of crystals warm and with thermal colors predominating, while the larger end was cold with blue predominant, the upper parts of plants and trees cold, the lower warm, etc. They could point out the main axis and its poles in crystals, by the

crystallic force itself, and in many crystals, especially such decided ones as " sulphuret of iron, selenite, fluor spar, heavy spar,
sphene granite, etc., they would also discover other axes, the
poles of which were much less strongly opposed." " Very frequently the main axis was not longer, but shorter, as in selenite."

IV. WARM AND COLD SUBSTANCES.

1. The sensitives in deciding what elements and compounds
were od-warm and od-cold, and thus arriving at their interior
chemical character more minutely than the chemists themselves have generally done, have proved irresistibly the importance of understanding these odic forces. Baron Reichenbach
enumerates 172 elements and compounds of every kind which
were determined by Mlle. Maix and Mlle. Reichel. Nearly every
metal and alkaline substance were declared to be warm, potassium being at their head in this respect, while the electro-nega-
tives generally, oxygen being at the head, and nearly every acid
were declared to be cold, thus being a grand argument in favor
of the correctness of the principles developed in the chapter, on
Chromo-Chemistry, and of the laws of chemical affinity, as explained in Chapter Third, XXXVII. *Sulphuric acid*, next to
oxygen is pronounced the coldest substance, and *water* is ranged
on the cold side, but very feebly so. The table is far more correct as giving the chemical power of substances, than those
giving what is called their *specific heat*, though, perhaps, presenting slight inaccuracies.

2. "Mlle. Reichel saw most metals red, almost as if red hot;
some of them gave a white light, some a yellow. Copper, as we
have seen, gave a green light. A delicate vaporous flame played
over all, undulating backwards and forwards. More complex
substances showed flame only at their points when crystallized.
Otherwise they were either surrounded by luminous vapor; or
were luminous in their mass as if red hot."

3. Reichenbach's sensitives constantly affirm that the sun's
rays and ordinary fire are odically cold, but I think this effect, at
least sometimes, comes from the thermo-electricity generated by
the warm rays, as electricity is always developed by heat, especially as the temperature of sunlight was frequently measured by
placing a metal plate in the sun, a few moments after which the

sensitive felt cold sensations, in other words, the cold was felt
after the plate had had a little time to get warmed and charged
by the light. The solar rays, as we have seen, must come
equally through both the electrical and thermal portions of atmospheric atoms, although the electrical rays are doubtless more
active in cold weather. The moon's rays were always pronounced warm. Its grade of heat is not coarse enough to be
measured by an ordinary thermometer, but it is known to be the
cause of nervous excitement in many sensitive organizations.

4. "The sensitive patient felt all radiations from electrified
bodies cold. The feeling of cold increased rapidly, the faster I
turned the plate of the machine, perceptible, not immediately,
but several seconds later than the electrical charge." This is
another confirmation of the statement so often made in this
work, that *electricity acts on the law of cold.*

5. *The roots of plants are stated to be warm, and the ends of
the leaves above cold.* The warm currents flow downward
through the plant, the cold currents upward. Most *flowers* were
found to be cool, but warm on their stem.

V. Influence of Solar and Lunar Rays.

1. *Sunlight.* Reichenbach put various plates in the sunlight
and connected them by a wire 13 yards long with Mlle. Reichel,
who held the point of the wire upward. The whole came through
darkened rooms. In less than a minute after he had put the
plates in the sunlight she saw a stream of light 10 or 12 inches
high emerge from the wire. When his daughter stood in the
sunlight in the place of the metal plate, the flame rose about 9
inches high. When he brought different metals from the sunlight into the darkened room, flames issued from them, especially from the sharp angles of the upper portions, green and
blue from copper, clear white from gold and silver, dull white
from tin, reddish white from zinc, etc.

2. *Objects charged with Sunlight.* I have already, in Chapter
Sixth, XVII, shown the great power of substances charged with
sunlight in healing, vitalizing or soothing the human system, including the discoveries of Dr. von Gerhardt, of Germany, which
consists of sugar of milk, charged with the electrical rays by means
of a prism, as a nervine and anti-spasmodic, and my own discov-

eries and inventions for securing the exquisite power of light, including a yellow-orange hollow lens, and a blue hollow lens, both of which when filled with water, and held in the light, answer as powerful lenses to focalize their respective rays upon the parts of the body externally, while the water within answers as a very soft, but subtile and penetrating influence to take internally, the former being a cerebral and nerve stimulant, vitalizing to the system, and laxative to the bowels, while the latter is cooling, quieting, anti-inflammatory, and soporific upon a system which is over-excitable and sleepless.   This healing power of the sunlight comes not only from the ordinary visible colors, but from the odic colors which form the next color-octave above the visible range, for the blue glass transmits a large amount of odic rays, and even those which are still finer, while the yellow-orange glass transmits a portion of them also.

3. *Moonlight.* The sensitives always felt a warm current from objects that had been held in the moon, and saw a flame 10 inches high arise from the wire held in the moonlight with a plate at the outer end.   Miss Maix felt an attractive force drawing her hand along the wire.   The fact that the thermal influences of the moon, especially in the range of odic rays, overbalance the electrical rays of the same, seems remarkably confirmed by authorities quoted by Dr. Forbes Winslow, in his " Influence of Light," in which it is shown that especially in warm climates such diseases as diarrhœa, dysentery, hemorrhage, fevers, convulsions, nervous irritability, lunacy, etc., are worse in the full of the moon (or sometimes in the new moon), just as we might expect from predominance of yellow and red rays.   " In India," says Dr. Winslow, " death has occasionally been known to arise from what is termed a *coup de lune,* or stroke of the moon ; and in Egypt blindness has often been produced in persons who have imprudently fallen asleep with their faces exposed to intense lunar light."   Blue glass or a blue veil would offset the exciting effects of moonlight, which in the negative condition of sleep, might at times be hurtful.   Dormant conditions would be benefited by moonlight, and walking under the open moonlight, would in most cases bring much more benefit than harm.

VI. Magnetism and Odic Force.

1. *Points in which they differ.* Reichenbach enumerates thirty points in which Magnetism and Odyl differ. Some of these are as follows :—1st, Odyl is in most cases developed without the aid of magnetism, but magnetism never without odyl; 2dly, clouds over the sun's face arrest odyl, nothing can arrest magnetism ; 3dly, all bodies may be charged with odyl, only a few bodies with magnetism ; 4thly, odyl cannot attract iron filings, the magnet can ; 5thly, magnetism, according to Barlow, lingers near the surface of bodies, odyl penetrates through and through them, making them translucent, sometimes transparent; 6thly, the odic flame of a magnet is sometimes extinguished by the approach of a living being, while the magnetic action remains in force ; 7thly, an iron bar placed horizontally in the magnetic meridian will have its north end odically cold and its south end warm, but if placed with its north end inclined downward at an angle of 65°, which is the true magnetic dip in Vienna, and the best position for magnetic force, then its north pole will be odically warm and its south pole cold, in harmony with the ascending electricities, and contrary to the descending magnetic currents, for, as we have seen, there are currents of electricity which move directly upward as well as other currents which move northward, a fact which Reichenbach was not aware of.

2. *The Magnetic Poles.* The odic light is described as being especially brilliant at or near the poles of a magnet, and those who have clear vision can see a fringe-work of light over the whole surface. From the north pole a brilliant white light ascends which merges into delicate horizontal layers of red, yellow, green, and lastly blue, which last is so abundant as to constitute the predominating tint of the whole flame. From the south, or negative pole, a still more luminous light, but of much smaller dimensions, descends with white and colored rays in which the red predominates. The sensitives generally would speak of the negative (south) pole as being red, the middle of the magnet green, and the positive pole blue. The reason the south pole is more luminous is because the red and yellow predominate, while the north pole is stronger in its electrical currents and consequently more blue. We have seen that a keen grade of mag-

neto-electricity rules at the north pole, while the weaker chemico-electricity issues from the south pole, but the greatest power of the magnet is in the former which, sending its blue forces in one direction, must naturally send its affinitive red in the other direction.

VII. Opaque Bodies become Transparent.

Mlle. Atzmannsdorfer in the " state of somnambulism " saw "the glowing steel transparent almost like glass." " Friedrich Weidlich saw the flame in air two inches long. I then sank the magnet, lying in a glass basin, into water. The flame (for the most part) instantly disappeared, but he saw the magnet glowing and translucent, almost like the glass itself." " Metals in the odylic glow, appear to sensitives translucent, glowing through and through hollow balls." A mercantile gentleman of my acquaintance, in New York, can become so *en rapport* with these finer grades of light, as to be able to see through the human body as though it were made of glass. Here, then, is the philosophy of clear-seeing or clairvoyance, although many have the faculty so feebly developed that they are liable to commit mistakes.

VIII. Is Odyl an Imaginary Power?

1. Miss Nowotny's hand, while she was in an unconscious cataleptic condition, would be drawn and held to the magnet as would a piece of iron. Reichenbach once had a person go into another room from where his patient lay, and open a magnet of 90-pound sustaining power unknown to her. She immediately became uneasy and " complained that a magnet must be open somewhere, desiring that some one would look and relieve her from the pain. The armature was replaced without her knowledge, and she became quiet again."

2. M. Baumgartner, Professor of Physics, desiring to see if imagination affected Miss Nowotny in her judgment of the power of the magnet, took out a magnet in her presence, which he said was the strongest one in his collection. She however declared that it was the weakest of all the magnets, and "it seemed to her almost without influence." Baumgartner then laughed, and said "that it had been deprived of its magnetism, before leaving

home, by friction in the reverse direction," so that it was little else than a mere plain piece of iron.

3. The *charging of water* and other objects by means of the magnet, by human hands, held or darted near the water, by sunlight, by crystals and other substances, was believed in by the great chemist Berzelius, of Stockholm, by Dr. Gregory, of the Edinburgh University, by the eminent Dr. Elliotson of London, by Dr. Lutze, a physican of vast practice in Germany, and very many others. "Nothing could be more disagreeable," says Reichenbach, "than the reappearance of apparently so absurd a thing which all physicists and chemists are horrified even to hear of. But in spite of this, I could not refuse to admit what I saw before my eyes as often as I tried it; namely, that the girl always determined and unfailingly distinguished a magnetized glass of water from an unmagnetized. The force of facts cannot be combatted by any reasoning; I was compelled to recognize what I was by no means able to comprehend, but when I again met with the same, subsequently, in Misses Sturman, Maix, Reichel, Atzmannsdorfer, and others, and saw it in a still stronger degree, I gave up all doubt and opposition." Speaking of Reichenbach's many experiments on the magnetizing of water and other substances, Dr. Ashburner, a prominent British physician, says :—" The facts stated in this, have been exhibited in my house hundreds of times. Water has been magnetized with magnets, mesmerized with the fingers, by breathing, by the exertion of the will: over and over again, the tumblers in which these specifically treated quantities of water have been contained, have been instantly detected by somnambulists in the lucid state of sleep-waking, who have been in another room when the fluid was charged." " I have darted my hands 200 times over the surface of water, and have been told that the blue haziness has overflowed the tumbler. Several persons have said the same thing. I have placed a watch before me while I held the tips of my right hand fingers in the mouth of the decanter. Several lucid individuals have separately indicated the precise hight of the blue haze in the water at the same interval of time. A few minutes were sufficient to charge a quart decanter. All concur in the fact that the fluid sinks in the water. Is it, then, imponderable ? "

4. In cool weather when the air is electrical, I can make one, two, or three strokes over tissue or other paper, and throwing it into the air within a foot of the wall, it will spring to it like a thing of life and cling there for hours, sometimes even for days. A mere stroke will make it attractive of everything around it, although it will generally repel another magnetized sheet, unless this sheet is magnetized with the same strokes as they lie together. Thousands of others can do the same thing, and some better than myself. I have made one magnetized newspaper lift and carry around another several times as large as itself. Now what is this power except the odic or vital force, combined with frictional electricity ? It is not the ordinary ferro-magnetism, as it will not influence iron filings in the least, but must be this finer power thrown into attractive curves on the same general plan. It is sometimes called animal magnetism, which name, although it has been abused, is not very improper, and yet so well known a physician as Dr. Brown-Séquard, in a course of lectures delivered in Boston, almost questions its very existence. But too many of our medical scientists are dropping behind the age in ignoring these finer basic principles of things directly in the face of the fact, that thousands of persons can see the luminous pathways of these forces, as they emanate from human beings or other objects, and hundreds of thousands can feel their influence.

5. In the light of such facts, the folly of attributing these phenomena to imagination, prepossession of ideas, or mere subjective conditions, as do Drs. Braid, Carpenter, and so many others, is too apparent to need comment, and shows that the diseased subjective conditions are not with Reichenbach's sensitives who constantly prove their own points by stubborn facts, but with the doctors themselves who cling to their own theories in spite of all facts. In Dr. Carpenter's late lectures on "Mesmerism," etc., he uses the following language about Reichenbach, which is almost the only point that would give any trouble to one who is enlightened with regard to these fine forces, although the whole book would tend to mislead the ignorant :—"The fact which Von Reichenbach himself was honest enough to admit— that when a magnet was poised in a delicate balance, and the hand of a 'sensitive' was placed above or beneath it, the magnet was

never drawn towards the hand—ought to have convinced him
that the force which attracted the 'sensitive's' hand to the magnet has nothing in common with physical attractions, whose
action is invariably *reciprocal;* but that it was the product of her
own conviction that she *must* thus approximate it." The sophistry of the above will appear, I think, from the following points:
1st, it is not the coarser forces of the magnet, which are known
as magnetism, that act upon a sensitive person, but the finer
odic and other forces which this magnetism wakens into action,
so that the attraction is not direct but secondary. These finer
forces have their attractive curves similar to the magnetic, which
are sufficiently subtile to act on the nervous system, as will be
shown in the next chapter; 2dly, it is probable that there is a
slight secondary attraction of the magnet, though not enough to
move a gross mass of iron. In the experiments with paper which
I have just detailed, the paper itself will readily be attracted to a
human being and will also attract sensitive human beings. 3dly,
the assertion that "it was the product of her own conviction that
she must approximate it," is overwhelmingly overthrown by
several facts given by Reichenbach, Ashburner, etc., in some of
which the subject was asleep or in an unconscious cataleptic fit,
when the hand would be immediately drawn to the magnet and
held rigidly to it. Dr. Ashburner speaks of persons who would
be drawn six feet to the magnet, and of a boy who, if the armature
was removed six feet off, would rush to it and fall asleep on the
way. But multitudes of cases could be given in which human
magnetism, crystals, and other objects have drawn unconscious
subjects in the same way; 4thly, the experiments which I have
just quoted with reference to Miss Nowotny and others, show
that these forces operate entirely independent of one's consciousness. But the fact that Doctor Carpenter could overlook a whole
volume of marvelous phenomena against his theory, and hitch
to some little weak point shows the power of a " prepossession of
ideas" in his own case quite similar to what he is fond of charging upon others. Wallace and Crookes having driven him into
a close corner, he writes an article in Nature, Oct., 1877, in which,
as he looks about for sympathizers, he makes the following remark :—" I asked my personal friend Prof. Hoffmann of Berlin,
whether the doctrine (of Odic force) any longer finds support

among scientific men in Germany.   His reply was a most emphatic negative; the doctrine, he said, being one which no man of science with whom he is acquainted would think worthy of the slightest attention." Is Prof. Hoffmann correct when he would thus indicate that German scientists are so deeply obscured in their perceptions that they utterly neglect these fine forces which are the vivifying power of all forces? I think there are many noble German thinkers who would consider this a slander upon their people.

VIII. Proof that Odic Light comprises Fluidic Forces.

1. Odic Light is manifested in flames which stream forth in various directions, and as the ordinary visible flames consist of luminous gases which are fluids, so must these odic flames consist of the finer fluids which we call *ethereal forces*.   While none can see the inner essence of odyl, or magnetism, or electricity, or the solar ethers, yet the luminous pathway which their flow enkindles may be seen, and, judging by all analogies of the known external universe, we must consider that some marvelously swift fluidic force is passing.   We have seen how the red odic fluid pours from the fingers of the left hand, and the blue odic fluid can be thrown from the right hand until a tumbler is filled to the top and made to overflow.

IX. Does Odic Light produce the Aurora Borealis?

Baron Reichenbach performed ingenious experiments to prove that odyl was the cause of the Aurora Borealis, but he seemed to forget that odic light, however intense, cannot possibly be seen by the ordinary vision, while the Northern Lights can be seen by everyone.   He has skillfully shown that the magnet working in connection with a hollow iron globe, with its north and south pole at the respective poles of the globe, sends forth its blue and iridescent lights at the north, its red, etc., at the south, much the same as does the Aurora Borealis, and thereby achieves the following grand result; namely, by showing just how magnetism on a small scale can develope such colors in connection with the odic atmosphere, he shows just how the mightier play of a world's concentrated magnetism at the poles may ignite the ordinary coarser atmosphere with its nebulous matter, and so cause a similar effect to the ordinary vision. See Chapter Fourth, IX, and X, 3, 4.

X. Terrestrial Dynamics.

1. In Chapter Fourth, X, we have seen that the law of heat awakens and propels thermo-electricity in two directions, namely, from the earth vertically, into the colder regions of the upper sky, and also from the warmer regions of the torrid and temperate zones towards the colder regions of the poles, the law of movement for electricity ever being from the warm to the cold. The sun's course, also, from east to west carries a line of luminous *force*, attended with some heat, westward, while in the east the tendency must be the other way. What, then, should be the colors that would naturally represent the main points of the compass, if we are to get at the real power of the earth's forces? Plainly blue for the north, with its kindred electrical colors on each side of it ; red for the south, with its kindred thermal colors on each side of it ; the luminous yellow for the west, and slight blue with some shadowy or gray elements for the east. This, we find, is exactly indicated by the odic lights and colors as discovered by Reichenbach's sensitives, although the Baron himself had not ascertained just why this arrangement in nature takes place. It being of vast importance that these great fundamental laws of force should be understood, it will be well to illustrate it at some length.

2. *Vertical Forces.* Let us commence first with electricity which moves from the earth vertically into the sky. If there is such a force of the cold principle, its manifestation must consist of the blue or violet as the leading element, while in the direction towards the centre of the earth the thermal colors, especially the red, must prevail. This we find to be the case with the odic colors, for when a bar magnet was placed vertically with the north pole upward, the blue would become more intense above and the red below ; when this direction was inverted, both ends would be so contrary to the forces of nature that their colors would be almost smothered. " When the bar was placed verti-

cally, she (Miss Zinkel) saw it, contrary to all expectation, glowing with a bluish gray light at the upper end and with a whitish red below." "When both poles stood pointed upward, the northward (blue) flame was increased, the southward diminished." "Blue predominated at the northward, red at the southward pole. But still the flames arranged themselves into a most beautiful iris on each pole." On the lower portion of Plate III, may be seen the general plan of odic colors as they appear at each pole, arranged as closely as possible after Reichenbach's description, although, of course, incomparably less exquisite than the tints of nature. The following is a description of colors emanating from an electro-magnet as seen by Mme. Kienesberger :—"Close to the (north) pole, which stood vertically, appeared a red stratum, next to that a stratum of orange, then one of yellow, then one of green, one of light blue, one of dark blue, and lastly one of violet-blue (indigo and violet), above which arose a gray vapor. At the same time, the positive (south) pole exhibited close to the iron a blood red stratum (probably thermel), then light red, and above this orange, from which a thick heavy smoke rose to the ceiling. She described the appearance as one of extraordinary delicacy and splendor. Some weeks later, I made the same experiment with Mlle. Zinkel. She described the appearances in the same way as Mme. Kienesberger, being about equally sensitive, and added that each colored stratum was not uniform, but subdivided into smaller strata of different shades of color, so that the whole iris had the appearance of a great number of colored bands overlying each other. Beyond the violet she observed *a narrow streak of pure red*, in which the violet ended, after becoming gradually redder, and which passed above into smoke." Here we have the whole scale of odic colors described, together with the thermel and red of a still finer scale above the violet, or in other words the psychic thermel and red. Next to the magnet comes doubtless the heaviest and coarsest color which would naturally be called red by most persons, but which is probably odic thermel, with a very slight tinge of blue in it, while the more ethereal psychic thermel and red naturally come in at the top, being more refrangible than even the odic violet. On the south or warm pole most senitives saw only the red or red and yellow, but under the aid of a strong battery Mlle. Zinkel

saw also the blue, and if her vision had been still clearer she
would perhaps have seen the other colors also, although the electrical colors predominate at the north pole, and the thermel at the
south pole. As we have seen, a weaker grade of electricity exists at the south pole, otherwise there could be no magnetic attraction there. If a piece of card board or glass should be laid
upon the sides of the poles as they lie horizontally, and sprinkled
with iron filings, the magnetic forces will arrange the filings into
curves resembling the dotted lines in the plate, and if a sensitive
look at these in the dark, they will coruscate like countless stars
on account of the currents that are passing through them. The
figures at the positive (north) pole represent colors as follows :—
1, gray-colored smoke; 2, psychic red; 3, psychic thermel; 4,
violet (odic scale) ; 5, indigo ; 6, 6, blue which predominates;
7, green; 8, yellow ; 9, orange; 10, red ; 11, thermel. N is
north pole, S, south pole. It will be seen on reflection how admirable is the law by which the cold currents are made to go
upward and thus prove cooling to the brains of human beings as
they stand or sit, while the warm currents pass downward and
thus help the feet. In the following paragraphs it will be shown
how a person may lie in sleeping so as to get the advantage of
still colder currents for the head and still warmer ones for the
feet.

3. *Horizontal Forces*. The great forces of the earth caused
by sunlight, heat, magnetism and electricity, and which are more
nearly horizontal, may be arrived at by studying the following
brilliant experiment of Baron Reichenbach, a beautiful illustration of which I have drawn up as nearly correct as possible, and
had engraved in the circular figure of Plate III :—" I now tried
the effect of *a circular surface or disc.* A disc of iron plate,
13.2 inches in diameter, was well flattened, and an iron wire folded
into its circumference, so that a smooth, round, clean border, one
twelfth of an inch thick, ran round it. It was suspended by a
small hook in the middle, horizontally above the pole of the
magnet, and could be fixed at any hight. I could now let it
down on the northward pole of the magnet which stood vertically. * * I showed the disc to Mlle. Pauer. The odylic glow
instantly spread over it. The colors were developed as might
have been expected ; on the upper centre, a blue spot, on the

lower, in contact with the magnet, a red spot, both upwards of two inches in diameter. They passed into a surrounding yellowish zone, faintly tinged with red on the under, with green on the upper surface, and this again lost itself in a gray zone. This last continued to the border, where it was surrounded by a downy fringe of light, 0.6 of an inch thick and colored gray, blue, yellow and red in east, north, west and south respectively. In north-west, south-west, south-east, she saw respectively green, orange and gray-red (red-gray) ; in north-east violet with a short patch of red. These colors formed a continuous wreath of tints passing into each other, and thus a kind of a circular rainbow.

"I varied the experiment as follows with Mlle. Zinkel ; I connected with the poles of a Smee's voltaic battery of more than two and a half square feet of surface, the two surfaces of the disc ; the wires being only separated by its thickness, about one twenty-fifth of an inch. Immediately the observer saw around the upper centre of the disc connected with the silver, a spot of blue glow forming more than two inches in diameter. At the same time a similar red spot appeared on the under surface, connected with the zinc. No flame appeared. But the whole disc acquired a colored glow, not merely on its border, but over its surface, blue, yellow, red and gray, appearing respectively in the north, west, south and east positions, green in the north-west, etc., as before. The blue and red central spots each formed a kind of a star of innumerable points, or rather ray-like prolongations, stretching out toward the circumference, and uniformly exhibiting the color corresponding to the point of the compass toward which they were directed. On the rest of the surface the colors were arranged around the central spot in successive zones, so as to form a rainbow of parallel circles. A luminous web of fine downy fibres, enveloped the border of the disc. Besides this border, the whole surface was covered with a similar downy light or flame, rising as high as the thickness of a thin quill." (p. 424–426.) I have taken the liberty to put a slight tint of blue with the gray of the east as the sensitives frequently described the eastern portion of a soft bar of iron, or other objects as " *blue gray*," or " gray with traces of blue," etc. The second red coming next to the violet will be recognized by the reader as belonging to the third or psychic grade of colors.

This second red so often spoken of by the sensitives puzzled the Baron. He made a hollow globe of iron, inserted a magnet through it at its poles—found blue at the north, red at the south, and other colors exactly as already given in describing the *disc*, with a *very brilliant red* just below the violet of the north-east. " This remarkable red," he remarks, " was very brightly luminous and strongly red, much brighter than any part of the red on the south side of the ball.   Red, therefore, occurred at both ends of the spectrum, on the one side from the yellow, on the other side from the blue. * * * Why this red, which in the ordinary spectrum appears only as violet in a.part of the blue, stands forth independently in the odylic, is a fact, the causes of which can only be ascertained by further researches of another kind." Reichenbach did not seem to have the least idea that there could be any spectrum of colors higher than the odylic, for which reason the facts thus presented are perhaps all the more valuable, as they are not warped by any theories, or rather are given contrary to his suppositions in the matter.

4. *Miscellaneous Points.* The principal direction of the earth's electricities as signified by the foregoing and many other experiments is north as shown by the blue, somewhat north-east as shown by the still finer violet, somewhat west of north as signified by the blue-green, and upward as signified generally by the intensifying of the blue and violet principles when the magnet is held vertically.   Mlle. Pauer saw the soft iron bar give out " to the south yellowish red, vertically upward, pale yellow (at a certain distance pale bluish), to the north blue."   Here it is said that pale yellow was the appearance which presented itself on the upward pole at a certain distance from the object, which may be true when the sun is high in the sky and throwing its luminous rays downward, but most experiments showed the power of the blue in that direction, though a more luminous and feeble blue than that at the north.

XI. Terrestrial Dynamics in Human Life.

1. *How Applied to Human Life.* Thus far we have ascertained how the great forces of the earth move—in what direction the electricities play, and whither the thermal rays tend. We

have also ascended one grade higher on the ladder of power than ordinary electricity, or magnetism, or thermism, or the visible rays of sunlight, even into the range of odic lights, colors and forces, which open up a new heaven and a new earth to man. We have seen that whatever may be the direct power of light, heat or electricity upon the human system, they call into action those finer interior potencies which almost take hold upon the very springs of life itself. In all this we have not been building upon dreams or mere theories, but upon an array of carefully established facts which to a candid and thorough mind should be irresistible.

2. *Physiological Adaptation.* The first question to be considered is—how shall we receive these terrestrial forces in a way best to harmonize with the natural constitution of the human system ? One thing is pre-eminently plain at the start, which is that the head is the warmest, and the feet the coldest part of the body, while nearly every inharmonious condition tends to bring too much blood or nervous action to the brain, and perhaps viscera, while the extremities are left too cold and dormant. For this reason the earth's magnetisms and electricities, which belong to the cooling category of forces, should move from the feet towards the head, while the opposite thermal forces should pass towards the feet ; consequently in sleeping, the head should be towards the north or north-east to receive the blue or violet forming currents, and the feet towards the south, or south-west to receive the warm currents signified by the red and orange. Another important matter to observe is to have the forces of the earth flow harmoniously with the same kind of forces in the human body. Thus it has been ascertained repeatedly that the cooling blue emanations flow from the whole right side of the head, arms and body, while the red emanations flow from the whole left side. In other words the electrical currents enter on the left side, and issue from the right side, while the warm currents must necessarily flow in the opposite direction. This was repeatedly demonstrated by the sensitives. To show that odic force was stronger than that developed by the earth's magnetism and illustrate the polarity of the body, I quote the following :—" I caused Mlle. Zinkel to hold between two fingers and *conformably* in the meridian a four-inch needle, not strongly

magnetic.   When I held the southward pole in my right finger
points, the blue northward became three times as long as before.
This showed the feebleness of the needle in comparison with my
hand.   But when I held the same pole with the fingers of my
left hand, the blue flame disappeared, and the red flame took its
place.   When I made the experiment at the other end of the
needle, with my left fingers on the negative (positive) pole, the
red flame of the opposite pole became brighter and three times
as long as before.   But when I applied the fingers of my right
hand to the same negative pole, the red flame disappeared and
was replaced by a blue one."   Such being the case it must be
evident that when the earth's electrical currents strike the right
side of a sensitive person, it must conflict with the natural currents of the system and give distress.   In illustration suppose a
person should lie on his back with his head to the west.   The
northward electrical and magnetic currents, which are strongest,
would then strike him in the right side, and, conflicting with the
natural electricities which move in the other direction would tend
toward inharmony.   Besides this the yellow forming currents
which flow westward must be highly exciting to the brain, and
thus the west-east position in sleeping must be doubly bad.
In proof of this and the first physiological law, I will now quote
some examples from Reichenbach, especially as even persons
who are not sufficiently sensitive to perceive the difference must
in the long run be injured by violating these simple laws of
nature, while persons of active brains and susceptible nerves
must at times be affected ruinously by such violation, for the
finer the force, the more deeply does it work either for good
or ill.

3. "*M. Schmidt*, Surgeon in Vienna, had experienced a chill
in his right arm, while traveling on a railway, and had for some
time suffered in consequence, from severe rheumatism in the
limb, with most painful spasms from the shoulder to the fingers.
His physician employed the magnet, which quickly subdued the
spasms ; but they always returned.   I found him lying with his
head towards the south.   In consequence of my remarks on this,
he was so placed as to lie in the magnetic meridian, with his
head towards the north.   As soon as he came into this position he expressed instantly feelings of satisfaction, and declared

that he felt, generally, refreshed in a singular degree.   The previously existing chilliness and rigors were instantly exchanged
for an agreeable uniform warm temperature ; he felt the strokes
of the magnet now beyond comparison more agreeably cooling and beneficial than before ; and before I left him, the rigid
arm and fingers had become movable, while the pain entirely
disappeared."

4. *Mlle. Nowotny* had intuitively sought out the north and
south position, that is, with the head to the north and feet to
the south.   She insisted upon occupying this position, and " it
had been necessary to remove a brick stove to allow of her wish
being gratified."   Baron Reichenbach had much trouble in per-
suading her to lie for a little while with her head to the south.
" Before long she began, to complain. · She felt uncomfortable
and restless, became flushed, and her pulse became more frequent and fuller ; a rush of blood to the head increased the head-
ache, and very soon the disagreeable sensations affected the
stomach, producing nausea.   We hastened to change the position of the bedstead on which she lay, but stopped when we had
turned it round to the extent of a quadrant, her head being now
towards the west.   Of course she now lay in the plane of a magnetic parallel.   This direction was to the patient absolutely intolerable, far more disagreeable than the former, that, namely,
from the south to north.   This was at half past 10 A. M.   She
was afraid, from her sensations, that she would soon faint or become insensible if kept in this position, and entreated to be
quickly removed from it.   She was now placed in her own original position, her head towards the north.   Instantly, all the
painful sensations yielded, and in a few minutes they had so
completely vanished, that she was again quite cheerful."   On
another day the same experiments were tried with still severer
results, causing " shuddering ; restlessness ; flushing of the face ;
acceleration of the pulse ; a rush of blood to the head ; headache ;
and finally pain of stomach, ringing in the ears, failure of the
senses, and the approach of fainting.   We were compelled to
bring her in haste into the north and south position, in order to
restore her, otherwise she would have fallen from the chair.
When this was done, the rapidity with which all these painful
sensations disappeared was astonishing."   The east and west

position also affected her severely, but more mildly than the others.

5. *Mlle. Sturmann,* of the Clinical Hospital of the University of Vienna, lay in the west-east position. When she was turned to the north-south position, everything was changed instantly. " The patient immediately gave signs of satisfaction ; the previous restlessness left her ; a painful smarting of the eyes, from which she had recently suffered, disappeared. Instead of the intolerable heat which had before tormented her, she felt refreshing coolness, and a general sense of relief pervaded her frame while we observed her. There followed a night of such quiet refreshing sleep as she had not for a long time enjoyed. From that time forward her bed was kept in the same position which she earnestly entreated." When she was turned to the south-north position all her bad symptoms returned, and these were removed by turning her head northward again.

6. *Mlles. Maix, Reichel* and *Atzmannsdorfer* found the same kind of improvement in the direction of north and south, the west to east position being the worst. *M. Schuh* had the singular habit of turning his head to the foot of the bed for his morning nap which was much more refreshing than all the rest of his sleep. " When he failed to obtain this he felt wearied the whole succeeding day." His bed was found to be in the south-north position. After he had turned it so that the head came north, he felt no need of the morning nap, and forever abandoned it, as his sleep was good and strengthening.

7. Another fact of vast importance with reference to sensitive patients was ascertained in these experiments, which is that *when they lay in directions contrary to the harmonious flow of forces such as the south-north or west-east position, all use of medicines or of the magnet for mitigating disease seemed to be either powerless or to have a very perverted action, giving distress rather than relief.* Ignorance of this fact has worked countless blunders in the medical world, and many mistakes in the effort to acquire a knowledge of the fine forces. Is it not criminal for physicians to neglect to inquire into these momentous facts, and thereby allow nervous patients and those of active brains and over-heated systems to languish and die from want of knowledge

of these resistless forces ?   To tell people that it is important to sleep with the head to the north is often to provoke a smile of incredulity.   There is no power that knocks them down when they sleep in other directions, and so they stupidly think that one direction is as good as another.   There is a force that is viewless and voiceless, and intangible, and a million times softer than the evening breeze.   Does that show that it is weak ?   It is vastly swifter than lightning, wafts all worlds on its bosom, and holds the entire universe in immutable chains, so that even a grain of dust cannot stir without its permission.   It is called gravitation.   Then kindling up all things are these glories of light and color, some of which are so exquisite as to conceal themselves from common eyes, and yet they are mighty in controlling human life, and their radiance reveals the secret hidings of power.   Although many persons may have that sturdy and coarser physical power which does not take direct cognizance of odic lights and forces, yet a long continued violation of their laws must demand their penalty.   For this reason I have striven to make the laws underlying these forces clear to my readers and have clinched them with this extensive array of facts.   I could give many more facts from acquaintances of mine, some of whom say they cannot sleep well at all except with the head to the north, or somewhere near the north.   When I have been in strange places and have found myself tossing in bed for hours without being able to sleep, I have noticed that I had been lying with the head to the south or west.   On changing my bed to the north or north east I would get to sleep in a short time, as the brain pressure would be gone.   I can sleep quite comfortably also with the head to the east.   I have taken pains in these remarks to show the philosophy of these directions, so that, aside from the facts, people may not consider it a whim.   When speaking to incredulous friends and urging them to change the position of their beds, I have referred them to the fact that the cold magnetic forces of the earth as they move northward, give the magnetic needle its direction, and as the head, being charged with blood, has need of the cooling element, and as I have fortified my theories with facts, I have not had much difficulty in getting thoughtful people to admit the force of the argument.

8. *Position in Sitting.* When it is convenient it is better to sit with the back to the north or north-east, or at least to the east, in preference to the other directions, especially when taking a sun bath, or receiving any kind of treatment. "All these patients," says Reichenbach, "now recollected how painful it had always been to them to remain for any length of time in the church. All Roman Catholic churches are built from west to east, so that the members of the congregation find themselves when opposite the altar, in the position from west to east; consequently in that position, which is to sensitive persons, of all others, the most intolerable. In fact they often fainted in that position and had to be carried out. At a later period Mlle. Nowotny could not even bear to walk in the street, or in the garden, in the direction from west to east, if her walk lasted but for a short time" (p. 71). There is no danger that people in general, especially in good health, will attain to any such extreme sensitiveness as this, but I quote it to illustrate a principle.

9. *Nervous Diseases.* Considering the great ignorance on this subject, and that there is scarcely a family but has one or more members afflicted with distressing nervous symptoms of some kind, the sweetness of womanhood and the dignity of manhood being too often turned to gall even when they are not innately hateful, would it not be well to turn for instruction and help to this beautiful radiation of light, including the finer as well as the coarser grades which seem to reach up more or less into the soul forces themselves, and attune them to greater harmony? *

10. *The North East Position.* I would recommend a direction for sleeping not exactly north-east, but some 30° east of north, or about one third of the way from the north to the east, as this would enable a person to receive the strong and cool northward currents over the head and upper body, and also some

---

* It occurred to me that the portly, rubicund Englishman should be more free from nervousness than ourselves, but after spending a year in their midst, I am not quite sure of this. At a private residence in London, I saw a lady rush screaming from the dinner table because some one remarked that there was a Sabbath school near by and it would be well for her to become a teacher in it. People greatly need more exercise in the sunshine and pure air, more calming of the brain forces by the blue and violet principles, and a more stern use of their will power to gain self-command.

portion of the eastern electricities. By looking at the circular plate it will be seen that this would bring the head somewhat into the violet odic rays, which are above all soothing to the nervous system.

A scientific gentleman, possessing exact habits of observation, has informed me that he sleeps better with head rather to the north-east than to the north, and for years I have slept with great comfort at an angle of 30° or more east of north. The main streets of New York inclining a little to the north-east and south-west are a very good model in this respect for a city. Reichenbach mentions a single case with whom the north-east position for the head disagreed, but the full north-east position, or a little farther around, would bring the head into a grade of red, and this of course is wrong. The advantages in laying out a city with streets which run as above recommended, east of north and west of south in one direction, and at right angles to these in the other, are as follows :

The beds can be in the best position and still be in harmony with the form of the rooms.

The sunlight can reach all sides of a house each day with its healing and purifying influence.

Every street at the different times of the day will have a sunny side for street walkers in the cooler seasons, and a shady side for use in the hotter seasons.

The front, back and side door-yards will each receive the sun some portion of every sunny day.

XII. MISCELLANEOUS POINTS.

1. *The Rapidity of Vegetable Growth* seems to depend much upon the intensity of its odic emanations as signified by the following, witnessed by Mlle. Maix :—" The *Calla* was most powerful, the *Aloe* the least powerful, so that it appeared as if the strength of the influence kept pace with the rapidity of the plant's growth. The rapid growing *Calla* produced a sensation greatly more vivid than the sluggish *Aloe*, notwithstanding the great size of the latter ; while the *Pelargonium moschatum* stood, in every respect, between the others " (p. 188).

2. *Hunger* and *weakness* cause feeble odic lights, and the

odic light emanating from the pit of the stomach is weakened during a pain. The *emanations* are more positive and brilliant during the positive conditions of health and strength.

3. *Sleep.* The state of shadow and darkness having a more quiet and negative grade of odic force than that which is aroused into action by the sunlight, renders night a more favorable time for sleep than the day-time.

4. The odic force from a powerful magnet could sometimes be *felt at a distance of several hundred feet* where no air was stirring ; the cooling effect of sulphur was felt 120 feet off, the warming effect of a copper plate of four square feet, 93 feet. An iron plate of 6 square feet gave warmth at a distance of 147 feet, and lead foil do., 75 feet.

5. Odic Light was seen to be more ethereal and pure when strained through glass, in harmony with what has been stated in Chromo Therapeutics.

XIII. Summation of Points in Chromo-Dynamics.

1. *This chapter demonstrates from actual facts, the existence of fluidic ethereal forces, and this is corroborative of the etherio-atomic law.*

2. *It demonstrates that other grades of color exist besides those we usually see.*

3. *The existence of Odic Light was demonstrated by years of experimentation by Baron Reichenbach whose thoroughness of method has never been surpassed, if equaled, in the records of scientific research.*

4. *Aided by a knowledge of atoms and chromo-chemistry we may perceive the real potencies of these interior forces.*

5. *Odic Light manifests the same phenomena of incandescence, flame, sparks, smoke, etc., as ordinary light, and must work in connection with a fine atmosphere of its own, just as common light works in connection with the atmosphere which we breathe.*

6. *Odic Force emanates from all known objects and manifests itself in the form of Odic Light when these objects are kindled into action by sunlight, moonlight, electricity, heat, magnetism, friction, etc.*

7. *Odic Flames have been witnessed of various lengths, from the fraction of an inch to about 6 feet.*

8. *Odic Force follows the law of polarity, and objects like crystals,*

magnets, etc., generally have one end more electrical, the other more thermal.

9. *Electrical or Cold Objects and forces were seen to be blue or bluish in their radiations, while most metals and the warmer objects had an extensive amount of red.*

10. *The Solar Rays will charge objects so that streams of odic light will flow from them and continue to do so for some time after the objects are removed. The Lunar Rays are somewhat exciting, especially at the full moon.*

11. *Magnetism, besides being coarser, differs from odic light in many points. The poles of a magnet, of crystals, and the ends of the fingers are especially luminous with Odyl.*

12. *The proof that Odic Light is not imaginary, is the fact that so many see and describe it in the same way, and can point out unerringly water and other objects which have been charged with it.*

13. *Opaque bodies are sometimes made transparent by Odic Light.*

14. *Odyl is shown to be a material emanation.*

15. *The Vertical Forces of the earth are cold and bluish upward, warm and reddish downward.*

16. *The horizontal forces of the earth are electrical in the following directions: 1st, in the direction of the north magnetic pole in which the thermo-electrical and magnetic forces predominate, and show a deep blue influence; 2dly, east of north in which the indigo, then the violet forces, rule; 3dly, west of north where the blue-green forces move, and lastly in the east, where a feeble electricity rules in the slight bluish gray. They are thermal in the south where the red is predominant, in the west where yellow forces rule, and in the south-west, south-east and north of west, in which the orange, red-gray and yellow-green respectively manifest themselves.*

17. *Physiology and many experiments show that in sleeping the head should be at the north or somewhat north-east, and the feet in the opposite direction to harmonize with the earth's cold and warm forces. Medical treatment is shown to be inefficacious or injurious with sensitive patients whose position is at discord with the earth's forces.*

18. *The direction of the streets of a city should be regulated with reference to lights, shadows and terrestrial dynamics.*

CHAPTER TENTH.

CHROMO–MENTALISM.

I. MENTALITY.

In considering the laws of visible light and color, we have been dwelling in nature's outer temple ; in unfolding the mysterious workings of the odic light and color, we have entered the vestibule of the inner, and have taken the first steps into the citadel of life itself. Shall we dare to open still another door farther within than the mere realms of physical life ? Nay, shall we approach the holy of holies and stand in the very presence chamber of MIND ? We gaze in awe upon a great temple, a mountain, an ocean, a world. But INTELLECT is greater than these, for it can measure and weigh the worlds themselves, and sweep a thousand times beyond their orbits. Intellect, or Mind, is the soul manifesting through the body, and the soul being a spark of the Infinity is itself infinite.

II. BEAUTY OF THE FINE FORCES.

I have been doubly impressed with the wonders of the Mind from the resplendent character of the forces which it uses, as manifested by a grade of light and color still finer than the odic, which may be termed the *psychic* or *third grade colors.* This, of course, is constituted of vibrations which are twice as fine as the odic or four times as fine as those of the ordinary light. In the year 1870 I commenced cultivating, in a dark room and with closed eyes, my interior vision, and in a few weeks or months was able to see those glories of light and color which no tongue can describe or intellect conceive of, unless they have been seen. Do you say it was imagination ? But no mere imagination can come half way to the reality of these things. Imagination itself must construct the warp and woof of its fabrics out of realities. The finest mosaic work and the most exquisite works of art are but trash by the side of these interior splendors. I have witnessed what have been called marvelous decorations in museums and palaces of Europe, but none of them are fit to be spoken of in comparison with these peerless colors and exquisite forms. Imagination is generally more dim and shadowy than realities, but these colors were so much more brilliant and intense and yet soft than any colors of the outer world, that when I opened my eyes upon the sky and earth around me after seeing these, they seemed almost colorless and dim and feeble. The sky no longer seemed blue, but blue gray, and a poor blue-gray at that. I saw so many grades of violet, and thermel, and indigo of wonderful depth, and blue, and red, and yellow, and orange, more brilliant than the sun, seemingly hundreds of different tints, hues, and shades which could be easily distinguished apart, that at first I thought there must be different colors from any that are usually visible, but finally concluded that we have the basic principles of all colors in external nature, though so feeble comparatively, that we scarcely know what color is. Sometimes fountains of light would pour toward me from luminous centers merging into all the iridescent splendors on their way. Sometimes radiations would flow out from me and become lost to view in the distance. More generally flashing streams of light would move to and fro in straight lines, though sometimes fluidic emanations would sweep around in the curves of a parabola as in a fountain. What was more marvelous than almost anything else was the infinite millions of radiations, emanations and luminous currents which at times I would see streaming *from* and *into* and *through* all things, and filling all the surrounding space with coruscations and lightning activities. I believe that if the amazing streams of forces which sweep in all directions could be suddenly revealed to all people, many would go wild with fright for fear they should be dashed to pieces. Several times I have seen untold millions of polarized particles of vari-colored luminous matter, changing their lines of polarity scores of times a second, like an infinite kaleidoscope, and yet never falling into disorder, for when a particle left one line it would immediately form in exact order in the next line. For sometime I was much puzzled to know what these could be, but it seems quite probable that they were the luminelles which fill the whole atmosphere and constitute under the solar power the basis of light.   The dust of iron filings, as seen by the coarser odic light by Mlles. Reichel and Zinkel, while animated by the magnet, caused exclamations of surprise at the extraordinary beauty.   Mlle. Zinkel " saw on the glass plate millions of little brilliant stars arranged in curved lines.   She testified the greatest pleasure when, by gently tapping the plate, I caused the stars to move and leap about.   The whole of the northward half had a predominating blue light, beautifully variegated with all other colors ; on the southward half an equally variegated and beautiful red light prevailed " (p. 357).   At the present writing, I have forgotten the exact direction of these lines, but think they were either perpendicular or slightly oblique to the earth's surface.   They were seen generally at night between 9 and 11 o'clock, and may have been excited into the fine grade of luminosity by the earth's radiations.

III.   This Finer Vision Exalts One's Conceptions.

1. These finer interior views of nature and her forces show us that *there are universes within universes,* and that the condition of things which we inhabit is not the real universe, but the mere shadowy outer shell of being, while the real cosmos is so much more intense and swift and powerful than the grosser grade of materiality around us that the latter compares with the former somewhat as a mist compares with a solid substance.   And yet there are those who think that this lower universe is all that there is for man, while the sublimer realms of existence are to go to waste as a worthless thing.   Even so low a grade of being as a chrysalis can awaken from its coffin and move off into the sunlight, but man standing upon the very pinnacle of nature, and the natural master of its domains, must vanish in eternal oblivion, according to these theorists, before he has fairly entered upon the possibilities of things around him.

2. After viewing these wonderfully refined lights, colors, and forms, my ideals of beauty and perfection became greatly improved, and my conception of the possibilities of man and nature grew far broader.   The gorgeous transformation scenes of the New York, Paris, and London theaters, which were generally pronounced magnificent, seemed tawdry and rude compared with

that soft and exquisite brilliance which so transcends the power of the outer world to equal, or of the external senses to perceive, while in many works of art or design I could observe features in which I think the artist could have improved upon his work if he had seen these higher manifestations of nature.

IV. Many Persons can see these Higher Colors.

1. Thousands of persons are able to see these finer grades of colors, and some much more easily and clearly than myself. Some can see them with the eyes wide open in broad daylight, and that while in the midst of company or surrounded by the turmoil of daily cares. A Mrs. Minnie Merton, of New York, informs me that she has always seen them from her childhood, emanating from all human beings, and is in the habit of reading the character of people especially from the emanations of the head. For some time in her childhood she supposed that everybody could see them. An eminent legal friend informed me some time since that he had seen these colors in all their splendor for many years, but at first he found it necessary not only to close his eyes, but to put a bandage over them before he could witness them. A lady in Chicago, whom I had never seen before, saw in a moment, as she met me, while I was still 15 feet from her, what my profession was or ought to be from the radiations of my person. A well-known judge informed me that he could often tell the general character of a speaker's thoughts before they were uttered, from the colors of the emanations. An eminent physician stated to me that he could see countless flashes, radiations and explosive forces all around the head, and that the ganglionic centers often emitted an explosive light, especially under excitement. I have seen a large number of persons who could see beautiful colors around persons or other objects, but could not tell what it meant. In giving an account of these, I do not include all persons who can see colors on merely shutting up the eyes, for in some cases this comes from a somewhat deranged nervous and bilious action, and in some cases, as in shutting up the eyes and turning them towards the light, the red blood of the eyelid gives a crimson hue as in ordinary light. Sometimes, when the intensity of this red is greater than that

which is ordinarily visible, it doubtless partakes more or less of the nature of odic light also.

2. *Reichenbach's sensitives*, as we have seen, *often saw the beginning of the psychic scale of colors, and probably at times they saw the full scale.* They often spoke of the beauty of the flames which they saw. Such expressions as the following are used: —"The columns of flame from each pole astonished her by their size and beauty;" "She described the appearance as one of extraordinary delicacy and splendor;" "Of uncommon beauty," etc. We have seen that in several cases they saw two grades of red as signified on pp. 393, 431, 436, etc., of Gregory's Translation. They saw shining emanations from the head and all other parts of the system, some of which must have been odic and others psychic.

V. These Colors Reveal the Higher Laws of Force.

1. The very fact that all objects radiate their own peculiar streams of light and color, while their interior potencies are revealed thereby, has given me the basic principles of the whole etherio-atomic law by means of which so many mysteries of force stand revealed. If, at first sight, the reader has deemed my positions at times as based on assertion with reference to the working of these different grades of ethers, without sufficient data of fact, it is proper that he should understand what a vast volume of facts could be given to sustain my positions, not only from my own experience, but from that of very many others. Besides this would it not be well for the reader to ask himself how I could have had the skill to hit upon those basic principles of force which so easily and naturally explain Attraction, Repulsion, Cohesion, Adhesion, Electricity in its various grades, Heat of various kinds, with the very law of movement required for its production, Light of different grades with the law of electrical and thermal colors, Chromo-Chemistry, Chromo Therapeutics, and many other points, if I had not been taught by seeing and feeling these wonderful fluidic emanations and radiations which are the law of all things? For this reason it strikes me as being exceedingly important to have these finer forces explained with some fulness not only as giving the fundamental principles of

the philosophy of this work, but of all philosophy of force both in external nature and in mental action, for, as we have seen, both the physical and spiritual universe are constructed on principles of absolute unity.

2. Many of our scientists, with a singular perversity of mind, grasp with all their souls after the grosser elements of nature, writing long treatises on a bug, a worm, a mineral, or a skeleton, but when marvelous facts are revealed with regard to these more beautiful essences of being, these lightnings of power without which the whole universe would be but a formless and lifeless mass of debris, they utterly fail to receive the glad tidings with philosophical candor, commence persecuting the discoverer as though he was an enemy, and return to the corpses and bones of the dissecting-room in preference to the radiant forms of the world of life. " We build on exact science and deal with tangible realities," is their watchword, and so they go right off in a carriage with one wheel into the pathways which lead to all confusion and inexactness of knowledge. Take, for instance, the common conception of a single ether which they conjecture must exist throughout all space. They have no facts to prove it, and have not the least idea of how the thousands of grades of force, luminous, thermal, electrical, magnetic, and molar are transmitted over and through it, but have endowed it with properties, as we have seen, at discord with all known law (Chap. Eighth, V). These exact men are immensely inexact. They cannot tell the cause of even so simple a thing as *muscular contraction;* are quite ignorant of *nervous force,* nervous diseases being confessedly the " scandala medicorum " ; have but a dim conception of the cause of *sensation,* the laws of *mental action,* of *chemical affinity,* of the *fundamental potencies of drugs,* and many other important matters which after all these ages might have been understood far better if they had but condescended to inquire into the basic principles of power as they exist in the fine forces. " The brain of man itself," says Tyndall, "is an assemblage of molecules arranged according to physical laws ; but if you ask me to deduce from this assemblage the least of the phenomena of sensation or thought, I lay my forehead in the dust and acknowledge human helplessness." (Amer. Lectures on Light). Ever grateful as an American for the simple and beautiful lec-

tures on light, and the donations in favor of scientific culture
which this apostle of science has favored us with, still I feel confident that if he had not pushed far from him the investigation
of these psychological forces, he could at least have understood
something of the processes of "sensation and thought." I believe, however, that he would be too truthful to do as did the
Vienna clique of Doctors with regard to Reichenbach's investigations, or as some British and American Doctors have done
since that time.   Referring to the Vienna Doctors, William
Gregory, M. D., F. R. S. E., remarks as follows : "It is painful
to think that parallel cases have not been wanting in England.
The spontaneous somnambulism, and apparent transference of
the senses, in Miss M'Avoy, met with precisely similar treatment ; as did the very interesting facts which occurred in the
case of Dr. Elliotson's patients, the Okeys.   There was the
same predetermination to find the patient an impostor, the same
utter absence of all cogency in the evidence adduced, and the
same rash and unjustifiable, as well as unmanly accusation of
imposture, brought against persons of whom no evil was known,
apparently because the authorities chose to assume the facts to
be impossible.   The still more recent case of Miss Martineau's
servant girl is another instance in point.   Having seen that girl,
and made observations on her, I can speak with confidence of
her honesty and truthfulness."   Alas! If scientists cannot rise
above prejudice into the pure atmosphere of truth, whom shall
we trust ?

VI.   This Light Renders Opaque Substances Transparent.

1. This transparency, however, appears only to those who
who can get *en rapport* with the finer light, and such persons are
sometimes called clairvoyant, or clear seeing.   In Chapter Ninth,
VII, we have seen that Odic light often made bodies transparent, or at least translucent to the sensitives, and we might naturally expect that the still finer psychic light would render bodies
still more generally transparent.

2. *Dr. Wm. A. Hammond* and *Dr. Geo. M. Beard*, of New
York, have declared positively that no person ever did or ever
will see through what we call opaque substances, or read with

blindfolded eyes. To make this assertion in itself of much value, we must first suppose these gentlemen to be omniscient and capable of grasping all the possibilities of man and the universe in order to know whereof they speak; and secondly, we must stultify ourselves by ignoring ten thousand facts which show that there are powers of vision in man aside from the external eye. I say ten thousand facts, but I believe I could collect in six months or a year, a million well-established facts from the records of England, France, Germany, Italy, Russia, America, and other parts of the world, and thus show that if these gentlemen are honest they are quite innocent of real knowledge of the facts. Both of them are very free in denouncing as fools or tricksters those who believe anything in this matter, but I have generally found that those who know the least of this subject are generally the most positive in denouncing those who know the most. In saying this I do not call them dishonest, but they simply possess such a materialistic bias of mind that all phenomena connected with the finer forces seem absurd to them, as they insist upon having them strained through their own imperfect spectacles. According to Dr. Leeds, " facts are the arguments of God," but Dr. Beard condemns the production of facts and the use of *induction* in this matter, and commends the exploded system of mere *deduction*. According to this the more we know the worse we are off, and *much* "knowledge is a dangerous thing," while *theories* only are safe. " The only way," says Dr. Beard, " to settle this question is through deductive reasoning," and this is his deduction which is to settle the point :—" No human being ever has, or can have any faculty different in kind from that conferred on the human race in general." Does not Dr. Beard know that the human mind takes hold upon the infinite, and that most men's faculties lie dormant, being developed as yet but little above the animal nature, while the faculties which are the very latest of development are those that deal with the fine spiritual forces? In Edinburgh, statistics show that 17 per cent. of the people are color blind, and in Russia a still larger number. Suppose Drs. Hammond and Beard should be cast upon some distant island where the whole people, or nearly the whole, are so undeveloped in the perception of colors that one is about the same as another to them. They show the people a red object, and tell them it is red, and holding up a leaf tell them it is green. "It is false!" the people cry; "one color is the same as another." "But we can see some colors which you cannot see," exclaim our visitors. "You are deluded! You are tricksters!" they cry, "for one man cannot see any more colors than another!" They are then receiving the very coin which they are in the habit of dealing out to others, and which they would be the first to complain of. To these gentlemen, and the many others who adopt their methods, I would say—*It behooves those who are blind to be modest and not to dictate to those of us who can see, but sit at our feet and learn.* On the other hand we will sit at their feet and learn of them concerning matters in which they may have a superior perception. Such must ever be the spirit of philosophers, to whom truth is supreme, while the use of severe epithets contrary to reason, must rebound boomerang-like upon the senders. I will now quote a very few facts from superior sources with reference to this higher vision, after which I will endeavor to state just how such vision is accomplished.

3. *From Boudois de la Motte, Fouquier, Guéneau de Mussy, Guersant, Itard, J. J. Leroux, Marc, Thillaye, and Husson, Committee of the French Royal Academy, in 1831 :*—" We have seen two somnambulists distinguish, with their eyes shut, the objects placed before them ; they have told without touching them the color and value of the cards ; they have read words traced with the hand, or some lines of books opened by mere chance. This phenomenon took place even when the opening of the eyelids was accurately closed by means of the fingers. We met in two somnambulists the power of foreseeing acts of the organism more or less distant, more or less complicated."

4. *From Wm. B. Gregory, M. D., F. R. S. E., Prof. of Chemistry in the Edinburgh University :*—(Some of the following I condense.) " Clairvoyance frequently commences by the sleeper's seeing the operator's hand. The eyelids, if opened forcibly, will show the eye turned upward and back so that the pupil cannot be seen at all in many cases, and when it can it is fixed and motionless, showing that sight must be caused by some inner vision." " The clairvoyant seems to go to a place mentally, or rather to ' float on the air,' for a while, when all at once he will exclaim,

'now I am there,' and will thus describe distant cities which he has never seen. He often reverses the points of the compass, but will describe people, streets, houses, colors, etc., correctly." " Some clairvoyants will give the time of the day at the places which they visit, getting it by means of watches and clocks, thus marking the different time signified by different longitudes." " He will often describe the wonders of his own body. When altogether ignorant of anatomy, he sees in all their beauty and marvelous perfection the muscles, vessels, bones, nerves, glands, brain, lungs and other viscera, and describes the minutest ramifications of nerves and vessels with an accuracy surpassing that of the most skillful anatomist. He will trace any vessel or nerve in its most complex distribution ; the whole to him is transparent, bathed in delicate light, and full of life and motion." " Major Buckley has developed the ability to read writing hidden away in nuts or boxes in 89 persons without inducing the magnetic sleep or affecting consciousness. Most of these belonged to the upper educated classes. The longest motto thus read contained 98 words. Many subjects will read motto after motto without one mistake. In this way the mottoes contained in 4860 nut shells have been read, some of them indeed by persons in the mesmeric sleep, but most of them by persons in the conscious state, many of whom have never been put to sleep. In boxes, upward of 36000 words have been read ; in one paper 371 words. Including those who have read words contained in boxes, when in the sleep, 148 persons have thus read." " A lady, one of Major Buckley's waking clairvoyants, read 103 mottoes contained in nuts in one day, without a pass being made on that occasion. In this and in many other cases, the power of reading in nuts, boxes and envelopes remained, when once induced, for about a month and then disappeared. The same lady after three months could no longer read without passes." " In this state the subject often possesses new powers of perception, the nature of which is unknown, but by means of which he can see objects or persons near or distant without the use of the external organs of vision," etc. (*Letters on Animal Magnetism*).

5. *From Rev. E. B. Hall, Providence, to Mr. T. C. Hartshorn, Translator of Deleuze's Animal Magnetism,* in which he speaks of a blind lady : " She described distant objects, whose

position in some cases I had just changed, whose existence in other cases I did not then know or believe, so truly, so wonderfully, that I could only marvel. At other times she has done the same with regard to my own house, and houses in other towns and states. I am convinced that she sees by some other organ than the eye, or with such rays of light only as can penetrate all substances, if there are any such. I have seen a sealed letter, containing a passage enclosed in lead, which letter she held at the side of her head not more than a moment all in sight, then gave it back to the writer, and afterward wrote what she had read in it. The letter was opened in my presence and the two writings agreed in every word, there being two differences in spelling only." The contents of the letter were as follows :—"*In these latter days, as in former times, the blind receive their sight.*" (*Appendix to Deleuze.*)

6. *Dr. Alphonse Teste, of Paris*, gives an account of some sentences which were read by Madame Hortense after they were locked up and sealed in a close box. The first was a passage from Lamartine as follows :—"*Le réel est etroit ; le possible est immense.*" The madame read "*le possible est immense,*" but skipped the rest. M. Amedée Latour then wrote a passage, placed it in the box and placed his own seals upon it. It was returned to him with the seals untouched with the following sen· tence :—"*L'eau est composée d'hydrogène et d'oxygène.*" "Well, you are the devil," cried he, "or magnetism is a truth."

7. The following fact with reference to *Swedenborg* is sanctioned by the great German metaphysician Kant, who remarked that it sets "the assertion of the extraordinary gift of Swedenborg out of all possibility of doubt." While in Gottenburg, on a Saturday night, he saw that a great fire was taking place in his native city Stockholm, 300 miles distant. On Sunday Morning he made a statement of it to the Governor, while on Tuesday morning the arrival of the royal courier gave full comfirmation of it. Other cases of his power could be mentioned.

8. *Alexis*, so well known in Europe, and who so often astonished the savans by his feats of vision and mental perception, has his eyes covered with thick masses of cotton, and then plays various games with experts, in which he usually wins. He is able to read the cards of his opponent and thus has the advantage.

9. *Miss Fay*, in 1856, in the presence of the Hon. Joshua R. Giddings and Stephen Dudley, Esq., in New York, exclaimed as follows : " I behold a sea of light extending everywhere, a never fading light. It is not of the sun or moon, or stars ; oh, that I had the power to describe it ! I must call it a divine light. It will never grow dim. I see no limit, but only an immensity of light. The sun fades beside it. The source appears like light creating light."

10. *Mrs. Mettler*, of Hartford, examined clairvoyantly some 40,000 persons during the first fifteen years of her practice, among which were many amazing triumphs of this finer vision. Dr. T. Lea Smith, from Hamilton, Bermuda, gives an account of an interview with her, in which he says she accurately described his island home and pointed out a weed which grew in abundance there, and which she declared would cure the yellow fever. In a letter written at Hamilton, Oct. 29, 1856, Dr. Smith says :—" During the last three months the fever has been making sad havoc in Bermuda, and we know not where it will stop; it is very bad among the troops, but I am happy to say that out of 200 cases treated by Mrs. Mettler's prescription, only four have died !" At another time he says she read an inscription on a tombstone in the cemetery at Hamilton. She was thus able, by the aid of this more exquisite light, to look something like a thousand miles and discover the real properties of a plant which the physicians on the spot had failed to do, and which was supposed to be a worthless weed. In another case related by Dr. S. B. Brittan in " Man and his Relations," Mrs. Mettler examined a gun-shot wound of a Mr. Charles Barker in Jackson, Mich., with which he had been suffering for months, and discovered a *piece of copper* in the wound, which she said would prevent it from healing until it was removed. " But young Barker was sure that he had no copper in his pocket at the time of the accident; and inasmuch as the medical attendant had made no such discovery, it was presumed that the seeress was mistaken. But some time after, the foreign substance spoken of became visible, when Mr. Barker's mother with a pair of embroidery scissors, removed a *penny* from the wound ! In such a case science is a stupid, sightless guide, and must stand out of the way. The doctors in Michigan could not see that penny

when it was within their reach and their eyes wide open ; but this seeress discovered it at a distance of 1000 miles with her eyes closed !" (p. 400.)

11. *Dr. Wm. B. Carpenter*, of England, has lately written a work disparaging the claims of clairvoyance, mesmerism, etc., to which Prof. Alfred R. Wallace has given a triumphant answer in the Quarterly Journal of Science, London, producing multitudes of overwhelming facts to show the reality of clairvyance. I quote simply the following : " I refer to the testimony of Robert Houdin, the greatest of modern conjurers, whose exploits are quoted by Dr. Carpenter when they serve his purpose (pp. 76, 111). He was an absolute master of card tricks and knew all their possibilities. He was asked by the Marquis de Mirville to visit Alexis, which he did twice. He took his own new cards, dealt them himself, but Alexis named them as they lay upon the table, and even named the trump before it was turned up. This was repeated several times and Houdin declared that neither chance nor skill could produce such wonderful results. He then took a book from his pocket and asked Alexis to read something eight pages beyond where it was opened, at a specified level. Alexis pricked the place with a pin, and read four words which were found at the place pricked nine pages on. He then told Houdin, numerous details as to his son, in some of which Houdin had tried to deceive him, but in vain ; and when it was over, Houdin declared it ' stupefying,' and the next day signed a declaration that the report of what took place was correct, adding, ' the more I reflect upon them the more impossible do I find it to class them among the tricks that are the object of my art.' The two letters of Robert Houdin were published at the time (May, 1847), in ' *Le Siccle*,' and have since appeared in many works."

12. The foregoing cases, though but a drop in the bucket of what might be presented with reference to this beautiful law of vision, are quite enough to demolish the rash remarks of Drs. Hammond and Beard. It is no wonder that Dr. Beard thought it best not to appeal to facts, in a matter loaded down with such an overwhelming array of them. My own powers enable me at times not only to see objects, but to look through them to objects beyond without the outward eye, while I have known a

great number of people who can do the same.   A lady in Chicago with whose family I resided for some time, could become quiet at any time and in a minute or two look into any residence of the city, or even of distant states, and tell whether the owners were at home or absent.   I knew of no failures, and a gentleman who had tested her for one or two years told me he had never found her mistaken.

13. *One of the eminent lady physicians of New York* received a salary of $3000 per annum from a Life Insurance Company, on account of possessing this finer insight which so transcends all ordinary perception, and saved her company tens of thousands of dollars.   I will simply mention one instance in proof.   A gentleman of remarkably vigorous appearance had passed the examination of the physicians of the company, and was pronounced as "sound as a bullet."   He wished to be insured for $10,000.   Before accepting of his case, however, they handed a little strip of paper with some of his writing on it to the lady.   Almost immediately, coming into rapport with the subject by means of the emanations from the paper, she declared that he would be a dead man within eight weeks, and warned them against taking him.   They asked him to defer the matter eight weeks, which he agreed to.   After seven weeks and two days the President of the company came with much excitement to the residence of the lady, and informed her that the gentleman had fallen dead with heart disease, on his own door step, that morning!   In another case, a southern gentleman applied for an insurance policy of $10,000.   This lady, on examining his autograph, saw a certain melancholy and diseased condition which she declared would lead him to commit suicide, and advised them against taking his case.   They concluded to risk it however, and so lost their money, as he committed suicide the same year in Virginia.

VII. Explanation of this Higher Vision.

1. The *Philosophy of Ordinary Sleep* consists in the withdrawal of the ordinary vital fluids from the *cerebrum* or realm of mental action, to the cerebellum or center of the physical forces. These vital fluids, which are doubtless a modification of odic

force, animate the external or gray portion of the brain, draw
the blood there, and thus bring about the ordinary grade of mental activity.   It is well understood by physiologists that a free
action of pure uncongested blood though the front brain is necessary to consciousness and thought, but how the blood itself is
enabled to move thus freely or what is its vitalizing principle, except that it must be properly oxydized, have sufficient phosphorus, etc., they cannot tell.   The clear seer, however, can actually witness the fiery streams of this invisible light, as they
kindle the blood and brain tissue, and can see that when all the
chemical conditions of the blood are proper, such as having a
sufficient supply of oxygen, cholesterin, etc., these animating
streams of nervaura, sometimes called animal magnetism, are
all the more brisk, and mental action all the more clear.   Wm.
B. Carpenter, M. D., F. R. S., says that " although the brain has
not ordinarily more than about $\frac{1}{40}$ of the weight of the body, it
yet is estimated to receive from $\frac{1}{6}$ to $\frac{1}{5}$ of the whole circulating
blood."   (*Principles of Mental Physiology*.)   He also says that
of the four arterial trunks which convey blood into the skull,
three may be tied and consciousness still remain, but if the fourth
is tied unconsciousness takes place.   One may become asphyx-
iated with depraved blood which has too much carbon in proportion to its oxygen, as chemical action of vital forces thus become
too dormant, and congestion takes place.   Persons of resolute will
can often fire up this odic force by the finer psychic principle,
and through that so animate the blood as to prevent many dis-
asters even when the blood has become more or less impure.   If
a part of the animating ether is drawn off to the back brain and
to the body, it carries a portion of the blood with it, and the front
brain becoming thus inactive, a quiet condition takes place and
a person begins to feel sleepy.   If a greater quantity is drawn
downward a dreamy kind of a sleep ensues, while a still greater
quantity will leave too little action of the cerebral forces to be
remembered at all, and so we call it perfect unconscious sleep.
Dr. Durham demonstrated, in 1860, that there was far less blood
in the cerebrum during sleeping than during waking hours.
Where he had cut away the skull in animals, the vessels of the
pia mater, which were full and red during wakefulness, became
contracted and pale during sleep.   The contrast was remarkable.

It must not be supposed, however, that the blood itself is the direct cause of mental action, but its free action through the brain awakens chemical affinity and constitutes a good conducting medium for the finer forces.   During this quiet of the cerebrum, the rest of the system is doubly active, building up its cells and tissues to make up for the combustions and waste which take place during the waking hours.   Ordinary Sleep, then, may be induced by whatever will draw this vital aura, and with it the blood, away from the front and upper brain, such as making passes downward from the head, laying the hand upon the back-head and back neck, warming the spine or feet, etc. *But how is it, if ordinary sleep thus stupifies, shuts up the faculties of the mind and renders it almost a blank, that the so-called mesmeric or lucid magnetic sleep opens up such new and wonderful powers of intellection which enables the sleeper to grasp the conditions of past, present and future with double power, and gives him a vision which seemingly penetrates through all substances and reveals the very soul of things ?*   I have not seen this point clearly answered, although the subject of psychology must ever have a misty aspect until it is answered.

2. *Somniscience, or the Lucid Magnetic Sleep, sometimes called Artificial Somnambulism, consists, not only in drawing away the blood and the vital ethers which usually kindle the phrenal organs into activity, but in calling into action the more interior, refined, swift and powerful psychic ethers that are more directly the handmaid of the spirit itself.*   In other words, when we abstract the coarser forces we can the more easily get *en rapport* with the finer, just as the sensitives by taking the ordinary light from a room, could the more easily see the odic light.   The outer and gray matter of the brain is the more immediate seat of ordinary sensation and mental action, while the more interior forces, quickened by the chemical affinities between the inner surface of the reddish gray matter and the outer surface of the interior bluish white matter, when called somewhat outward, produce a higher grade of mental action than the slower and coarser forces which are usually predominant, while if they are called still more outward and wrought up into still greater action, until the whole brain is suffused with this diviner light which blends with the same grade of light in the external world, this

higher vision takes place and a wonderful illumination of the mind is the result. I will illustrate by the process of outward vision. This is accomplished as follows :—The rays of light fall upon the retina of the eye where they stamp their image, which image is carried to the external sensorium by a grade of vital electricity that is just suited to it, and thus we get the effect of vision. *Bell's Telephone*, by which the human voice is transferred hundreds of miles, operates on much the same principle. The waves of sound strike an artificial diaphragm at one end of the line, and are transferred by means of electricity through a wire to another diaphragm and human ear at the other end. In human vision the first diaphragm is the retina at the back of the eye, the conducting wire is the optic nerve, the second diaphragm is the external sensorium in the outer gray matter of the brain aided by refining processes, and the ear of the listener represents the human spirit itself which takes cognizance of the whole. In certain magnetic conditions the eyes are wide open, but the ordinary light cannot make much impression as the internal corresponding vital electricity is withdrawn to other parts of the body. But the finer psychic ethers, having full play, receive the finer light that emanates from, or penetrates through all substances, and carrying it to the inner sensorium, which, according to the magnetic vision itself, seems to have its culminating point at the junction of the gray and white matter of the brain, the mind receives the exquisite images thus conveyed, and so the higher vision is perfected. By means of ordinary light we may see through all transparent bodies because the light itself can penetrate them, but by means of the psychic light, the vision may pass through nearly all bodies as easily as ordinary vision passes through glass, which accounts for what is called clairvoyance.

3. It is by no means necessary to get into this magnetic sleep in order to have this finer vision. Many can so cause the finer ethers of their brain to gain the ascendency over the coarser as to be able to see almost immediately, and that without even closing the eyes. Some learn to throw the animal forces away from the front brain by their will power, meantime assisting the action by throwing their eye-balls upward and back as in a sleeping condition. Those less developed in the matter

will frequently have to look at some object in front or above
them, or thinking of some place intensely in order to draw the
psychic forces sufficiently outward, and this in many cases a
half-hour, an hour, or more at a time.

VIII. How to Develop this Finer Vision.

1. These finer ethers are so swift, penetrating and powerful
that it is a very great achievement to be able to wield them for
the sake of the wonderful powers of vision which they give, as
well as for the great control of both bodily and mental forces
which can be gained thereby. I will give some brief hints for
the culture and control of these agencies.

2. When convenient it is quite desirable to have a person
who is already well charged with these fine forces and who can
himself see clairvoyantly, make passes over the head downward
and especially over the eyes and forehead, and thus impart his
own power to the subject. Sometimes these passes can be made
from the head to the feet along the face and body, and sometimes one or two inches from the body.

3. Dr. Braid, of England, who styled this magnetic sleep
hypnotism, was in the habit of having his subjects look steadily
at an object placed in front and somewhat above them, for some
time. Such a process will answer very well for awhile, after
which downward passes will be useful.

4. One of the most practical methods of developing these
forces is to sit somewhat reclining in an easy position with the
back to the north or a little north-east, have merely a dim light
rather than otherwise, close the eyes, turn the eye-balls a little
upward, if they can be held so without pain, and then steadily and
gently make an effort as if to see. This can be practiced for a half
hour to an hour or so each time, and while doing so the thoughts
should not be allowed to wander, but the aim should be to see
if lights, colors, forms, and motions make their appearance. If
colors do not appear in a few days, the prospect for clairvoyance
is poor unless assistance can be imparted by persons already developed. Dr. Fahnestock, of Pennsylvania, has developed what
he calls *statuvolence* or *artificial* somnambulism, which he says
can be acquired by all in from one to twenty sittings, while most

of the persons who attain to it gain the *clear vision*. This will be described in X of this chapter.

IX. THE PSYCHIC FORCE A GREAT POWER TO BLESS MANKIND.

1. *Because it brings into action this sublimer vision* which reveals the wonders of both the interior and exterior universe in a way that entirely transcends the power of the telescope in the distance of its scope, the microscope in the minuteness of its power, and throws both into shadow by its ability to reveal the realm of intellect and that finer radiance which can never be seen in the external world. When its powers have become more developed, mistakes of vision will be more rare, and discoveries of vast importance in psychological and physiological phenomena will be made.

2. *Because through the Mental Forces it is able to build up and heal the physical system* in a way sometimes which would seem almost too marvelous for belief. Dr. Gregory says " an immense number of magnetic cures have been recorded ; " Dr. Elliotson commends it highly and enumerates cases of Epilepsy, Insanity, Hysteria, Paralysis, Chorea, Hypochondriasis, Sick Head-ache, Convulsions, Nervousness, etc., and a severe case of Cancer, as having been cured by the human magnetic (or psychic) forces. The Zouave Jacob of France who was wonderfully charged with these forces, cured multitudes by a mere touch of the hand, and many times without touching his subjects at all. This was done when they were in their normal condition, by a powerful effort of his will. Sometimes a score of policemen were required to regulate the crowds who pressed forward to be healed by him. Downward passes over the body soothe and quiet excited nerves, and upward passes arouse dormant and cold portions of the body.

3. *Because it has a remarkable and unequaled power in improving imperfect mental and moral conditions.* I have charged and regulated the psychic forces of different parts of the brain and their negative poles in the body in a way to quell the appetite for liquor in several persons, to abate their animal passions, and to stimulate to much greater activity the mental and moral forces. The achievements accomplished under the form of Psychic influence, called statuvolence, will be described shortly (X). I will

quote a passage from an eccentric writer, named P. B. Randolph, which will apply here :—" We have known a sweet Miss only six years old, to thoroughly mesmerize her great burly uncle, a man capable of knocking a bull down with one stroke of his ponderous fist, and who was one of the roughest sea tyrants that ever trod a quarter-deck, and yet the little lady rendered him not only helpless, but clairvoyant by repeatedly manipulating his head, while he held her in his lap in his daily calls.   She had witnessed a few experiments, believed she could do the same, tried it four times and accomplished it in great glee on the fifth attempt. But the greatest miracle of all was, that the captain's nature became entirely changed, and to-day a better or a gentler man does not sail out of New York harbor ! " (*New Mola.*)   In the case of this captain, the finer forces of the man, combined with a gentle pure element from his little magnetiser, were doubtless made to permeate and refine the region of his external brain. " In the highest stages of the magnetic sleep," says Dr. Gregory, " the countenance becomes irradiated and heavenly beyond the power of art to picture, and the language becomes exalted."   I have several cases in view in which persons have dated the commencement of a nobler and truer life from the development of these higher elements.   That some fortune tellers may really have the ability at times to use them and convert them to a low end, does not argue against the holier purposes to which they ever may and should be consecrated.

4. Because it begets a keenness of vision and mental perception, which when it becomes widely developed will so penetrate through all fraud and hypocrisy as to greatly destroy their practice.   A lady of New York traced out a thief and recovered diamonds of the value of $10,000 for one party, and has found a large number of stolen watches and other articles by this superior vision.

X. STATUVOLENCE, OR SELF-PSYCHOLOGY.

1. Statuvolence is a phase of power brought about by these same psychic ethers, wielded and developed on a somewhat different plan from those which we have been considering.   Dr. Wm. B. Fahnestock, of Lancaster, Penn., has devised the name

and method of operating, and has wrought some remarkable
cures and effects even on the mental system by its means.   It
is, moreover, one of most effective methods of developing the
higher vision, and of assisting a person to gain control both of
his physical and mental forces.   Dr. Fahnestock does not seem
to understand the philosophy of this power any more than did
Dr. Braid and most others who have writen upon this and similar subjects, but is deserving of credit for his successful experiments.   He and Dr. Braid, and Dr. Brown-Séquard, and very
many medical men, deny that there is any magnetic fluid because
these singular phenomena seem to come from *belief* or *imagination*, or the *mind* in some of its manifestations.   This is simply
on a par with denying the existence of sunlight, because the
sun itself shines.   How do these gentlemen suppose the *mind*
or *imagination* can do these things without some instrument to
do them with ?   The sun starts vegetation into life because it
sends its light to the earth.   Mind or volition wields the human
system because it sends out its psychic and animal ethers.

2. The process which Dr. Fahnestock uses to bring about
the state is simply a method of drawing the interior forces outward.   I quote his own words:—"When persons are desirous of
entering this state, I place them upon a chair where they may be
at perfect ease.   I then request them to close their eyes at once
and remain perfectly calm, at the same time that they let the
body lie perfectly still and relaxed.   They are next instructed
to throw their minds to some familiar place, it matters not where,
so that they have been there before, and seem desirous of going
again, even in thought.   When they have thrown the mind to the
place, or upon the desired object, I endeavor by speaking to them
frequently to keep their mind upon it.   This must be persevered
in for some time, and when they tire of one thing, or see nothing,
they must be directed to others successively until clairvoyance
is induced.   When this has been effected, the rest of the senses
fall in at once, or by slow degrees.   If the attention of the subject is divided, the difficulty of entering the state perfectly is
much increased, and the powers of each sense while in this state
will be in proportion as that division has been much or little."
Sometimes as the especial condition approaches, the subject will
feel that he is falling away or floating off, but there is no occasion

for alarm. The thoughts being intensely concentrated on the place or object, he will begin to feel that he is there in person and can see what is going on, hear the words that may be spoken hundreds of miles distant and take cognizance of the very thoughts. When thoroughly in the state, the subject, at the request of the operator, can use these forces with a wonderful power, can will a certain disease to depart and it will very frequently leave, can determine to be strong, firm, self-controlled, after waking from the condition, and he will find himself in possession of a new strength ; can will to have his head in the ordinary conscious condition, and have all sensation leave his hand, or foot, or any other member, and it will be so to such an extent, that he can look on and see it amputated without any pain, and can determine to have a certain condition of mind permanently, and it will be very likely to take place. By a little practice, after once getting into this condition, he can throw himself into it in a few moments and be master of himself. I know of a lady who, when she goes to have a tooth pulled, can put herself into the condition immediately and, willing all sensation from her jaw, will feel no pain when the operation is performed, which signifies that this mighty psychic force under the mind can hold the sensory nerves entirely in check. Some of these statuvolists become remarkably clairvoyant, profess to look in upon different parts of the world, or even other worlds, and describe their people, although their astronomical ideas are not always reliable, as they see people in worlds which evidently possess no people, which shows that they are looking at the wrong world, or else have their vision but partially developed. In many cases their clairvoyance is proved to be entirely correct. I had a lady patient who would describe what was going on at her home in another state, and she said she was not quite sure whether she really saw her people and certain neighbors, or whether it was imagination, as she was but partially in this condition, but on writing home she found she was exactly correct. One day she stated that a certain acquaintance of hers was treating her too familiarly, and he held her under a kind of a psychological spell so that she had no power to resist him, and grieved over it, confessing also that she had been in the same helpless state before in the presence of another gentleman. I

told her that that weak condition of the will power must be
changed, and getting her into the statuvolic condition not fully,
but so much so that she could see her home and friends, I then
impressed upon her the baseness of an attempt to exercise an
improper control over another, and the grandeur of having self-
command, and asked her to will with all her power to be now
and afterward strong and self-poised, which she did most earnestly.   She found no trouble afterward in holding her annoyer
and all other persons at a proper distance, and during the months
after that in which I met her, I saw she had more independence
and force of character than before.

3. *Case of Melancholy from unrequited Love.*   I will quote a
single case of mental control from Dr. Fahnestock's work on
"Statuvolence or Artificial Somnambulism":—" Miss —— had
been desponding for many years.   She was induced to try somnambulism for her relief.   She entered the state perfectly the
first trial, in less than ten minutes ; and after she had been in it
for some time, I asked her, as is usual in such cases, whether
she did not think it was better for her to forget an attachment
that could not be returned ?

" She said ' Yes I believe it would.'

" I asked her whether she was perfectly satisfied to do so and
to become lively and happy hereafter ?

" She said ' Yes ; and I am resolved that it shall be so.'

" With this understanding I requested her to awake.   She
awoke and retired with a friend.   I have since been informed
that she has banished the circumstance from her mind entirely,
and has become lively, contented and happy every since."

4. *A merchant of Boston* informed me that in the quiet of the
morning, when his mind was in a calm state, he would generally
will to be in a certain frame of mind all day, and in this way
gained such a control over himself that nothing would disturb
him.   He also possessed a marvelous control over others without
uttering a word, holding fifty men who were under his employment in absolute harmony with his wishes.   He once caused a
man to leave an audience and follow him through the streets,
and into his own home, by mere volition without a spoken
word.   This and a host of other examples which could be given
explode the idea that this power is imaginary, and shows that

human beings can throw out their magnetic curves to *hook around*
and influence others, just as a magnet can attract iron, only with
a finer power.   In his younger mischievous days, he broke down
a clergyman in the midst of his sermon by looking steadily and
strongly at him, which fact is explained by clairvoyants who can
see streams of fiery light issuing from the eyes.   It is well known
that Daniel Webster's gaze once completely confounded a young
clergyman in the same way, so that an older clergyman present
had to rise and finish the sermon for him.   On being asked
afterwards what was the difficulty, he said "he couldn't endure
those great terrible eyes."   But this was not to be wondered at,
for the lightning from those eyes combined with that which went
forth with his voice and accompanied with great ideas, had en-
chained many a listening senate before that day.   As orators
become more refined by living noble lives, and learn more about
the control of these divine forces, they will have the greater
skill in swaying an audience and inspiring them with great purposes.

5. *Dr. Fahnestock mentions the cure of six cases of Epilepsy,
besides other cures of Rheumatism, Erysipelas, Scarletina, Chorea,
Amaurosis, Hysteria, Fevers, Labor-pains,* etc., and shows its remarkable use in obstetrical cases.   In my own practice I have
found it also a great assistance.

6. *In Psychology and ordinary Mesmerism,* the operator generally comes near to or even touches the subject and makes his
own forces predominate in the subject's brain.   In this better
method of Self-Psychology, the subject develops his own powers
and becomes strong of himself as the operator sits outside of the
coarser magnetic sphere, part way across the room from the
subject.

7. Mr. Thomas C. Hartshorn, translator of Deleuze, gives a
number of accounts of persons who were placed in the ordinary
magnetic sleep and then required to decide against the use of
tea, coffee, snuff and various articles of food which were hurtful
to them, with the proviso that if they were taken any more they
should create nausea.   When they awoke they knew nothing of
what had been determined upon, but could not take the articles
without their becoming sick, or did not wish them and so they lost
all desire for them.   Dr. Cleveland of Pawtucket caused several

somnambulists to become far more cheerful, hopeful, and orderly, which remained as a permanent quality afterward. In one he induced a charitable spirit towards one who was intensely hated. What a heavenly transition it would be if a few million people could be magnetized and then made to abandon selfishness, hatred, gossiping, jealousy, overreaching their neighbours, etc. An intelligent New York merchant, who is highly charged with these psychic forces, informs me that many persons addicted to intoxicating beverages have lost all desire for them after being with him a few times. While with them he would feel an aversion for these intemperate practices, and his own strong forces must have penetrated theirs sufficiently to constitute a controlling power there. A person who thus aspires after the high and good can radiate silently and unseen an influence which shall bless and beautify the natures with whom he associates, while another, who yields to low and impure desires, sends out a subtle virus which tends to contaminate those who are not firmly grounded in principle.

8. The *Hundreds of Lives Lost* in the burning of the Brooklyn Theater, and the multitudes more which have been destroyed in church panics and elsewhere, could in many instances have been saved if the people had ever gained any proper psychological control over themselves. Fear being appealed to starts the animal forces into a mad rush through the brain, and these not being held in check by the psychic control which should ever be masters of the castle, confuse the intellect and destroy the common sense until the people rush over and crush each other and block the way, thus leading to their death. Dr. Williams, the Psychologist, told the members of an audience in St. Louis that he would give any man $10,000 if he would remain quiet every morning for a year and use his will-power 20 minutes before rising, if at the end he did not admit that he had received vast advantages therefrom. A gentleman did so and gained such additional power of mind and body that he said he would not take $10,000 for it. This will-power should be used in throwing the animating forces to all parts of the system, and in determining to be calm, just, gentle, and yet self-possessed through the day, whatever excitement may occur around him.

XI. The Colors and Forces of the Brain.

1. The *Encephalon* embraces such an almost infinite diversity of colors, centers of Luminosity, of volition, emotion, sensation, consciousness, intuition, nervous action, of animal, mental and spiritual power, and the positive poles of all human forces, that if an ordinary mind could possibly look in upon it and see all its amazing machinery, he would find it more complicated and containing a greater number of distinct objects than his present conception of a world.   And yet, although man in his infinite unfoldings, capacities and parts is thus a study for an eternity, still by the aid of philosophy and this wonderful grade of light, we may at least arrive at the great general principles of vital and mental action, and grasp many details of these diviner laws of power.

2. *Different Forces of the Brain.*   Dr. J. R. Buchanan, Professor in the New York Eclectic Medical College, is perhaps the most eminent of Neurologists and Cerebral Physiologists, and one method by which he has gained his superior knowledge has been by consulting this finer vision and also by charging with the finer ethers which flow from the end of the fingers, different portions of the brains of sensitive persons, each portion of which caused its own peculiar manifestations.   In 1842, he made a number of experiments in the presence of the poet William Cullen Bryant, Dr. Forry and Mr. O'Sullivan.   When he touched the organ of self-esteem in a lady, it became active under the vital fluid thus communicated, she kindled into importance and began to proclaim woman's rights ; when he touched what he calls the organ of Humility, she at· once changed her tone and said that "she was but a weak woman after all."   When he touched another lady's self-esteem she left the room from feeling herself too good to remain with such company, but was induced to return when Humility was touched.   When he touched a section of the brain which he terms Infidelity, she would believe in nothing and denied all things.   They asked her if she did not think that the stove was hot.   She immediately declared that it was not hot at all, and would have put her hands on it to prove it, had her husband not prevented her.   Thus he could seemingly play any tune he pleased on the human instrument.   A sensitive young man touched the poet Bryant on his Ideality, and thereby

his own ideality became so charged with new fire that he soared off into the most glowing language, and many other effects were produced. Similar experiments were tried by Dr. Elliotson of England, and by O. S. Fowler and others in this country. Dr. H. H. Sherwood gives an account of a lady whose "sense of hunger, produced by exciting the organ of Alimentiveness, was so great as to require a considerable force to prevent her from eating the flesh from her own hands ; and the sense of the ludicrous, produced by exciting the organ of Mirthfulness, was such as to make it necessary to remove the excitement immediately to prevent her from laughing herself to death." These facts show 1st, that different parts of the brain have their special mental and emotional characteristics ; 2dly, that these get their activity from the vital or psychic aura which passes through them ; 3dly, as much of the character and conduct of human beings come from adventitious circumstances and conditions of the brain which, in their present ignorance, they do not know how to remove, they should not be held up to scorn and considered as so severely accountable therefor, but those who are physicians should see to it that by becoming acquainted with the working of the psychic lights and forces, and the phrenic organs through which they move, they should be able to correct and control these perverted conditions by reaching their causes ; 4thly, the vast diversity of effects produced on different portions of the cranium should lead physiologists to abandon at once the absurd position that "there are no special organs of the brain for special qualities of the mind." I shall presently add another proof of the diversity of the functions of the brain by showing the different colors which emanate from them, and which exactly harmonize with the nature of the organs themselves, as ascertained by phrenologists.

3. I will quote some *cases from real life* as illustrative of the importance of these great fundamental principles. A lady of New York became more and more melancholy in spite of religious consolation or kind friends, and, baffling the power of her physicians, she was fast becoming insane. Going to a lady physician who possessed this psychic vision, it was discovered that the region of cautiousness was over-active, while that of hope had too little radiation of the psychic ethers, showing that

it was too dormant.   She at once drew off by passes the super-
abundant forces of cautiousness, and charged with her fingers
the organ of hope, and paid some attention also to the portions
of the body which correspond to the same.   I saw the patient after
a week's treatment.   She had become exceedingly cheerful, and
was attending to her daily duties, seemingly a well woman.   I
have myself worked on the same plan in a number of cases and
with admirable results.   I have taken persons whose strong
animal passions were leading them into excesses, and worked
great and radical changes in their disposition and feelings.   Such
are generally heated and sometimes diseased in the lower back
brain at and below the region which phrenologists generally designate as amativeness, and those who can see the color emanations from the head, discover a muddy red light issuing from the
same portion in such cases.   My process has been to draw the
hot forces of the back brain by passes of the hand over the part
and down the arms to the hand, also to draw the heat of the
negative pole of the same organ which Dr. Buchanan has located
in the lower spine, between the lumbar and sacral plexuses, down
the hips towards the feet, and to equalize the system generally.
The passion for alcoholic stimulus I have frequently quelled as
follows ; 1st by drawing the heat away from the portion directly
in front of each ear ; and 2d, by scattering in different directions
the heat of the epigastrium, and sometimes cooling it off by fingers wet in cold water, especially as an inflamed gastric membrane is a great cause of the burning thirst for liquors.   The fact
that I am strongly charged with the vital magnetic power was
no doubt a help in the matter, as I was able to infuse through the
patient a healthier flow of the life currents, but nearly every one
could do something in mitigating such evils by knowing how.
A person of stupid perceptions can become quickened by animating the region over the eyebrows, by passes with the hand, each
day ; his reasoning powers can become quickened by holding
the hands over the forehead ; his moral powers by charging the
whole upper head.   At the same time the whole system should
be exercised and kept in as healthy a condition as possible, as the
bodily organs react upon the brain.   One thing should be remembered, which is, that a person of fine reasoning powers and
high-toned moral nature is especially desirable as an operator to

stimulate the nobler intellectual and moral forces in another.
For want of space here I must leave this subject only partialy
explained, meantime reserving it for a much fuller explanation in
a future work on *Human Development*, which I hope to prepare.
Reformers and religionists have been trying for centuries to bless
and save the human race, but the wrecks of humanity which
cover the world, and the vice and corruption which fill society
on every hand, proclaim that our methods have been false, that
we are simply dealing with the surface of things and neglecting
those interior basic principles upon which the structure of human
life must be built if its foundations are to be eternal. The people in general are not only grossly ignorant of the proper pre-
natal conditions requisite for producing a magnificent manhood
and womanhood, but more than this, having started a race full
of imperfections, they are quite ignorant of the methods of making them over into something higher. The Medical world, the
Pulpit and the Academy of learning are grossly culpable if they
fail to impress these momentous laws upon the people, and a
future bar of public opinion will hold them severely responsible.
They may do something in laboriously bailing out a vessel which
is full of leaks, but they would act much more like philosophers
if they would deal with causes and stop the leaks themselves.

4. *The inspired Plato* well understood the basis of mental
action which many physicians of the present day seem to be unacquainted with. " It is not art," said he, " which makes thee
excel, but a *divine power* which moves thee, such as is in the
stone which Euripides named the *magnet*, and some call the He-
raclian stone which attracts the iron rings."

5. *Dr. J. R. Buchanan* has arrived at an excellent perception of these finer life-ethers, and admits the gradation of forces
as follows :—" The action of the brain and nerves upon the muscular system is affected by an agency strikingly similar to the
galvanic. This agency or fluid which is evolved by the bàsilar
portion of the brain, the spinal cord and the ganglionic system,
is one of the lower species of nervous fluids. The nervous fluid
or emanation, which may be most appropriately termed NER-
VAURA, is essentially different in the different organs. While
the nervaura, or influence of the basilar portion of the brain, directly and powerfully stimulates the muscular system, that of the

anterior region is incapable of producing muscular contraction, and tends to soothe or arrest.   The nervaura of the basilar part of the middle lobe, in front of the ear, excites the digestive organs, that of the superior organs adjacent to firmness, diminishes the gastric activity. Thus, every portion of the brain originates a distinct nervaura, producing different and peculiar physiological effects, and producing also peculiar psychological effects upon others.   The influence of the basilar and occipital organs is chiefly expended upon the constitution of the individual; that of the anterior and superior organs is more diffusive. * * * In the vast interval between our spiritual nature and the solid forms of inorganic matter, we have traced a regular gradation from solids to liquids, from liquids to gases, from gases to imponderable substances and agencies, from the imponderables to the various species of nervaura, coming from the basis of the brain to the higher forms of mental emanation, proceeding from the anterior superior portion of the brain. * * * Matter in a fluid form manifests more extraordinary, active powers (than solids), and presents phenomena which are the subjects of chemical science.   It is only in consequence of the existence of fluids that vegetable and animal life are possible. * * * In Caloric, Electricity, Galvanism, Magnetism, etc., we find the moving powers of the physical world.   Partly in these, but chiefly in still subtler agencies—in the vital forces and nervauras—we find the moving powers of the physiological world.   The subtlest of these agencies again conduct us into the Psychological world. In other words all physical phenomena, all life and all thought— in a word, all POWER comes from immaterial sources." (*Anthropology*, 1854, p. 194.)   These are noble thoughts, but the expression "all power comes from immaterial sources," would be better I think, thus—"*All power in its positive or primary principles comes from spiritual sources,*" for as we have seen, spirit and matter are correlative, and neither can ever work without some grade of the other.   The word *immaterial* is now being dropped by thoughtful writers, and I presume Dr. Buchanan himself does not use it at present.

6. *The Color Radiations of the Brain.* " Human beings are luminous almost all over the surface of their bodies," says Reichenbach, "but especially on the hands, the palms of the hands,

the points of the fingers, the eyes, different parts of the head, the pit of the stomach, the toes, etc. Flame-like streams of light of relatively greater intensity flow from the points of all the fingers, in a straight direction from where they are stretched out." Reichenbach's sensitives were not sufficiently developed to see the higher color radiations of the brain with much distinctness, although they saw some of them. The following description of the Psychic colors was written out by Mrs. Minnie Merton for the author's " Health Guide," from which work I extract it :

" In the base of the brain (the animal loves), the colors are a dark red, and in persons of a very low nature, almost black, while in the upper brain the colors assume a yellowish tint, and are far more brilliant. In a high nature, the colors over the moral and spiritual powers are almost dazzling, with the yellow tint nearly merged into white, and far more exquisite than sunlight. In the higher front brain, in the region of the reasoning intellect, blue is the predominant color, and is lighter as it approaches the top brain, and a darker blue as it comes down to the perceptives (over the brow), and a little touch of the violet in its outer edges. Benevolence emits a soft light green of indescribable beauty. Over firmness the color is scarlet, and over self-esteem, purple. As you move down the sides of the head, from the moral powers towards the lower loves, it becomes orange, then red, then dark (at the bottom). Very low natures sometimes emit such a dark cloud from the base of the brain, that it seems as though I could scarcely see them. When a person laughs or sends forth happy thoughts, it causes a dancing play of bright colors ; but when in violent passion, a snapping and sparkling red is emitted," (p. 55). An eminent clairvoyant informs me that this description is mainly in harmony with the colors as he has seen them, and it also coincides nearly with my perception of the same. In saying firmness was of a scarlet color, I think it is an oversight, as I heard her in private conversation admit that there was a blue on the upper head behind the yellow which would bring it about over firmness, in accord with my own perception. Firmness seems to form the upper end of a mass of polarized lines of force which run down through the whole spine, and thus, when active, causes the whole being to become braced up into a rigid and powerful condition, hence the effect which we call *firmness*. But these firm conditions, or polarizations, come from electricity, and electricity is the blue principle, so that both theory and observation agree in the matter. I have drawn the colors and had them engraved in Plate IV., according to Mrs. Merton's description, modified and completed by my own observations, assisted somewhat by others. The combination, as in nature, is so soft and indescribably exquisite, and the variety of tint is so vast that it is impossible to give anything more than the general plan of colors, and that with materials many times as coarse as the radiations themselves. The eyes, perceptives, and reasoning powers radiate blue emanations, the animal energies, including Amativeness or sexual love (A), a dingy red, what Dr Buchanan calls the higher or more celestial grade of Love, LL, is a most beautiful grade of red; Benevolence (B) is an exquisite green; Religion (R), is yellow; Firmness (F), is blue; Self Esteem (SE), is purple, etc. Dr. Buchanan places Hope just above LL, and Patience and Integrity in front of Firmness. The blue of the Reasoning powers is a grade higher than that of firmness, the red of the front lower face is finer and more brilliant than that of the back head, and the red of LL is possibly a grade higher than the psychic, as is the yellow of Religion or Veneration, as it is sometimes called. These would then belong to the fourth grade of colors, and the same celestial grade may, in the greatest exaltation of mind, be used in the reasoning powers also. The nose has a green emanation, the lips yellow, below the lips orange, the chin scarlet, the temporal region below LL violet, merging into the finer red above and the coarser red below. This violet section includes Ideality, Sublimity, etc., according to Dr. Buchanan, but is slightly lower than these organs, as placed by the Gallian Phrenology. I have laid off the head in general divisions mainly after the plan of Dr. Buchanan. The anterior upper brain con-nects with the Thorax, or rather has its negative poles in the Thorax; the Higher Energies connect with the Brachial Plexus of nerves (B P); the occiput generally connects with the Dorsal nerves, the lower occiput with the Lumbar and Sacral plexuses at the lower spine, the lower cheeks with the abdomen, etc. The part of the head in front of the dotted lines rules the Visceral system, that back of them rules the muscular system. It will be seen that the opposite parts of the head seem to be polarized or arranged quite generally with affinitive colors, the red of ama-tiveness balancing the blue of the Reasoning organs, etc. The front brain has a higher grade of colors than the back, and the upper front brain still higher, as the most exquisite ethers, being the lightest, must naturally gravitate to the highest point. Dr. Buchanan ascertained by experiment that the highest part of all organs is nobler than the lower, the upper part of Self-Esteem, for instance, causing a person to have pride of moral character, and the lower part pride of power ; the upper part of Ambition (approbation), tending to moral achievements, the lower part to military achievements, etc. The colors as witnessed by a clair-voyant harmonize beautifully with this idea, growing more pure and brilliant as they approach the upper brain, and being far more magnificent in a high and noble nature than in a low and selfish one. *This shows that refinement of mental or spiritual qualities manifests itself by refinement of physical emanations.* The region of Religious aspiration (R), pointing heavenward, is the sunrealm of the human soul, and the most luminous of all, being in a person of noble and spiritual nature of an exquisite golden yellow, approaching a pure and dazzling white. The front brain being the realm of Reason and Perception, manifests itself naturally in the cool and calm color, blue, while the love principle, typified all over the world by warmth, finds its natural manifes-tation in the red. Such faculties as those of Ideality, Spiritual-ity, and Sublimity, combining as they do both thought and emo-tion, radiate the violet, or the union of blue and red, while such faculties as Patience, Firmness, Integrity, and Temperance, have more to do with coolness than heat, and have a predominance of the blue. According to Buchanan's arrangement they are all situated in a group. The letter V is a vitalizing center, and N a center of nutrient nerves, as designated by Buchanan. The nerves of both centers may be roused to greater action by holding the hands on the place, or by rubbing with the ends of the fingers.

7. There is a great resemblance between the colors of the human head as to their direction, and the colors which flow from a bar magnet when turned over vertically, as seen by Reichen-bach's sensitives, thus showing the harmony between man and the outward universe.

I give this after Reichenbach, and it will be seen that the face corresponds most nearly with the north, the occiput with

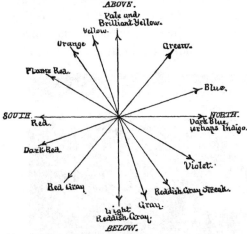

the south, the top of the head with the zenith, and the lower head and face with the downward direction. A little below the north is the violet which is not imitated in the face except at the sides, while the blue of the upper occiput is omitted in the magnet, but the head of course is more complicated than the simple forces of nature and is modified more or less by the body of which it is the capital.   In the foregoing figure the brilliant yellow above melts into the green, then into blue, then into dark blue, which is exactly imitated in the head and face, commencing with the yellow of the top head, and ending with deep blue at the eyes which correspond with the north.   Below and above at the south and the north, and at several intermediate points the resemblance is almost exact.   Thus we have the finer and the coarser forces, spiritual emanations and physical emanations, and the laws of nature and man all working together on the same wonderful system.

Fig. 185. Odic Colors from the North Pole of a Magnet made to revolve vertically in the Magnetic Meridian.

8. There are two great leading styles of radiation from the human system, one of which consists of straight lines that .emanate in all directions and are not sufficiently deflected by counter currents to form into curves, while the other consists of systems of lines which have been deflected and formed into magnetic curves that pass round and round in and out of the brain in endless circuits.   Fig. 186 gives a few from among the millions of straight line radiations, while fig. 187 presents a few of the magnetic curves which also circulate in almost infinite numbers in a vast variety of directions, only a few of which I give in the engraving.   There is a system of efflux curves or

positive radiations from the right side of the head and face which
sweep around and become influx curves on the left side, and
there are circuits behind, which enter on the right side of the
cerebellum and emerge on the left, just contrary to the directions of the frontal forces; and there are systems of straight

Fig. 186. The Angel of Innocence.

line forces which enter at the left and emerge at the right more
strongly than they do in the opposite directions, and other systems which glide conversely through the whole body from head
to feet, and feet to head, and far beyond into space, and still
other systems which are influx behind and influx from the fore-

head and face, and in fact too many other divisions to mention
here, although I have named some of the more important.
When I speak of the forehead and right side as strong in positive and efflux forces, I mean in electrical forces, although the
thermal radiations are just in the opposite directions as signified
by the colors and other phenomena.   I make these statements
from the observations of Henry Hall Sherwood, M. D., of Baron

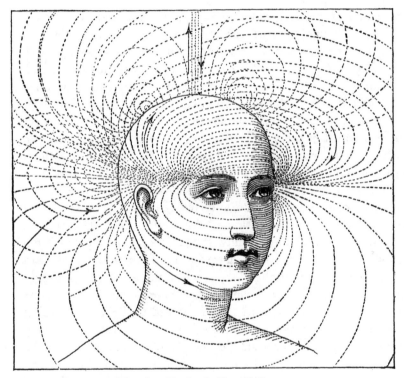

Fig. 187.   The Psycho-Magnetic Curves.

Reichenbach and other persons, as well as from my own experience, and the reader will find confirmation of several of them in
what is still to follow.   Not only are there curves encirling both
hemispheres of the brain, but systems of curves in each hemisphere.   Persons of psychological power can sometimes throw
these curves of force around others at a great distance and
influence them.   An eminent German singer informed me that
he had often made persons turn around while forty yards away,

and a New York gentleman of my acquaintance often amuses himself and a friend, who is with him, by willing and causing ladies at some distance ahead of them, to turn around so that they may view their countenances, and says he can generally tell what ones he can influence thus, and what ones he cannot affect. I could give various examples of ladies who have the same psychological power, especially those who possess health and vital force. A man is a magnet, only of a higher grade than magnets of steel, having power to attract and repel sensitive human beings just as the steel instrument can attract its like, only with a compass a thousand times as far-reaching.

9. *Perversions of Psychic Forces.*—All things, however excellent, can be perverted, and the grandest things can sometimes be perverted the worst if people will remain in ignorance of their real nature. A flock of sheep will wear certain pathways and then travel in them even if it takes twice as many steps to reach a certain point as it would to move in another direction ; and so human beings have carved out in their own mental and psychological conditions, ruts of all kinds, such as the medical, religious, social, and political, and are ready to fight almost to the death those who dare to chisel out any other style of ruts than their own, and especially those who, emancipated from such slavery to old opinions, dare to stand upon the mountain top in God's free sunlight and welcome all truth, however contrary to preconceived opinions. There are always some men and women that can be psychologized to believe anything under heaven, however monstrous, if only persons of some ability or magnetic power shall earnestly inculcate it. A gentleman once made some children cry out of sympathy for "a poor broomstick that had been left out in the cold and snow all night alone," while millions of grown-up children are easily made to believe that certain persons are prophets or vicegerents of God who have a right to tyrannize over them. A community of the ignorant class of Europeans, settled in Illinois, have a leader who professes to be God himself, and is revered and obeyed as such by the people, who dare not even marry or do any other important thing without his permission. What hundreds of millions of Brahmans, Buddhists, Mohammedans, as well as one thousand different Christian sects, are absolutely sure that

they alone are right, while perhaps their neighbors, who may be better in life and practice than themselves, are doomed to destruction because they do not walk in the same rut of belief. As people become broad in their culture, and their intellect gains control of their impulses, and they attain the grandeur of a free manhood and womanhood, they will learn to weigh all things in the scale of reason and not be governed so slavichly by the psychological bias which has been fastened upon them in the helpless and plastic period of childhood.

But how many cases of bargain and sale take place in which one party is unconsciously misled by a kind of psychological spell thrown over him by the other party. How many marriage contracts are made under the subtle charm, as it were, of the aura which the parties throw around each other, unconsciously perhaps, or which the more positive party may throw around the more negative, possibly with wrong intentions. What multitudes of seductions are thus brought about. For this reason all should become skilled in these fine and mighty agencies, should know their laws and be able to hurl back indignantly all base influences that shall be attempted, or if they are physically too weak at once to do this, they must grow strong by means of light and air and exercise and the help of vital magnetism.

XII. The Right and Left Brain, etc.

1. *It is the usual law for the blue and violet streams of the electrical psychic forces to sweep into the left side of the head and out at the right, both in curves and straight lines as we have just seen.* There is a coarse animal magnetic sphere of radiation in the case of all persons, extending usually some three or more feet around the body, but these finer soul forces often extend many miles, and can be thrown by a powerful volition hundreds of miles, as can be thoroughly proved by facts. Mental telegraphing between sensitive persons has taken place at a great distance apart. M. Dupotet magnetized persons at the Hôtel Dieu, Paris, through a partition, by simply using his will, and that in the presence of very eminent physicians who admitted the fact, while in various cases which have taken place in this country and elsewhere, magnetizers have put their subjects to sleep while many miles distant and while walking around

engaged in their daily duties, entirely unconscious of what was to be attempted. How much imagination is there in such cases? Mr. J. Mendenhall, of Cerro Gordo, Indiana, stood a number of rods behind a wood-chopper, unseen by him, and using his will powerfully, gradually made his strokes grow less and less frequent until at last the uplifted axe was stopped in mid air and the man stood like a block of marble transfixed by these mighty streams of force. The stronger magnetic flow from Mr. Mendenhall entered the brain of the chopper, became master of his nerve channels, and through them paralyzed his muscles.

2. The *left brain* is the portion especially strong in the interior forces, especially potent in discovering the properties, relations and proprieties of things, and thus, being the receptive brain, must naturally be more skilled in its intuitional character, while the *right brain* is the realm of positive efflux power, of executive skill and of vitalizing character. This we might naturally expect to be the case from knowing the law of the influx and efflux forces. Dr. Brown-Séquard has shown that memory and intellect and the perception of how to control the tongue and larynx and muscles of the chest to produce articulate voice, and the remembrance of how to use the hand in writing words, come more from the left than the right brain, while the right brain "serves chiefly to emotional manifestations, hysterical manifestations included, and to the needs of the nutrition of the body in its various parts," and " has more to do with organic life." If disease attacks the right side of the brain, paralysis is much more apt to take place than when it attacks the left side, which accounts for the fact that paralysis occurs on the left side of the body more than on the right side, as the right brain rules the left side of the body, and the left brain the right side of the body. The left brain causes right-handedness, and the fact that it rules the more masculine, or positive side of the body, shows that of itself it is more feminine, being the chemical affinity of that side. When Dr. Brown-Séquard talks about our having one side of the body developed up to the same strength and skill as the other, he seems to be unaware of the fact that positive and negative conditions must forever rule in nature, and can never be wholly obliterated.

XIII. RADIATIONS AND LAWS OF POWER.

1. A beautiful lesson can be drawn from these radiations
from the different parts of the head, a hint of which was given
in Dr. Buchanan's Anthropology. Each part of the head radiates more or less in all directions, but the plate gives simply the
predominant direction. Notice the lines of polarity extending
from the perceptives. Their direction is somewhat downward toward the earth and their leading purpose is to take cognizance of
the outer world to mirror forth the material conditions around.
Their color is blue, indigo and violet as they move earthward,
but the very lines of polarized atoms which carry these colors
to the earth, have an especial affinity for the red, orange and
yellow which emanate *from* the earth towards the perceptives,
and which, being of the luminous order, are especially fitted
to reveal the character of the objects from which they pro-
ceed. A little higher are the radiations from the domain of
Reason which point upward, downward and forward as if to
weigh and balance all things above and below. The moral and
spiritual faculties radiate principally upward, and drawing their
inspirations from the celestial, tend to lift man above the gross-
ness of earth. The radiant yellow emanates principally from
the median line and comes from the higher portion of both the
right and left brain. Firmness with its co-operative elements of
Energy, Integrity, Patience and Hardihood, sends upward a shaft
of blue electricity, a portion of which comes doubtless from the
spine, thus holding the body and mind up to a rigid polarity of
forces which, when strong, will bend neither to the right nor the
left. Self-Esteem sends its purple light partly upward and partly
behind, and tends to draw the head backward, just as Benevolence and Reason, as balancing principles, tend to draw the head
forward, and lead to the esteem of others. Firmness, Self Esteem,
etc., are the executive forces of volition and can never lead to
selfishness or wrong, if balanced by the coronal and frontal developments. Below and behind are the more violent passional
developments with their red phases pointing mainly downward.
These are in the lowest and darkest parts of the brain, but
although placed thus in the most inferior part of the scale of
being, they have their divine elements of use which, when

regulated by their opposite polarities on the other side of the head, become harmonious and good. The trouble is that mankind in its average present grade of development, constitutes this animal portion the captain of the ship, while nature has placed Reason at the helm and the Spiritual Forces at the highest lookout above the whole.

2. *The great law of perfection in human development is to have a harmonious balance of all the faculties.* The back head has great propelling power and must be active in order to vitalize the body and give physical force, but if not cooled, refined and guided by the front and upper brain, the forces become too gross, over-indulgence and warmth burn out and exhaust the system, and the end is fearful suffering, insanity and death. This sort of preponderance fills the whole brain with a cloudy red, and colors all thoughts and sentiments until truth and purity finally become impossible. On the other hand, however beautiful Reason and the Inspiration of the upper brain may be, their excessive development to the neglect of the lower brain will draw the forces too much away from the body, and by exhausting the physical system lead to disease, insanity or death. The disease and insanity caused by the over use of the higher brain, is however of a milder kind than that caused by beastliness. *We do not want a blue brain, or red brain, or yellow brain, but one which like the union of sky, water and landscape, gives us the beautiful diversity of nature. Holiness, or wholeness includes the full development of the Perceptive, Reasoning, Esthetic, Spiritual, Social and Animal man, the deficiency of any part of which leads to unholiness.* Tried by this standard we see that asceticism, exclusiveness of religious devotion, intellectual culture or excessive animal desires are each and all but different grades of unholiness and onesidedness.

3. *The greater the radiation of the Vital Ethers to any one place, the more the blood is drawn there as a general rule, and hence the greater the increase of the tissues, and consequently of the size.* Thus if the muscles are used, the vital magnetism and blood cause them to increase in size; if the psychic ethers are drawn to the forehead by the hand or by study and thought, the Reasoning powers increase in power and the forehead becomes more prominent; if the Perceptive powers are animated by

vital ethers from the fingers or by constant observation they will enlarge the prominence of the ridge above the eyes. I knew a young man who increased the circumference of his head, measured around the eye-brows, a half an inch by one year of travel and observation. The treatment of the Moral, Spiritual and Esthetic Faculties on the same principles, will give the forehead and upper head, a higher, broader and nobler appearance. Other portions of the brain may be increased in the same way by mechanical appliance of the hand, the fingers being highly magnetic, and by psychological use of the faculties. We should remember, however, that some persons may have much intensity and power in certain phrenal organs without necessarily building those organs up into a large size, from deficiency of their nutritive system.

4. *The emanations from the brain are not always seen as straight lines of radiation,* or in just the appearance given in the plate. If the brain observed is absorbed actively in thought, the blue element for the time being will swallow up the other colors; if love, or the emotional elements are most active, a red cast will predominate. A lady informed me that as she observed a public orator, a great variety of brilliant and flashing coruscations of every kind of color made their appearance. Sometimes under the excitement of powerful thought and feeling, a thousand flashes of light are seen around the head, caused probably by the explosion of brain cells brought about by the chemical action of the psychic ethers. If these cells thus destroyed by mental action during the waking hours are not replaced by sufficient food and sleep, the system begins to decline.

5. *The Ganglia* or knotted portions of certain nerves are seen clairvoyantly to emit explosive flashes of light, especially when the forces of a nerve are excited into action, as by pricking or pinching the flesh. Suppose the flesh to be pricked by a needle. The animal electricities being aroused flow in streams of light towards the brain in the pathway of the sensory nerves. When a ganglion is reached an explosive action takes place, caused by the chemical affinity of the bluish white nerve fibres with the reddish gray matter in the ganglion. What is the necessity of this ganglion? One advantage of its existence seems to be that it continues the action which has already been commenced by the needle with all the

more distinctness to the brain.   The merest touch of the foot
with a hair starts a stream of vital flow which may not be sufficiently strong to go all the way unassisted to the brain in a
way to produce sensation, but coming to a ganglion, the chemical
action intensifies the stream and the effect is the more easily accomplished.   This is nature's method of economizing her forces,

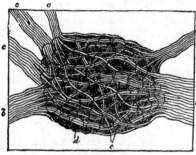

for were it not for the ganglia, the apparatus for producing an equal degree of
sensation would have to be
more complicated.   The interior ganglia of the sympathetic nerves must also produce a very vitalizing effect
on the surrounding viscera.
Fig. 188 will show how the
nerve fibres pass through the

DIAGRAM OF GANGLION.—*a, b, c.* Nerves. *d, e.* Cells.
Fig. 188.

nerve cells of a ganglion, thus bringing the bluish gray and
reddish gray matter into connection so that chemical affinity
may produce its explosive action and send the currents of nervaura onward to other centers.

6. Reichenbach and others repeatedly describe the streams
of light which radiate from the ends of fingers, or of a magnet,
or of a crystal, or from the angles of a substance.   The human

Fig. 189.   A Sphere.   Fig. 190.   An Ellipsoid.

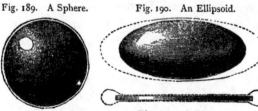

Fig. 191.   A Disc.

system has not
only its centres
of luminous action
where masses of
nerves are found,
but also from its
angular or project-

ing portions, on the same law that electricity is known to gather
at points rather than at the larger expanses of surface.   This
fact will be shown in figs. 189, 190, 191, which I take from Guillemin's Forces of Nature.   The sphere shows a diffused electricity over its whole surface, the ellipsoid shows the increase of
electrical tension near its narrower portions, while a flat disc
shows a still stronger tension at its edges.   A bar or tube would
perhaps show a more intense electrical action at its ends than

the disc.   These facts will furnish a hint of how it is that nature, in building up the human system, has sent the nerve ethers out to the ends of the fingers, tip of tongue, etc., with such an intensity as to carry a large amount of their affinitive nerve matter with them in the shape of tactile corpuscles, by means of which sensation becomes so acute.   As streams of water, rushing to any particular point tend to carry the soil and other light substances suitable to its style of power along with it, until it builds up its little points and promontories, so will streams of nervaura, assisted by the galvanic action of the blood, sweep nerve cells and tissue more and more outward until a projection called a tongue or other organ is formed.   Thus is the fluidic theory ever coming to our aid in the solving of mysteries, and making difficult things more simple.

XIV. Intuition, and the Relation of the Sexes.

1. Now at last we may understand the mystery of Intuition, that wonderful method of reasoning by means of which the mind is said to mount at once to the top of the ladder, and come to definite conclusions without going up the intermediate steps. In the usual methods we reason by the aid of comparatively slow and coarse ethers ; in the case of Intuition, we come into more direct use of these amazingly fine and swift ethers, by means of which our thoughts can move on the wings of lightning.   No links in the chain of reasoning are omitted, but the mind dashes through them so rapidly that it is impossible at times to remember them all.   This is woman's favorite method, and the fact that she gets into rapport with the fine forces more easily than man is the reason.   In mathematical demonstrations and slow laborious reasoning, man is the superior.   In the impressions of truth which flash upon the mind in a moment, woman is the superior.   Coleridge once had a lady of fine intuitions in his family, and having got into a difficult maze of thought left the study and asked her for her first impressions on the subject.   She immediately answered him, and commenced telling her reasons for her opinion, when Coleridge, interrupting her, said: " Never mind the reason, Madam, I will find out that when I get into my study."   I have myself submitted to certain intuitive ladies dif-

ficult questions which they had never considered, their first impressions of which would be correct, but in some cases I found I could confuse their minds and lead them to doubt by presenting arguments on the opposite side.

2. While the *Education given to Women* is even yet much inferior to that which men receive, thus leaving her mental faculties less perfectly developed than would be desirable, yet by means of her intuitional nature she possesses various advantages over her masculine competitor. Applying this remark to only one subject it is safe to say that if medical science had sooner received the co-operation of women with their quick practical insight into conditions and their sympathy with suffering, we should not have had so diseased a world as we have to-day, and a more common sense system of methods would have been adopted.

3. The Sensitives of Reichenbach always perceived much longer and larger odic flames around men than women. Miss Reichel saw flames from the tips of all men's fingers darting up and down like other flames, but women's fingers emitted little or no light, and her own, especially, no light. This signifies that *woman's forces, being more negative than man's, are more of the influx order, while the latter is stronger in his efflux radiations. All forces from surrounding conditions are received into the system of women more than into that of men, which accounts for their sensitive and sympathetic natures.* The fact that the sexes are thus constituted on the plan of positive and negative forces shows why it is that when they dwell in each other's atmosphere they often find themselves refreshed, strengthened and harmonized, as each intensifies and balances the action of the other. It can be proved that boys and girls, educated in the same schoolroom, grow stronger, wiser and better than when educated apart.

4. In woman's lower occiput and chin the love forces manifest themselves in the red tint as in man, but with somewhat less of the dark element.

5. Another mystery is made clear by these Psychic forces. It has often been a matter of wonder that *women in spite of their physical weaknesses live, on the average, longer than men,* as shown by statistics. In speaking of statuvolence, we saw the remarkable power over both disease and mental conditions which persons could wield in proportion as they went into the condition.

Woman in her weakness may bend like the willow, but being able to call the swift forces to her aid more easily, can weather a storm which would sometimes destroy a man. In the sick-room, or in a severe siege of suffering she is ever the mightier of the two ; and suicides are far oftener masculine than feminine, which looks much as though the latter had the greater moral courage.

6. It has puzzled Dr. Brown-Séquard somewhat that *Americans are longer lived*, as he admits, *than the people of European nations*, especially as they do not seem so sturdy as their brothers over the water.   This cannot come wholly from the universality of education among our people, for Prussia, perhaps, can even surpass us in that respect.   If we remember the nervous activity of our people, which makes the movements of other people seem rather slow to us, we may easily understand that these finer ethers must have a considerable prominence among us, and hence the power of recuperation.   Our business men and our politicians in their fierce rush for pelf and power, should remember that when these active forces are too constantly used without sufficient rest, they are liable to burn the system entirely out and make wrecks of themselves physically as well as morally.

7. The *Wonderful Rapidity of Mental Action* possessed by certain persons is easily accounted for by the fact that these interior forces, when brought into predominance, must necessarily make all perceptions remarkably swift and clear.   Zerah Colburn when a boy, could in a moment multiply in his head a number requiring six figures to express it by another equally large, and young Safford, of Massachusetts, now Professor in a Chicago College, when only nine years old would multiply still larger amounts together, while whirling around on his heel in an intensity of excitement.   At the same age or a little later, he would calculate eclipses mentally, and that by methods one-third shorter than those in ordinary use.   Mr. Hutchins, of New York, known as the " Lightning Calculator," in the process of addition, can sweep immense columns of figures on a blackboard from top to bottom, almost as swiftly as the shooting of a meteor, and give a correct answer before any ordinary eye can even see the figures to read them.   But this amazing velocity of mental action cannot be practiced with safety too long at a time, and great pre-

cocity in children must be guided with care, and a powerful
physical system built up to prevent the blaze of thought from
burning up both brain and body.   Safford, when a mere boy, was
handed over to the care of Harvard Professors, and was thus
guided with sufficient wisdom to prevent h' remature death.

8. *The power of using these fine forces in the process of clairvoyance, etc., is supposed by many superficial students of this subject
to betoken weakness and disease.*   Never was a greater mistake.
While it is true that some delicate and diseased persons, from
having almost none of the coarser forces to interfere with the
finer, are able to see clairvoyantly, yet many clairvoyants entirely
lose their power when they become sick, and I have known
many persons to rise from a condition of ill health into great
power as they cultivated and received these influences.   A lady
in New York who treats patients by powerful manipulation and
giving out of the life power all day and nearly every evening
until midnight, for weeks or even months in succession, is
more or less clairvoyant all the time, feels the fine fluids animating her whole system, and is a superb specimen of physical
power.   Some of the most powerful men in the country would
be like wilted leaves if they should attempt such an exhausting
practice for three days.   My own case is an example in point.
Before cultivating these subtler agencies, I was often sick, sometimes dangerously so.   Since I have learned how to receive
and use them, I have possessed a very strong physique and
have never been sick a day.   My weight is 180 pounds.   One
of the best clairvoyants in the country is a Mr. Wilson of
Illinois.   He is almost a giant in size and power, weighs 265
pounds, and is never sick.   I could quote a multitude of similar
cases, some of whom possess a marvelous stock of vitality and
force.   Is it reasonable to suppose that the most powerful
forces, like these fine agencies, compared with which the common coarser life currents are slow and sluggish, will have a
tendency to weaken ?   Never, if managed with any care, for the
mind, if persevering, can easily learn how to hold them under
rigid control, bidding them when, where, and how far to go and
making them mighty for good.   The truth is that nearly all
have untold treasures of power locked up in the inner being, in
fact are *millionaires*, but their priceless treasures will remain

useless to them, until some one informs them of their own pos-
sessions, and hands them a key with which to unlock them.
For this reason I have written this volume, striving to reveal
to dear struggling humanity, whose interests I would ever sub-
serve, the blessed qualities of that light which illumines external
nature, and the still holier light of man's inner temple where
dwells immortal spirit itself.

XV. Positive and Negative Poles.

1. As has already been stated the positive poles of the human battery are generally in the head, and the negative poles in
the body. Up to this time I have not been able to get a very
clear view of the colors of the body, but in the lungs orange and
red are well developed, and to some extent the yellow; in the
stomach I think the ruling color is yellow, with a sufficient
amount of blue to give it a yellow green cast. The sexual organs are surrounded by a reddish brown, being of a somewhat
darker cast than the region of amativeness on the head. The
position of the negative poles on the body corresponds very generally with the position of the positive poles on the head, the
front and upper head matching the front and upper body, etc.
It will be seen that the color of the lungs constitutes a chemical
affinity with that of the forehead and bridge of the nose, which
connect so directly with the breathing apparatus. Amativeness,
with its red elements, corresponds with the bluish portion of the
lower spine, which is its negative point of manifestation, etc.

2. Since writing the foregoing I have received through the
inner vision of Mrs. Dr. Somerby, of Syracuse, a full confirmation of the points there stated, together with still other points.
Mrs. Somerby remarks that she first began to observe these
psychic manifestations of color in connection with human beings, at a time when two gentlemen who sat part way across the
room from each other were engaged in a warm argument. The
one was somewhat dark and rubicund in complexion, and
strongly of the arterial or vital temperament; the other was
pale, slender, and more intellectual. The former would send
out coruscations of light which was tinged with red, thus reasoning, as it were, from the blood and from his emotional na-

ture; the other more cool and surcharged with thought, would
radiate blue emanations towards his opponent. She was greatly
amused at seeing these emanations darting back and forth and
sometimes clashing.

I have taken down the following from her description of the
colors of the human body :—The central portion or pole of the
brain was described as being very brilliant like a sun, or a calcium light; the stomach was pronounced a deep yellow; the
lungs, yellow and orange; the heart, a dark red; the bowels,
yellow, with the lower part greenish mixed with some red; the
back lower brain, a dark red which merges gradually into bluish
white as we move down the spine; the spine, a bluish white as
the ruling color, with also a reddish or reddish brown cast at the
lower part, while in fact the whole nervous system showed
streams of bluish white light coursing through all its channels,
just as the arteries exhibited currents of red light, and the veins
a grade of color less luminous than the arteries. Pointing to
the pit of the stomach beneath which the solar plexus and semi-
lunar ganglion lie, she says she saw all the colors radiating in
brilliant rainbow style, and remarked that by placing a magnetic
hand there it would have a healing effect on all below it, but not
so much above. She saw a considerable variety of color in the
region of the hypogastric plexus also. She saw different poles
at the heart, liver, the bottom of the feet, etc. The feet send
out quite a variety of colors with the warm colors in predominance, just as the head, being the opposite pole, on the plan of
a bar magnet, has a variety of colors with blue predominating,
especially at the back and front upper portions.

XVI. The Interior Machinery of Life.

1. Henry Hall Sherwood, M. D., of New York, a man of
scientific culture and original force of thought, published works
in 1841 and 1848 on the *Motive Power of the Human System*,
which being too much in advance of his time to be appreciated,
are now out of print. I have in my possession a fragment of
his leading work which is considered so remarkable that a physician has offered ten dollars for it. By the aid of clairvoyants
he was able to penetrate more deeply into the philosophy of life

than most others, and made numerous experiments in magnetism
and electricity which confirmed the revelations of this clairvoyance. I will give in fig. 192 a general view of the interior radiations of the brain as seen by his experts. It represents a section as cut from the upper part of the forehead at the organ of
Causality, *a b*, through the
brain longitudinally, sloping
to the lower occiput through
the cerebellum, thus bisecting
the organ of amativeness, *c d*.
Five great leading poles were
discovered, one very splendid
and powerful at the center of
the brain in the third ventricle, one each side of the forehead, *a b*, constituting the two
sides of Causality, the central
reasoning function, and one
in each portion of the cerebellum, *c d*, constituting Amativeness, or the function of
procreation and certain motor
impulses. Minor poles were

Fig. 192. Interior Radiations of the Brain.

also discovered in each of the other organs of the brain, between
which and the great central pole were constant radiations. The
outer convolutions of the brain in which the organs are situated,
are reddish gray, the inner mass of the brain is bluish white, and
has a vast number of fibres or striæ which radiate outward in all
directions, as conducting lines doubtless for the interior ethers,
and the third ventricle at the center is also bluish white, which
according to the laws of chemical affinity must cause an admirable harmony and activity between this center and the reddish
gray matter of all the organs in the outer brain. The anatomy
of the brain shows that there are special striæ radiating from
the front brain corresponding to the organ of causality, and
others corresponding to the organ of amativeness. The two
stars between the organs of amativeness in the cerebellum,
were seen by the clairvoyants to have much to do in regulating the motions of the body in harmony with the discov-

eries of physiologists, though not the only ones that operate thus.

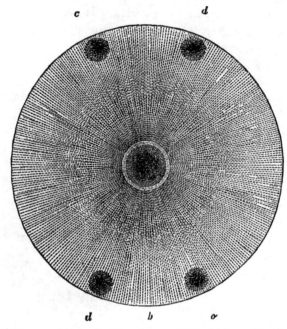

Fig. 193. A magnetized Steel Disc sprinkled with Iron Filings.

2. This system of the brain in which five leading centers were discovered both in its physical structure, and in its luminous radiations, was shown to be in harmony with the forces of inorganic nature by Dr. Sherwood, as follows :—" This was seen to be an extraordinary number and arrangement of the poles, as we have been accustomed to the number and arrangement of two poles only —of a positive and negative pole. We must therefore see whether the magnetic forces would of themselves, without artificial aid, produce five poles in this order of arrangement, and for this purpose we may use a circular plate of steel which would correspond with a middle horizontal section of the brain. A circular saw plate eight inches in diameter, and the tenth of an inch thick, with a hole in the center of one inch in

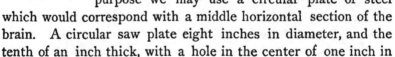

Fig. 194. Geo. Combe. The Phrenologist, representing the Location of Causality on the Forehead.

diameter, was accordingly subjected to actual experiment in the following manner :

" The middle of the plate or disc was carefully let down in a perpendicular direction on the middle of the positive pole of the galvanic battery, and after having remained there a moment, was raised from its position in a perpendicular direction, turned over, and the opposite side of the plate placed upon, and then removed from the negative pole of the battery in the same manner. The plate was then covered with white paper, and fine iron filings were strewed over it, and they were immediately arranged by the forces in the plate in the manner seen in fig. 193.

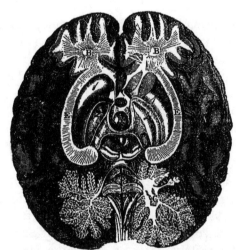

Fig. 195. The Brain laid open. AA, Anterior portion ; CC, Ganglia of the Cerebellum ; EE, Corpus Collosum ; A, Third Ventricle ; 1, 1, Great Superior Ganglia ; 2,2, Great Inferior Ganglia ; 3, Interior of Fourth Ventricle ; 4, Medulla Oblongata.

" This experiment was repeated eleven times on plates of from four to fifteen inches in diameter, and always with the same result. It may therefore be inferred to be constant. It presents one large and strong pole in the center of the plate, and four smaller and weaker poles in the circumference, like those in the brain.

" On applying the dipping needle to these poles, that in the center and those in the circumference at *cc* were found to be positive, and those at *dd* negative poles. When, however, the order of magnetizing on the different poles of the battery was reversed, the character of the pole in the center was changed from a positive to a negative pole, and the positions of the positive poles in the circumference were also changed ; the positive occupying the positions of the negative, and the negative those of the positive poles."

This last arrangement would be an exact representation of the poles of the brain as seen by the arrows in fig. 192, although the

great central pole must combine the character of both the positive and negative conditions, as it receives forces from all
quarters internally, and radiates them to all quarters externally.
Fig. 195 shows two radiating centers BB, with striations in all
directions, situated in the anterior portion of the brain; also the
two centers of physical life CC situated in the cerebellum, together with the location of the third ventricle A, etc.

3. *The Poles of the Body.* Dr. Sherwood had a lady, who
had been blind from her infancy, examine the whole system
while in the somniscient state, as he calls it. He says her "extraordinary revelations excite the greatest astonishment among
anatomists and physiologists," and she could not have read Dr.
Sherwood's mind for she had her own positive vision of the interior parts of the body more clearly even than could be impressed upon her by those present, and sometimes differed from
them and taught them. She could see the five leading poles of
the brain, could see lines of light running along the nerves,
could see bright spots or poles in all the ganglia and in all the
organs of the body. What was curious was the fact that she
would send fresh illumination into an organ by placing her own
fingers over it and by getting Dr. Sherwood to place his fingers
over certain parts of the spine which had nerve connections
leading to it. Thus when she was asked to examine the
left lung and heart, she placed Dr. Sherwood's hand "on
the left side of the space between the last cervical and first
dorsal vertebra," and then her own hands over the front of
the chest. To examine the liver she would kindle the interior
light so that she could see it the better by placing the Doctor's hand "on the right side of the space between the
seventh and eighth dorsal vertebræ." Another lady examined
the poles of the body clairvoyantly "with precisely the same
result. She confirmed in the most minute manner the number and situation of the poles in the brain, lungs, heart,
stomach, pancreas, plexuses, mesentery, liver, spleen, kidneys,
uterus, ovaries, tongue and orifices, and the connection between
the left kidney and spleen, and also the connection between
the uterus and breast, etc. Mr. Sunderland then commenced an
examination of the joints of the limbs and spine, each of which
she said had too poles, the one for extending, the other for

flexing the body and limbs, when he commenced demonstrating the fact, by exciting the different positive and negative poles of the elbow joint, situated at the points of the insertions of the muscles, one near the upper and the other near the inner side of the condyle of the humerus, when she would extend and flex her arm alternately by exciting in the slightest manner the different poles."

"He then held the point of a pen-knife near the organ of Causality, on the right side, when she began to move her head from it. He then held it near the same organ on the left side, when she began to move her head toward it, and on inquiring the cause of her doing so, she answered. 'It pulls, oh! take it away.' He then held the point of the knife near the organ of amativeness on the right side when she again observed 'it pulls.' He then held it near the same organ on the left side, when she soon began to move her head from it, and on inquiring why she did so, she observed, 'it pushes.'"

This confirms the statement which I have already made that the forces sweep into the principal brain from the left side, which thus by their suction drew her head forward in a way to make it pull, while they pass outward at the right side in a way to make it push. In the back part of the small brain, called the *cerebellum*, the forces move in just the other way. The doctor has well represented these currents by the direction of the arrows in fig. 192. I will now quote Dr. Sherwood's synopsis of the number of the poles in the different organs as signified by these young ladies, and also as signified by two boys and one young lady examined by Mr. L. N. Fowler, the Phrenologist, while they were in the somniscient state.

"*Number of Large Poles in the Organs.*--Brain, 5 ; eyes, 2 ; ears, 2 ; lungs, 2 ; heart, 5 (like the brain) ; stomach, 2 ; liver, 2 ; spleen, 2 ; pancreas, 2 ; kidneys, 2 ; bladder, 2 ; uterus, 2 ; ovaries, 2 ; vagina, 2 ; breasts, or mammæ, 2 ; solar plexus, 2 ; mesentery, 2.

"The *Orifices* have each one large pole, namely :--Tongue, 1 ; larynx, 1 ; pharnyx, 1 ; cardiac orifice of the stomach, 1 ; pyloric orifice do., 1 ; ileo-cœcal valve, 1 ; anus, 1 ; and 1 in each convolution of the intestines.

"The *Ganglions of Vegetative Life*, or those connected with the great sympathetic nerve, including those of the solar plexus, have each one small pole.

"The *Ganglions of Phrenic Life*, or those of the brain and cerebellum, including the olivary bodies, and ganglions of the spinal nerves, have each one small pole.

"*Secreting System.*—The lymphatic glands of this system, including those of the mesentery, have each one small pole. These poles are alternately negative and positive, and not only secrete a fluid in these glands, but change its negative and positive character alternately, and at the same time attract the fluid secreted along the lymphatic vessels to the heart.

"*Excreting System.*—There are no poles discovered in the mucous glands of the mucous membranes or in the skin, in the somniscient state, but numerous nerves are seen to terminate in these membranes and in the skin.

"The *Convolutions of the Brain*, or phrenological organs, have each one small pole."

4. *The Direction of Human Polarization.* Faraday says man is diamagnetic, *i.e.* if his body should be suspended from a pivot between the poles of a great horse-shoe magnet, it would not arrange itself in the magnetic meridian, with the head at one pole and the feet at the other, but at right angles to this direction, or in the magnetic equator. This would show that the strongest forces are transverse and agrees with Reichenbach and with my own experience, the front and right side being positive, while the back and left side are negative. Sherwood thinks the lines of polarity in man are between the head and feet. That there are such lines is doubtless true, but the transverse lines seem the strongest and are very distinctly indicated by the opposite poles of color. We have seen that the lower occiput reverses the order of currents which prevail in the front head, the influx or negative currents being at the right, and the efflux currents at the left. This may occur from the fact that the right and left hemispheres of the brain decussate at the region of the *pyramids* (*corpora pyramidalia*) and carry some of their influences to the cerebellum. The legs have been compared to a horse-shoe magnet, the positive pole of which is at the right foot; the arms to another magnet, with the positive pole at the right hand, while the fingers of each hand and the toes of each

foot constitute a series of magnets. Thus the human body is diamagnetic as a whole, but magnetic in its parts. The fact that the heart is located somewhat towards the left part of the body, may have had an influence in bringing the red thermal light on the left and the electrical colors most strongly to the right. On account of the polarization of these different magnets of the body many sensitive persons find that they cannot cross their own hands or legs without interfering with the regular play of forces and causing uneasy feelings. Reichenbach states that M. Schuh, a physicist of Vienna, will have a headache if he puts right and left hands together a few minutes, while some are so feeble and sensitive as to go into spasms when hands and feet are crossed.

5. *Muscular Action.* Physiologists are much puzzled by the fact that nerves of motion, or those that act upon the muscles, and nerves of sensation which carry the vital ethers towards the brain, are composed of exactly the same material. The etherio-atomic law makes this clear, and shows that the same material can conduct both the thermal and electrical forces, and also the same kind of forces both ways, and as the nerves are but the wires which connect the different poles of a battery, the principal effects which are communicated through them depend not on the conductors but on the elements and forces at each end. Thus if the reasoning forces of the front brain in which motor nerves are in predominance should decide to close the fingers, they can instantly, by causing an explosive action at the poles, send an electrical force through the motor nerves which connect with the flexor muscles and it will cause these muscles to contract and bend the fingers. Why will it *contract* the muscles? Because it is electricity, not the coarser grade, but vital electricity, for every grade of electricity is contracting in its nature. To intensify this electrical action all muscles are provided with a mucous membrane and a serous membrane, the former having a predominance of alkali, the latter of acids, and both acting as the opposite plates of a galvanic battery, the blood being the connecting fluid. At the same time the brain sends down a thermal force to the extensor muscles on the opposite side of the fingers which, of course, causes them to expand, as all thermal action is expansive. This point will be explained more in detail in a future work on Human Development.

XVII. PROCESSES OF MENTAL ACTION.

1. *Thought and Feeling.* We have already seen that thoughts, emotions, etc., cause a great rapidity of action among the ethers of the brain, thought sending its blue radiations, love its red, etc. This by no means signifies that we can see thought, but simply the action of some of the coarser ethers which its processes awaken, and demonstrates also that no mental action is possible without motion, or in other words without some active instrument through which it works. Dr. Sherwood's somnis-cients saw streams of light going to and from the great central pole of the brain while thinking, and also lines connecting with each other. The outward world radiates its light, including col-ors, forms, sizes and motions upon the mind through the eye, its voices, tones and sounds through the ear, and many of its subtler forces directly into the brain itself. These may be supposed to pass on to the central pole and by that be reflected to all quarters of the brain, so that each faculty can take cognizance of them and pass its appropriate verdict. Suppose for instance a choice stone has been discovered. Its image is carried first to the retina, then modified and carried to the central pole, then reflected to the various organs or gray convolutions of the outer brain for them to pass their decision upon it, such as that of Form which takes cognizance of its shape, and Color which dis-criminates with reference to its tints and hues, and Acquisitive-ness, which considers its value as a possession, and Ideality which considers its beauty, and Comparison which measures its qualities with other similar substances, and Causality which traces out its origin, laws of formation, etc., and Benevolence which asks what good can be done with it? and so on, the fine ethers echoing and re-echoing from center to circumference, and from circumference to center of the brain, and making their impressions on the inner tablets of the mind just as really as impressions can be made in plaster of Paris. That this play of mental forces has a reactive effect on the whole system is too well known to need illustration here, as physiology shows how the fibres of the nerves pass through the medulla oblongata and elsewhere to the heart, lungs, stomach and all the other viscera, producing sometimes an animating and sometimes a depressing

effect, according to the nature of the force communicated. Persons of violent impulses will frequently have the lower and back brain in such a hot and perhaps diseased condition as to radiate their ethers powerfully over the front and upper brain, and thus becloud and overpower the voice of both reason and conscience in case of any excitement.   Such are not to be cured by severe means, but by remedying the physical and psy. chological causes of the difficulty.   We need fewer prisons and more institutions that shall combine the character of a *work-house, hospital* and *school* in one, for sick minds should be treated as tenderly as sick bodies, if we are ever to save the world, or in other words, sick minds always include sick bodies, or imperfect bodily conditions, for we cannot have a thought or an aspiration, or even an inspiration while in this life, without using a physical brain and physical aura as the negative instruments.

2. *Psychometry*, literally *soul-measuring*, is a term adopted by Dr. J. R. Buchanan over a third of a century ago.   It recognizes the fact that all things radiate their own character upon all surrounding objects so that sensitive human beings can often describe them minutely.   Thus Prof. Denton gives an account of two ladies who, on holding a piece of matter from the ruins of Pompei, saw belching fire and smoke and seemed to be almost frightened at the excitement and turmoil which was indicated thereby, and this when the object was covered with a paper and they were entirely unconsious of where it came from.   Dr. Buchanan has shown in many cases in his lectures before medical classes, how drugs merely held in the hand, will produce the same symptoms on most persons that they would if taken internally, only in a milder form, and has found in very many places, persons sufficiently sensitive to read the character of another from an object which they have handled, especially from a letter which they have written.   Bayard Taylor, the celebrated American Traveller, who has had a vast experience in observing mankind, writes as follows to the Cincinnati Commercial, of Mr. Brown, the Mind-reader : " Mr. Brown, is giving what he calls ' mind readings' at Chickering Hall.   It is nothing but a marked instance of natural clairvoyance—a power which, in greater or less degree, is known to at least one-tenth of the civilized human race.   But the materialistic philosophers are bent

upon giving a purely materialistic explanation of the phenomena;
and it is curious to what incredible lengths they go, in order to
avoid admitting the existence of a ' spiritual sense.' The last
explanation is that Mr. Brown is a 'muscle reader'—that is,
that he detects from the muscles of the face the particular
thought, name or object in the mind of the person which he
professes mentally to read.   This is very much like inventing a
miracle to account for a natural occurrence.   I see nothing extraordinary, or even unusual, in all that Mr. Brown does.   In him
the sense is more finely developed, but tens of thousands have
it in common with him.   I know an artist, who, with bandaged

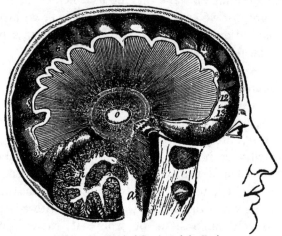

Fig. 196.   Vertical Section of the Brain.

eyes, and a letter in a blank envelope placed between his two
hands, will presently describe the character of the writer.   In
one instance, one of his own letters was thus given to him, and
the result was such an astonishing, unconscious revelation of
himself, his weaknesses and faults of character, that the experimenter hastily removed the letter, feeling that he had com-
mitted a wrong."   I see by our New York papers that Mr.
Brown, while at Chickering Hall, on Fifth Avenue, has lately
shown his ability to find any object, secreted as carefully as
possible, without leading by the hand the person who has hidden
it, and has thus taken the last plank of the carpers from under
their feet.

3. *Vertical Section of the Brain.*   While fig. 192 gives a

general plan of the lateral radiations of the brain, fig. 196 gives a vertical section of the brain through the reddish gray convolutions, the bluish white interior portion, the great inferior ganglion in the cavity of the third ventricle *o*, the cerebellum *n*, with its arbor vitæ, the cerebellar ganglion 1, and the medulla oblongata *a*, constituting the upper end of the spinal column. The convolutions of the brain here given, representing the functions of intellect, sentiment, etc., are as follows, according to the usual plan, which differs somewhat from Dr. Buchanan's nomenclature :—*n*, Amativeness, or sexual love; 2, Philoprogenitiveness, or love of offspring; 3, Inhabitiveness, or love of home; 4, Concentrativeness, or power to concentrate one's thoughts and forces; 5, Approbativeness, or love of approbation; 6, Self-Esteem, or dignity of self; 7, Firmness; 8, Reverence, or Religious and Spiritual Aspiration; 9, Benevolence; 10, Human Nature; 11, Comparison, or faculty of seeing analogies, etc.; 12, Eventuality, or power of observing actions and events; 13, Individuality, or faculty for observing individuals and existences; 14, Language, or power of remembering words. This, when large, pushes the eye outward and gives it a full appearance. Causality is on each side of 11, or Comparison. Thus we see that these striations extend in every direction and connect with the external brain on a beautiful law of unity and diversity. But there are many other series of striations and modifying portions of the brain which cannot be shown in the cut.

4. *Gray and White Brain Substance.* Dr. John Hughes Bennett, F. R. S. E., speaking of the white matter of the brain, says :—" On carefully examining a thin section of this structure, prepared after the manner of Lockhart Clarke, and steeped in carmine, the white substance in the adult may be seen to be composed wholly of nerve tubes. These become more and more minute as they reach the gray matter of the convolutiohs, and are gradually lost in it. * * * The gray matter evolves that force or quality which is essential to mind, and the conditions necessary for this are evidently connected with the molecular and cell structure. The white matter, on the other hand, conducts the influences originating in, and going to, the gray matter." (*Clinical Lectures, p.* 139.)

In the foregoing excellent remarks the learned doctor has

evidently omitted a very important factor connected with the intellectual processes, as the gray nerve cells alone cannot "evolve the force necessary to mind," or to sensation. He might have received a very valuable hint from the following, which I quote from Dr. Sherwood's work :—"On a third examination in the same somniscient state, Mr. Sunderland inquired what she felt with, or what the sense of feeling was in; whether in her skin, flesh or bones; when she answered, 'No, it is not in either of them.' What then do you feel with ? 'I don't know.' I then took hold of her hand, and when pinching one of her fingers inquired, where does the sensation of pinching go to ? 'It goes along up my hand and arm to my head.' How do you know it goes there ? 'Because I can see a motion along the nerves from the pole where you are pinching my thumb to the brain. How can you see a motion along the nerves? 'Because it is lighter where it is moving along.' What part of the brain does the sensation go to ? 'To the middle of the brain, I believe.' Well, the magnetic forces move along the nerves as you have before described ? 'Yes, they do.' Are not the sensations, then, in those forces ? 'Yes, to be sure they are.'" Even this idea is not quite exact, as sensation does not come from the magnetic forces alone, nor from the brain cells, but from both combined.

5. *Special Organs for Special Mental Qualities.* The following is from a lecture of Prof. Agassiz, and is in harmony with the opinions of many physiologists of the day:—"The attempt to localize the mental faculties of men and animals, to connect them with the superior organization of special parts has failed." It is supposed by Dr. Brown-Séquard that there are no special organs for special mental characteristics, any more than the bottom of the foot can be called the *tickling organ*. On this principle a man might have a magnificent dome of thought in his front brain with expansive brows and forehead like a Lord Bacon or Daniel Webster, and it would have no more significance than the low sloping forehead of an idiot, which would be contrary to all human observation. To say that the mind, whose more immediate realm is the brain, has no special organ for *reasoning* with, or for *perceiving*, or loving, or calculating with, is on a par with saying that we can walk without legs, or see without eyes, or hear without ears. Such is the logic, such the exactness of

our men of *exact science.* Phrenology, of course, is too vast a science to have all its details perfected, and like all other departments of human knowledge, must exhibit many imperfections and seeming inconsistencies until the forces of life are more widely understood, but its fundamental principles must be eternally true, and its leading details must also be correct; 1st, because our principal phrenologists have examined multitudes of cases and given their characters minutely while blindfolded; 2dly, the color radiations already described show the variety of powers and qualities in different parts of the brain, and these colors just harmonize with the leading qualities of the brain as discovered by phrenologists; 3dly, all organs of a sensitive brain can be charged with the hand or otherwise, and the subject, without knowing anything of the organ so charged, will manifest its especial quality in the most unmistakable manner. We have already seen how a lady was brought to an insanity of hunger by touching Alimentiveness, and thrown into convulsions of laughter by charging Mirthfulness, and how Dr. Buchanan, in the presence of Bryant, the poet, and others, could produce any mental phenomena he chose by charging different portions of the brain. Dr. Ashburner would arouse uncontrollable passional impulses, even in ladies, while in somniscence by touching Amativeness with the pointed (warm) end of a crystal, while he could immediately change the feelings by presenting the blunt or electrical end to them. I once placed my hand over the religious and spiritual portion of a young man whom I had in a magnetic state, and he uttered a rapturous expression ending with a prolonged "oh!" He saw visions of sublimity and unutterable splendor, but soon his spirit seemed to be so abstracted from the body that he was sinking into a death-like stupor, which I immediately ended by removing my hand, and making upward and outward passes. The late Dr. Elliotson, some years ago, read before the Phrenological Society of London, an account of a young lady, wholly ignorant of phrenology, who, when mesmerized, pointed out the different parts of the brain in which she *felt anger* (destructiveness), *kept a secret* (secretiveness), *felt hunger* (alimentiveness), etc. I will quote some of the account :—
"Upon my exciting her organ of *tune,* she said, ' That makes me feel so very cheerful—it makes me feel like hearing some sing-

ing.' I requested her to sing. She persisted in asserting her inability until I energetically excited *self-esteem*, when she said, 'I'll try,' and she forthwith hummed an air. When her organ of *Color* was excited (in nearly the middle of each eye-brow), she exclaimed with animation, 'Oh, oh! I see green, yellow, purple, etc., such beautiful colors.' If when she was unable to distinguish an object, I excited *individuality*, she instantly perceived it distinctly. The organ called *wit*, or *mirthfulness*, being excited, she fell into a continuous fit of laughter, exclaiming as well as she could, 'I shall die of laughing.' Upon exciting her organ of *destructiveness*, her whole aspect and tone gradually underwent the most marked change ; the 'milk of human kindness' gradually turned to gall and venom ; she pouted, frowned, threatened, stormed, clenched her fist, and finally became exasperated. Thinking I had gone far enough I breathed upon the organ * to reduce its activity, and she very soon became calm, losing every symptom of anger." The experimenter in this case was a Mr. Gardiner. Under the light of such facts, and of many others, of a physiological and psychological nature, which cannot be mentioned here, the arguments in favor of this science seem irresistible, and of vast importance, as it opens up the true science of man, and shows how to develop human life on a grander scale. It is a wonderful key to the insanities and idiosyncracies of mankind, as it is plain to be seen that when some phrenal organ or bodily organ corresponding with it, becomes over-excited or diseased, there must at once be that overaction of the mental forces developed by it which constitutes a grade of insanity : if the organs of the front brain be demagnetized by passing the currents away from them it develops a temporary idiocy—if other parts of the brain are treated thus, the conception becomes strangely perverted. Dr. Sherwood and Rev. La Roy Sunderland witnessed the case of a mesmerized lady in New York, who, when *tune* was charged and reverse passes made over *language*, could give the music, but no words, and forgot even her own name ; but when language was charged and tune demagnetized, she remembered the words but not the tune ; when *eventuality* was demagnetized she forgot all events, even her own age.

* A breathing which resembles blowing, is electrical and calming in its nature while a gradual emission of breath near a person is warming.

VIII. THE ORGAN OF THIS HIGHER VISION.

1. That odic and psychic colors and objects may be seen by some other faculty than the outward eye must by this time be sufficiently established for most reasonable persons, and this must be accomplished by means of a different grade of light from that which illumines the external universe. If the following idea is sufficiently remembered it will save a great deal of trouble and many mistakes :—*No grade of vision can ever be accomplished without an eye to see with, or without light adapted to this eye.* We have seen in Chapter First, III, that the unity of law is everywhere so complete that we are safe in judging of the unknown by the known, and hence our rule. But nearly all persons treating of this superior vision have been misled in this matter, and the fact that so many scientific minds have wandered off wide from all fundamental law, led me to try to ascertain, in the beginning of this work, what are the great basic principles that rule immutably in nature. Writers will constantly affirm that the well known Seeress of Prevorst could see with the pit of her stomach, and Dr. Gregory, of Edinburgh, says that "Clairvoyants sometimes see with the epigastrium, top of head, occiput, fingers and even toes." That these great luminous centers where the nerves are so abundant, act as windows for admitting this finer light and conducting it to the inner vision at the brain, is no doubt true, but it would be a most useless thing and a vast waste of material to have eyes with their almost countless parts all over the body where more necessary organs are required. Suppose I view the moon through a telescope 20 feet long; the act of vision does not occur at the end which receives the light, but 20 feet away from it where my eyes are.

2. But what is the location of these interior eyes? And if a man possesses a finer interior eye he must naturally possess interior ears and all other parts of the body. Is not this the logical sequence of this admission? Have we not seen that there is a grander universe within the universe, and has not St. Paul spoken of "a natural body" and "a spiritual body?" And have not many persons been conscious of a second self which at times could look down upon their outward body?

Varley, the eminent English Electrician, once did this, and the doctrine of "the *double*," so well known in Germany under the name of "*Döppelgangers*" argues in this direction. In my own experience I have met several who at times have been able to look upon their own bodies which were lying near them, and occasionally have found difficulty in re-entering them. These would be connected by shining life-cords with their own bodies, and sometimes would see the indescribable radiance of the inner world. Dr. Cleaveland, of Providence, in the translation of Deleuze, speaks of a carpenter who fell from the staging of a building to the ground. "As I struck the ground," said he, "I suddenly bounded up, seeming to have a new body, and to be standing among the spectators, looking at my old one. I saw them trying to bring it to. I made several fruitless efforts to re-enter my body, and finally succeeded." (p. 367.) Is not this a most cheering thought, giving tokens of the immortal life and of a more beautiful existence to those who have become innately beautiful? Our outward flesh easily becomes corrupt or worm-eaten, and at death is disintegrated. But this inner body is finer than light itself or any known ethers, and having no elements of decay in it must continue to live. The materialist says that thought and mentality are absolutely impossible without a physical brain to think with. Well, I am not denying their proposition. Here is not only a brain but a whole body which are material in their nature, although of a very refined materiality, but still back of these must be the animating spirit itself. So that we have this finer eye about at the same point as the outer eye, only perhaps a little farther within, and the same with the other organs. This will account for the fact that so many persons who have had a leg or arm amputated will still continue to feel pains at times in the toes or fingers whose coarser counterpart is absent.

3. H. Helmholtz, Professor of Physics in the University of Berlin, and one of the eminent names of Europe, is an illustration of how weak in philosophy a man may sometimes be who is very skillful in science. He uses the following language in a lecture delivered at Frankfort and Heidelberg:—"We know that no kind of action upon any part of the body except

the eye, and the nerve which belongs to it, can ever produce the sensation of light. The stories of somnambulists, which are the only arguments that can be adduced against this belief, we may be allowed to disbelieve." Certainly! The learned Professor may be allowed to disbelieve in the existence of the Rhine, or any other immutable fact of nature, if he choose; but as long as this river will continue to exist and roll on towards the sea, it would be unwise to do so. Should he attempt to walk across its channel under the impression that no water exists there, he might fall into great danger, just as he does when he ignores these subtile forces of life which have such a bearing on all science. He then proceeds as follows, which shows that he has already got into a very dangerous pathway of thought: "But on the other hand, it is not light alone which can produce the sensation of light upon the eye, but also any other power which can excite the optic nerve. If the weakest electrical currents are passed through the eye they produce flashes of light. A blow, or even a slight pressure made upon the side of the eye-ball with the finger makes an impression of light in a dark room, and under favorable circumstances this may become intense. * * * Under these circumstances, at least, there is not the smallest spark of actual light." If Professor Helmholtz had properly studied the work of Reichenbach, written in his own language, he would have seen that there are hundreds of cases given in which sentitives could see the odic light under the stimulus of electricity, friction, &c., with its flames, sparks, and smoke as an actual entity, as real as the light of the sun. The fact that many persons can be stimulated to see these lights and colors by having their eyes electrized or pressed, should not lead him to banish all perception of light from the earth in its objective phases, as we shall soon see that he does, but should make him understand that there is more light than he at first thought there was, for similar effects must have similar causes. He then goes on to say that the "most complete difference offered by our several sensations, that, namely, between those of sight, of hearing, of taste, of smell, and of touch, *does not, as we now see, at all depend on the nature of the external object, but solely upon the central connections of the nerves which are* *affected.* * * * These elementary sensations of color, can only be called forth by artificial preparation of the organ, so that, in fact, they only exist as *subjective phenomena.*" The Italics are mine. If all these sensations "do not at all depend on the nature of the external object," then a rose or a piece of carrion are alike to the sense of smell, pepper and sugar to the sense of taste, or the red and blue colors to the sense of vision. If the Professor had studied these fine laws of force, he might have ascertained the very laws of chemical affinity between the red light, for instance, and the nerve fibres which receive it in the process of sensation, and the entirely different chemical process between the blue light and the nerve fibres which receive it, and so with the other colors, which process will be treated of in the next chapter. He would see very clearly, too, that action and reaction being equal, the object acting upon the nerves of the retina, has exactly the same importance with reference to these nerves that the nerves have with reference to the object; or, in other words, the nerves of sensation depend as much upon the nature of the object as the object does upon the nerves of sensation. His theory makes the sensation every-thing, the object nothing, and tends directly into that system of idealism which pretty much annihilates the outward universe and sets up human consciousness as the all-embracing thing. But we ascertain at once how he has been misled when he affirms that his opinions " are clearly expressed in the writings of Locke and Herbart, and they are completely in accordance with Kant's philosophy." It is high time that these mere specula-tive systems of philosophy were laid on the shelf, and a system founded on nature substituted in their place, so that science shall no longer be kept in the back-ground. For other opinions on these matters, see Chapter Second. I will simply add that had I followed such principles I could never have discovered any laws of atomic action, of the chemical affinity of colors, or their therapeutical or other potencies, or a multitude of other things, for if I had believed that force or the perception of force "does not depend at all upon the nature of external objects," but rather upon something merely in the mind, I should have looked upon only one side of matters, and this is the best way to learn neither side correctly. Many of our scientific men,

however, including Helmholtz himself, are superior in practice
to their theories, and so in spite of all deficiencies the world
owes many great achievements to their discoveries.

4. I must be pardoned for telling a little story at the expense of these idealistic scientists :—

Alphonso, a young man who was fond of philosophy, became
quite enamored of a certain silver-tongued reasoner by the name
of Sophistes.

"My boy," said the would-be sage as they met for conversation, "there is nothing but the immortal mind, nothing but the
conscious *ego* in the whole universe that has any real or absolute
existence. Look at yonder sky. It appears to be a dome of
blue sapphire, but go up into it, by means of a balloon, and the
blue can never be found ; it is all delusion. In your childhood
you were sure the rainbow rested on a distant hill, but when you
chased it the whole thing turned out to be deception.* You say
that yonder rep cushion is green. That is entirely owing to
what kind of light touches it, for look, as I throw the light
through a prism, and see how one part becomes red, another
yellow, another violet, etc. Where, now, is your green ?† My
friend, the color is 'all in your eye.' If color is anything at all
why cannot we photograph it ? " ‡

* A similar style of sophistry was perpetrated by Dr. Geo. M. Beard in a lecture before a body of physicians in New York, in such language as the following :—
" So far as the senses are concerned they deceive all of us every hour and every moment. * * * The sight is on the whole the best of the senses, but in civilized lands
only fools trust it. If any man wishes to blunder, let him open his eye and believe
what he thinks he sees." That is the way a man reasons who has a theory to prove,
namely, that we should not reason inductively from facts ascertained through the
senses. The truth is that not once in a million times will a person be deceived
in reaching out the hand or foot to touch an object, but he will find it just where
it seems to be. Animals are often still more acute in their perception, and thus
vision is next thing to perfection in its accuracy, except when the eye is imperfect
or diseased.

† This absurd argument has been advanced by eminent writers, but instead of
showing that light is a nonentity, it proves with especial force that it must be a real
substance that can thus rest upon and conceal the color beneath it.

‡ One reason, doubtless, why artists have not yet succeeded in photographing the
chromatic colors in connection with their pictures, is because of the dynamic theory of
force which, if true, would show the folly of attempting to photograph a nihility.
Building on this theory, a New York paper has declared that color, not being a substance, cannot, of course, be photographed, hence the uselessness of trying. But we
have seen in Chapter Fifth that it is a substance, and has been photographed imperfectly already.

"But," interrupted Alphonso, "are not metals, woods, liquids, etc., actual substances?"

"Put a powerful heat upon gold, silver, and platinum even, and they can be vaporized and passed away from your vision forever."

"And still their parts must continue in some form."

"Do you not see that if these hard elements can be thus dissipated and made invisible, it is quite easy to suppose that if a heat sufficiently great were brought to bear upon them they might be entirely annihilated? Reasoning from analogy with these other so-called objects which I have just spoken of, it must be so, and in reality they are shadowy nothings. As colors, then, and solids and liquids have thus no fundamental basis of substance, the same is true of sounds, and odors, and heat, and cold, and everything in the realms of being. Intellect and sensation and consciousness are the only entities and potencies which a philosopher can recognize. Does not Locke say that 'what in our sensation is heat, in the object is nothing but motion?' Does not Count Rumford also prove that there is no such thing as caloric, heat being a mere motion? Let us be keen enough, then, to rise above these phantasies and delusions around us, and dwell on the eternal rock of being within."

These and many other points were inculcated upon the young student, and he, becoming spell-bound by the teachings of Sophistes, was impressed with the grandeur of being a philosopher and the folly of heeding the material conditions around him to such an extent that he concluded not to take any more food or drink. "Such things," he said, "would do for ordinary stupid mortals who know no better, but so long as he knew them to be mere shadowy nothings, what folly to pay attention to them." His motto was, "Be strong in immortal thoughts and control all surrounding conditions by the might of volition." Reasoning thus, he became weaker and paler every day, and when his distressed friends entreated him to eat he proved to them their shortsightedness and said that when he had brought his mind into harmony with surrounding motions and conditions he should be all right. He, however, continued to waste away, when a friend, by the appropriate name of Llewellyn, which interpreted means *lightning*, determined to break the spell that was destroying him. He made an arrangement to accompany Alphonso to see his mentor Sophistes, whom the young man had pronounced one of the greatest of philosophers, quite able, as he felt sure, to wind up Llewellyn in five minutes. "We shall see who will get the best of the argument," said the strong man who, by name and nature, was charged with a good stock of the principle of lightning.

Having reached the room of the wonderful teacher, Llewellyn remarked to him that his young friend here had spoken of his remarkable wisdom, and that he was anxious to hear his explanation of that which we usually suppose to be matter. Sophistes felt flattered, and went on in his most eloquent style to demolish the whole external universe, leaving not a vestige of it behind. Alphonso was pleased to see the wrapt attention with which Llewellyn seemed to swallow every word, and chuckled at the thought that he was already conquered. As Sophistes was about finishing up his glowing exposition, a terrific explosion took place, seemingly under his chair, which made him spring out upon the floor in great alarm, with staring eyes and a flushed face, declaring that somebody was trying to blow him up with a bomb-shell. Alphonso, too, being in a weak state, was very much frightened and rushed for the door. Llewellyn spoke up and said : "Friends be calm ! I beg of you be calm ! I defy any bomb-shells to hurt me ! Have you not just proved irresistibly that sound is a nonentity, and heat a nonentity, or at most a mere motion, and that the thing which just exploded is really no thing at all ? Why, then, this alarm ? You surely believe your own theories ?"

"Of course I do," said Sophistes, " but that was motion, a terrible motion, my dear Sir ! Can't you understand me ?"

"Certainly," replied the man of lightning, " and have been charmed by your beautiful language, but you see I am not in the least afraid of any motion so long as there is nothing to move. You have shown me very eloquently that what people call solids, liquids and gases are really mere moonshine, mere diluted nihilities, so of course the infernal arrangement that somebody placed under your chair could not hurt anybody, for there was nothing of it."

Sophistes tried to stutter out an argument and seemed quite excited, when Llewellyn exclaimed : Please be seated, my dear sir, and I will show you by a practical illustration what a bound-less faith I have in your philosophy.   Have you a piece of gold coin, Sir ?"

Sophistes handed over a half eagle.

" Have you also a handkerchief with you ?"

Sophistes passed a neat white handkerchief to him.

Holding them up, Llewellyn exclaimed : "Very pretty indeed! I once thought they were real substances, but now I find out otherwise.   What dreamers we all are, living in a vain delusion ! I don't wonder you look with pity upon the great vulgar crowd who are ever clinging to the shadowy nothings around them as if they were something genuine.   I used to think that heat was a severe reality, but now I find it is a mere matter of sensation, a subjective matter, being nothing but motion in the object. Now if I should throw this handkerchief into that fire, it would not give you any sensation of heat, and therefore there would be only some motion going on in the handkerchief, which, of course, would not amount to anything.   To prove it, I will try it and see," at which the lightning man had the handkerchief in the fire in a twinkling.   Its owner sprang forward with a groan and clasped the burning article, but not before some ugly holes had been made in it.   His face was as red as fire as he exclaimed :

" Sir ! are you crazy ?"

" Well," said Llewellyn with a puzzled look, "either I must be crazy, or you must be, for there is a powerful objective some-thing somewhere, else how could those holes have come?   I think I had better not make any more experiments, as I have had bad luck, and so I believe I will go home."   Saying this he started off and beckoned to Alphonso to follow him.

" But stay !" said Sophistes, " I will take that five dollar gold piece if you please."

" Excuse me," said the man of lightning, " you have proved conclusively that gold and other solids are mere diluted moon-shine, or in other words simply nothing at all.   Since you know this to be the fact, and since my last experiment has shown me that there may be a reality in these objects, I will just take this piece along with me and see how it turns out."

" Saying this he started out into the street followed by Sophistes, who cried " Police ! Police."   A policeman immediately made his appearance. The reader, I presume, will perceive that Llewellyn had prearranged all matters, including the explosive, as well as the policeman who had been informed of the programme.

"Explain this conduct, sir," said the policeman to Llewellyn, with some show of sternness.

"Certainly. This is the explanation:—This gentleman is a *philosopher*," emphasizing the word philosopher—"and he has proved to me very powerfully that gold and other substances have no real existence as distinctive objects—that they are shadowy elements which may be dissipated, and consequently are mere nonentities. Now I am not quite sure of this fact, and so I wish to take it home and experiment a little upon it. As he is sure that there is nothing in it, he certainly should not feel that he is losing anything.

"If you don't consider that the gold is any special object," said the policeman to Sophistes, "why do you object to his taking it?"

Sophistes quibbled some and showed much excitement, and vowed that he would not be robbed by wrong applications of his principle.

By this time Alphonso, who had been silent so long, became so indignant that he could hold in no longer. Rushing up to the sophist, he exclaimed:—" Sir, your fine words turn out to be nonsense when put into practice. The truth is you and I are both fools, you a dishonest one from not acting up to your own theories, and I an honest one who have already starved myself nearly to death as a proof of my sincerity. I shall hurry off and get something to eat, for I feel now as though a good beef steak would weigh down a hundred of your arguments."

He was hurrying off, when Llewellyn caught him and bade him wait a moment, as it was necessary for him to attend him and prevent his over-eating. Turning to Sophistes, Llewellyn exclaimed:—

"Sir, my purpose has been accomplished. I shall trifle no more with this subject; I came here to show this young man that a few simple facts would scatter your theories to the winds. So far as my methods have seemed rude, I beg your pardon, and my excuse is that when men wall themselves about with very absurd channels of reasoning, they can only be liberated from it by some rather hot and explosive styles of facts.   I have not had the most distant idea of wronging you, and now offer you the gold, which is one of nature's eternal entities, and a dollar more to pay for the handkerchief destroyed.   Let me beg you not to further mislead people's minds by attempting to destroy the whole outward universe, especially so long as you cannot prove that the most minute particle of matter has ever been or ever can be destroyed."

These words were hardly finished before the indignant sophistical philosopher had withdrawn into the house and slammed the door.

5. Does my reader say that the foregoing is an extreme view of things, and that such a philosophy has not been held by any one?   Is it not the logical sequence of even the reasoning of Helmholtz, and especially of Kant and others whom he follows?   To show that the mystic schools of Germany go even beyond what I have represented, I will quote a little from Dr. J. R. Buchanan :—" Kant, in opposition to the cosmologists, denied our ability to know anything of the world, or of being exterior to ourselves, because of the limitation of our faculties.   He affirms that space and time are mere conditions of *our own perceptive faculties*, and that if we would understand external objects we must conceive them independent of space and time ; and, as we cannot do this, we cannot know anything truly, but can recognize certain delusive appearances.   * * *   Fichte, equally absurd with Kant, decided, by a course of inconsequential reasoning not worth repeating in its jejune tediousness, that *man exists*, but *nothing else*.   The supposed reality beyond man (the universe and Deity), is merely derivative from man ; in other words, is merely an affection of our consciousness.   Of course, then, each human being must consider himself the universe, and all other human beings being an effect of his consciousness, as he is but an effection of their consciousness—which seems logically to annihilate the substantial existence of man, leaving only ideas.   It was with reference to such a philosophy that a Boston transcendentalist was said to have pronounced it very unphilosophical to say, ' It snows,' or ' It rains.'   It would be more philosophical to say, ' I snow,' or ' I rain.'   * * *   The next step in misological absurdity is to deny, with Kant, the existence of time and

space, affirming that they appertain only to our minds. The next beyond Kant is to deny all perception, with Fichte and Schelling, and affirm that nothing exists but our own consciousness or thought. The very *ultima thule* of absurdity is reached with Hegel in ignoring our positive consciousness of self and observation, to affirm a limitless consciousness—unlocated, undefined, and commingled with being and unconsciousness, in a *tertium quid* which defies description or even conception." (Brittan's Quarterly, July, 1873.)

XIX. THE MEDICAL WORLD.

1. *The lack of knowledge of these Fine Forces* is constantly apparent in the medical profession. When they wish to get up an action in certain parts of the system, they know of no better way than to produce new diseases in those parts, by blistering, burning with hot irons, leeching, lancing, drugging, using setons, etc. If they would keep up with the progress of the day they would ascertain that counter irritation and counter diseases are generally unphilosophical, as passes and friction from a warm magnetic hand can draw the blood powerfully to any desired part of the body, or call it away from any part, and that in a way to cause no local harm but to animate the whole system. They should learn also that by means of sunlight, aided by lenses, as well as by electricity and water, they may in many cases produce the same result, and that without any severe after effects. More than this they would see that the barbarous practice of *transfusing blood* from a living human being or animal into the veins of a patient, is far less scientific than the transfusion of psycho-magnetism and vital magnetism through the whole nervous system, and thence through the whole vascular system, by means of which a pure and fine flow of blood can be developed on natural principles, and the life forces made strong from the very foundation. If you tell them about this higher science of life, these diviner essences of power, they cannot see them or clasp them in the hand as they can drugs or lancets, and so very many of them will pronounce such methods "*quackery*" or "*fanaticism*." They however seem to be so afraid of the rising power of these "quacks," and are so anxious to protect the interests of *the people*, which

expression being interpreted means the *medical people*, that
they will sometimes raise heaven and earth to have laws en-
acted against allowing them to practice until they have passed
through the same false systems of collegiate medical training
as themselves. These quacks cure thousands of cases that
baffle the power of drugs and surgery, and I could fill large
volumes with their achievements which would be considered
almost too remarkable to be credited. I am no advocate of
ignorance and would glory in a true system of medical education founded on nature's higher methods, but *an ignorant healer
who deals with the fine forces will in most cases do more good
and less harm, than a so-called learned physician who practices
only with the coarser elements.* I will quote a very few of
the admissions of eminent physicians themselves, as the best
proof that the cruder elements of nature are not suited to build
up so refined a being as man, and also to show that those who
build so much upon such forces, are quite conscious of their
failure in arriving at the true elements of power, or in attaining to a scientific basis of cure :—

"Our remedies are unreliable." *Valentine Mott, M.D.*

"Of all sciences, medicine is the most uncertain." *Dr. Willard Parker.*

"I have no faith whatever in our medicines." *Dr. Bailey.*

"Medicine is so far from being a science that it is only conjecture." *Dr. Evans.*

"Mercury has made more cripples than all wars combined." *Dr. McClintock.*

"So gross is our ignorance of the physiological character of disease that it
would be better to do nothing." *Dr. Magendie.*

"Digitalis has hurried thousands to the grave." *Dr. Hosack.*

"Blisters nearly always produce death when applied to children." *Prof. C. R.
Gilman, M.D.*

"Drugs do not cure disease ; disease is always cured by the *vis medicatrix na-
turæ.*" *Prof. J. M. Smith, M.D.*

"Opium diminishes the nerve force." *Dr. Davis.*

"The older physicians grow, the more skeptical they become to the virtues of
medicine." *Dr. Stevens.*

"The action of remedies is a subject entirely beyond our comprehension."
Prof. John B. Beck, M.D.

"I fearlessly assert, that in most cases the patient would be safer without a
physician than with one." *Prof. Ramage, M.D., F.R.S.*

"Let us no longer wonder at the lamentable want of success which attends our
practice, when there is scarcely a sound physiological principle among us." *Dr.
Magendie.*

"The science of medicine is a barbarous jargon, and the effects of our medicines
on the human system are in the highest degree uncertain, except that they have
already destroyed more lives than war, famine and pestilence combined." *Dr. John
Mason Good.*

The uncertainty and failure signified by the above expressions of high toned and honest physicians must ever continue until men shall learn the dual relations of matter and force, the law of atoms and ethers, and through them the principles of chemical action as applied not only to the coarser elements of external nature, but to the finer physiological and psychological phenomena of man. I do not protest against medical science, but against the lack of science, and against that arbitrary spirit among the lower ranks of our medical men which would make laws to fine and imprison all who practice on a plan different from their own, although their own is admittedly very imperfect, while the men whom they would enchain might prove to be the Galileos and Harveys of a new and grander medical dispensation which shall yet give joy and power to the world. The intelligent people of Massachusetts have triumphantly defeated the attempt to enact these despotic laws which would crush out the freedom of the people to choose their own medical advisers. On the same principle they should make laws to determine what clergymen, what teachers, what merchants should be employed, what churches should be considered safe to attend and what style of schools should be allowed, and having thus put the people in swaddling clothes as being incapable of self-government, should appoint guardians over every family to tell them what they may graciously be allowed to eat, drink, or wear. The laws of Illinois and California on this subject, are a disgrace to those States, and even those of Ohio, New York, and some other States, though of a milder type, show that their people have not been sufficiently acute in their perceptions, or manly in their love of liberty, to prevent their legislators and designing physicians from getting the advantage of them. In making these remarks I am not condemning all physicians by any means, for very many of them are grand men who rise above their schools, seeking for truth in all directions, and following nature's diviner teachings. Such ones have no hand in persecuting others.

2. *The Drinking of the Blood of Animals*, newly butchered, is a disgusting practice which also arises from ignorance of these finer forces. In New York, and perhaps other cities,

many refined ladies and gentlemen are in the habit of going daily to places where cattle are butchered, and imbibing glasses of freshly drawn blood. This in some cases is found to be beneficial, but why, they cannot tell. The truth is that when the blood is first drawn, before the subtle magnetic life fluids escape, there is an animating principle in it which may strengthen and vitalize to some extent. This vital element is what keeps the blood fluidic and active, and when it escapes the blood stiffens into clot. The folly of these *blood-thirsty* persons consists in the fact of their not knowing that they could get a far more refined and potent life power from the touch of many human beings, some of whom can rival the galvanic battery in immediate effect and far outdo it in the fineness and durability of their power. This power of psycho-electricity was well tested by Prof. S. B. Brittan, in Saratoga, before an audience of several hundred persons some years since. A Mr. Cook who, from his knowledge of electrical science, had been employed by the government, denied that there was any such thing as vital electricity, and stated that he could knock a man down with his electrical apparatus ; and when Prof. Brittan " would do the same with his mental electric battery he would believe that electricity had some-thing to do with the phenomena in question." Two worthy young men, strangers to Dr. Brittan, were chosen by the audience and sent upon the platform. After manipulating them a little he directed them to stand firmly, 12 or 15 feet distant from him. He then made a powerful effort of the will and forward thrust of his hands towards them which struck them to the floor as though they had been shot. Mr. Cook immediately left the audience without saying a word, which was a confession of defeat. Some account of this may be found in Brittan's " Man and his Relations," p. 40.

3. While *disease*, according to the old schoolmen, has gen-erally been treated as originating and developing in material conditions, according to Hahnemann and the modern idealists, it has its origin wholly in spiritual conditions. While the latter have done great good by refining the conceptions of the peo-ple, my readers by this time have seen an overwhelming array of facts to show how matter and spirit must work forever in

correlation, while the attempt to build on matter alone, or spirit alone, is like driving a carriage with one wheel.

XX. MISCELLANEOUS POINTS.

1. *The Universal Unity of Things* is apparent from the whole tenor of this work, all things in their basic principles resembling all other things, so that we may judge the whole by a part, the unknown by the known, and the invisible by the visible. We have seen that one great difference in the methods by which this unity manifests itself is, that there is an infinite stairway of degrees reaching from the coarse to the fine, progressing from solids to semi-solids, to liquids, to gases, to ethers, and, finally, to that inconceivable fineness, and subtlety of principle which we term *spirit.* Thus we have the spiritual and material ever blending, ubiquitous, eternal and necessarily correlated in all things as the positive and negative principles of force, or as the basis of all action and reaction. We have seen how the material and spiritual are simply the two ends of the same immeasurable scale of being and both subject to the same laws of chemical action. Does my reader say that the spirit can *think* and *perceive,* while the material or bodily portion of man cannot? This is a great error which should be laid on the shelf as soon as possible, as I have already shown perhaps a score of times, that all possible action must have its dual relations, spirit not being able to act without connection with some grade of matter as a reactive element, nor matter without being potentialized by spirit. Seeing, then, that there is such an absolute unity and interblending and correlation throughout the universe, it is evident that Herbert Spencer is mistaken in declaring that there is a realm of the "unknowable," and many philosophers of the day are mistaken in asserting that we can gain no possible conception of infinity. While we can gain no proper conception of the vastness of the infinite whole, yet, building on the foregoing principle, we may gain a clear conception of the constitution of the infinite, for if we take the smallest atom and mount from that up to a drop of water, which is a huge globe in comparison, and then expand

our view until we take in a world, a solar system, a cluster
of solar systems, or in fact the whole known universe, we
find not a particle of difference in their great fundamental
principles, such as unity, diversity, gradation, contrast, etc.
So far, then, we may be said to grasp infinity itself, and *qualita-
tively* considered there is no absolutely unknowable realm, however short we may come in the *quantitative* grasp of things.

2. *The Magnetic Needle.* Having this conception of the fraternity of all things, the philosophy of much that is now obscure
becomes comparatively simple. Suppose we ask why it is that
the magnetic needle points to the north magnetic pole? We
know that a vane is swept around in a certain direction by currents of air, and a stick of wood, by currents of water, and that
all known displays of force are caused by a current-like or wave-
like flow of some fluid, and so we may be sure that certain currents or ethereal winds of force drive the needle around in their
own direction. In Chapter Fourth we have seen just how and
why certain magneto ethers are drawn northward on the law of
thermo-electricity, and thus made to turn the needle northward,
and how certain magnetic curves or whirlwinds of force, sweeping into the earth, deflect the needle downward in what is called
the *magnetic dip*.

3. *Mental Action.* How does mind control matter? Let us
again come right to nature's simple method of operating. We
have seen that no mental action can take place until the convolutions of the brain have been awakened into life by the sweep of
fine ethers as well as blood through them just as in a landscape
a tempest brings all surrounding objects into action. But volition and mental action of various kinds can send the ethers and
with them the blood to various parts of the body ; can make the
maiden's cheek blush; can send these life currents to the
heart and cause paleness under an impulse of fear ; can send
electric currents to contract muscles, and thermal currents to expand them, and bring about a hundred other kinds of effect.
Many persons, including the author, have learned to will the vital
electricities to the hands or other parts of the body with a power
that causes them to thrill and burn. A magnetic physician once
informed me that he had treated a tumor on one of his limbs for
months without any special effect, until finally he concluded to

fasten his will upon it while treating it, when to his surprise it immediately commenced going down and soon became entirely well. How does spirit accomplish such a movement among physical conditions? Exactly on the same principle that the body can do the same. If a human hand can dash water into eddies or currents in any direction it pleases, so can the human spirit dash those spiritual and psychic ethers with more than lightning speed in whatever direction it pleases, and through them waken the animal ethers and nerves and blood and muscles and the marvelous forces of the brain itself. If a physical hand is moved, this motion requires the play of certain chemical and galvanic action. Does not the spirit also have its marvelously fine play of chemical forces? Have we not seen from the color radiations of the brain and body, that all mental as well as physiological action involves exquisite grades of chemical affinity and chemical repulsion? Seeing, then, that these fine forces, guided by this simple generalization, can thus open up the pathway of divine wisdom and reveal so many secret hiding places of power, why shall men stupidly shut their eyes and ears to them, and groveling among the grosser conditions of matter, declare that nothing can be known of the basic principles of molecular, or chemical, or physiological, or psychological action?

4. *Memory.* How can the mind bring up and retain *images* of past or distant events in the way which constitutes *memory?* Just as a photographic plate can receive and retain images of objects which are thrown upon it. The photographic image is formed by sunlight aided by proper chemicals. These mental images are formed by the higher grades of light, aided as we have seen by the interior chemical forces of the brain. Psychometrists and clairvoyants can, at times, so come into rapport with this finer light as to see these mental images and read the events of a lifetime to the astonishment of the persons thus read. Thoughts, imaginations and passions also stamp actual images on this wonderful tablet of the soul, which thus constitutes a book of life that at some future time may cause great mortification to the owner, unless the gross and selfish imaginations may be sufficiently covered up or erased by those of a nobler kind.

5. *Self-Psychology.* Dr. Fahnestock, following the lead of Dr. Braid, Dr. Carpenter, and many other physicians who, from

their mental constitution and bias, are unfitted to perceive or explain correctly the working of these fine psychological forces,
contends that there is no such thing as any magnetic or fluidic
emanation which may pass from one person to another, but that
all mesmeric, somnambulic or similar phenomena are caused by
imagination, or *suggestion*, or *volition*, or some other action of the
mind. This is on a par with saying that Goliath was not smitten
by a stone from David's sling, but by David himself. In other
words it declares that the mind does something, but quite ignores
the instrument through which it works. In my little work addressed to Dr. Brown-Séquard,* I supposed that I had given
an array of facts which would entirely destroy any such hypothe-
sis, as they showed the power of these forces to work at a distance upon adults and sometimes upon infants who were entirely
unconscious of their exertion, but it makes no difference how
often you kill these theories, they will come to life again the
next day in some other form. The method by which the doctor
beclouds his own and other people's vision at present is, by asserting that a person may put himself into the mesmeric or
statuvolic condition, and therefore this is conclusive proof that
he never receives any emanations from another person. By
similar reasoning we may say that a man can dash water upon
himself, therefore no one else can dash water upon him. I have
already shown that the mesmeric or lucid sleep consists not only
in having the vital ethers and blood of the brain drawn away into
the body by means of passes from some other person's hand, or
sent away by one's own volition, but in drawing outward the finer
and more powerful psychic ethers by means of looking at some
object, or thinking of some object, outside of one's own brain.
A person who is finely magnetic can assist in charging another's
brain and putting it in rapport with these fine forces, a man like
Major Buckley, whom Dr. Gregory describes, being able to charge
people so powerfully that multitudes became clairvoyant, while
other persons would impede clairvoyance. Many persons, however, can learn to control their own forces without the aid of
others at the time.

* Vital Magnetism, the Life Fountain ; being an answer to Dr. Brown-Séquard's
Lectures on Nerve Force; the Magnetic Theory defended and a better Philosophy
of Cure explained, by E. D. Babbitt, D.M. Price, postpaid, 25 cents. Babbitt &
Co., 141 Eighth St., N. Y.

6. *The Stupidity of Investigators* of these fine forces may be seen in the case of a number of positive skeptical persons as they get around a sensitive subject, and perhaps taking him by the hand will laugh and jest and show their incredulity as they require him to see through solid matter. Sometimes they will practice deception upon him, for a sensitive is generally in so negative a condition that he can easily be psychologized to believe and admit almost anything that a positive mind may desire, and so when they sometimes succeed in making him admit a falsehood, they chuckle over the matter and declare that *imagination* or *suggestion* is all there is of it. Instead of exulting thus in their own supposed shrewdness, they should mourn over their supreme folly, and ignorance of law, and the wrong they do to a divine cause. The author, in most cases, cannot see clearly with this inner vision if a single person is in the room, and while charged with these lightning ethers sufficiently to see the glorious colors and lights of the interior world, the tension of his system will be so great and his sensibility so keen that a sound like the dropping of a pin will sometimes make him start and will completely dissipate all colors and forms. I have seen a lady while in this sensitive condition, thrown into spasms by the falling of a small article of furniture, and very few sensitives in the world can exhibit their powers before a noisy audience with any success. Investigators should have a supreme love of truth and should be able to remain entirely passive at such times.

XXI.   Summation of Points in Chromo-Mentalism.

1. *Intellect is the culmination of power, and may be affected indirectly by ordinary light, still more by odic light, and most of all by the psychic light which is the direct messenger and servant of the spirit in its relations to the outward world.*

2. *The psychic lights and colors are inexpressibly beautiful and manifest the infinite activities of nature unseen by ordinary eyes.*

3. *This higher vision exalts the conception and shows that there is a grander universe within the visible which is the real cosmos.*

4. *Thousands of persons are able to see these psychic colors.*

5. *They reveal the primary laws of force. When scientists dwell only*

among the coarser grades of matter, they deal with the outer shell of things, and fail to find the richer kernel within.

6. *This light renders opaque substances transparent from its power to penetrate them, and hence those who can get in rapport with it become what is called clairvoyant. The Committee of the French Royal Academy recognized this fact, and Major Buckley developed 148 persons so that they could read sentences shut up in boxes or nuts.*

7. *Ordinary sleep is caused by drawing the vital ethers, and with them the blood away from the front brain into the cerebellum and body, thus leaving the mental powers so inactive as to be unconscious, while somniscience, or the lucid magnetic sleep not only calls these coarser vital ethers away, but brings into action the finer interior forces which being more swift and penetrating cause greater keenness of mental power, and, when sufficiently developed, clairvoyance itself.*

8. *This lucid condition is often induced by fastening the mind on some near or distant object to draw the finer ethers outward, and is sometimes assisted by downward passes to draw the coarser ethers away from the brain.*

9. *These psychic forces can bless mankind by opening up a sublimer vision of the possibilities of the universe and of human life, by controlling physical, mental, and moral diseases in a very remarkable way, and by circumventing fraud.*

10. *Self-Psychology, or Statuvolence, is a condition which is brought about by getting in rapport with these psychic forces, when by the power of the will the subject can cause all sensation to cease in a part or the whole of his body, or cure disease, or permanently correct many of his mental and moral deficiencies.*

11. *Every part of the intellectual, moral, or passional nature can be aroused into greater action; or subdued into a feebler action by charging different portions of the brain and body with these psychic forces with the hand, or otherwise, or by drawing them off. When the subject is in a somnambulic or otherwise sensitive condition, each part of the brain so touched will arouse a special and intense kind of thoughts and feelings entirely different from every other part, thus showing that the brain has its special organs, or regions of special mental characteristics. The psychic colors which vary in different parts of the brain in harmony with these organs, also confirm the same idea.*

12. *The fine forces of the brain radiate colors on much the same principle as the odic forces in nature.*

13. *The left hemisphere of the brain receives the blue and electrical forces and radiates the warm red forces more strongly than the right, while the right brain radiates the blue forces and receives the red more strongly than the left. The left brain is stronger in the domain of intellect; the right, in that of organic life.*

14. *The highest faculties radiate their forces most strongly upward; the lowest, most strongly downward. The Intellectual faculties radiate their forces both upward and downward in front, the Propelling faculties, both upward and downward behind, and the color radiations are beautiful and pure about every person in proportion as his mental and moral character becomes refined and ennobled.*

15. *Intuition is large in proportion as the psychic forces gain activity in a person, and small in persons whose brains use mainly the ordinary slower ethers. Geniuses, and prodigies of swiftness in mental action, abound in these finer ethers. Woman is more intuitive than man on the average, and being more subject to influx ethers is more sympathetic. Systems strong in the psychic element are especially elastic and recuperative in their vitality.*

16. *The poles of bodily organs, so far as examined, radiate colors which form a chemical affinity with those of the brain, hence the attraction between them.*

17. *The brain has been seen to have five great leading poles, or centers of luminous radiation, the greater of which is in the center, besides which it has minor poles in all the organs, which connect with the central pole. Besides these all of the ganglia and organs of the body have each one or more poles. All sensations and perceptions cause luminous streams of force to pass to the great central pole of the brain from which they are reflected to the external gray matter that constitutes the organs of thought and feeling.*

18. *The reddish gray matter of the brain and nerves, and the bluish white matter of the same, constitute those elements of chemical affinity without which the psychic ethers could not act, and hence all sensation must cease.*

19. *The motor nerves are strong in the intellectual, and the sensory nerves in the passional and emotional portions of the brain.*

20. *A human being must have special organs for special operations of the mind as truly as for walking, seeing, hearing, etc.*

21. *No vision can ever take place without an eye, or without a grade of light adapted to that eye, as Nature never works without instruments, and never violates in one department of being the general law which she follows in another. This finer vision then shows that we have a finer eye than the outward, to which this more exquisite light is adapted, and having eyes of this superior interior character we must have a whole body to match them, a fact that is abundantly proved by the revelations of this diviner light itself, which has often portrayed the human double.*

After giving all these facts and deductions, will not the reader indulge me in one little speculation? As we have this finer body within the coarser, and composed of materials which are never known to decay like gross matter, and which, as we have seen, must be vitalized by a spirit incomparably finer still, is it not reasonable to suppose that when it lays aside the outer garment at death, it must rise by its own gravity, in case it has been sufficiently refined by a true and pure life, into higher realms of space, some distance above the earth, where all things exist in a much more ethereal and exquisite condition? In Chapter Fourth, VII, we have seen that in the ever refining and radiating processes of nature, the more ethereal portions of all matter are being thrown off into space, that exquisite light and fine elements of oxygen, carbon, sodium, lime, silex, hydrogen, nitrogen and other elements of our earthly soil send their emanations upward into the atmosphere, and becoming still more ethereal must rise even higher than what we usually call our atmosphere, for all things must rise in proportion as they become light and airy. Now is it not reasonable to suppose, nay, must it not be almost a certainty, that the immense play of chemical forces through these upper realms, must have segregated and aggregated vast masses of these exquisite particles of earthly matter, until islands, continents, and perhaps almost a continuous belt-work of this divine Kingdom of the Father have been thus constituted? Reichenbach's sensitives ascertained how much more brilliant were the odic lights and colors when the atmosphere was removed, and we may imagine how superbly fascinating must be the psychic grade of light where no gross elements intervene. Does it strike you that this celestial zone would interfere with the brightness of the sun's light on our earth ? So far as it would affect it at all, it must increase this brilliance, for we have seen that we cannot get any effect of light except when the luminous ethers pass through chemically formed particles of matter which we call luminelles, and which float in our atmosphere. Thus we have our radiant celestia crystallized and developed on natural principles. But we have no heavenly realm yet until we can get landscapes, and flowers, and trees, and lakes. Can we get these on natural principles? Why not? We have simply a more exquisite soil, made up of the emanations of the earthly soil itself. If flowers and trees will grow from our coarser and more inert earthly soil, how much more rapidly should they grow from this very soil in its fine and more active conditions when transferred to these more powerful realms, and if the water of the earth is beautiful, how much more beautiful must its finer counterpart be in the higher lakes. Think you it would be too cold there for vegetation and human life? But the coarser grades of heat and cold which rule here, have no effect on the finer conditions. The fine thermal and electrical rays that radiate from everything would be just suited to the conditions there. The light of the sun, moon, and stars would not be visible in its present form. Only their subtler rays would be seen and felt. Thus at last, may we not have some conception of Heaven, how it has been formed, and what its materials, glorious conditions, and locations are ? Locations, I say, because there must be portions far higher and finer than those I have been describing suited to conditions of advancement, for man must ever pass onward and upward towards the Infinite Perfection as eternity glides along. Is not this the realm that John of Patmos saw with his inner vision, a portion of whose sublime simplicity of language I will quote : " And I saw a new heaven and a new earth : for the first heaven and the first earth were passed away. And I John saw the holy city, now Jerusalem, coming down from God out of heaven. Having the glory of God : and her light was like unto a stone most precious, even like a jasper stone, clear as crystal, and the city was pure gold like unto clear glass, and the foundations of the wall of the

city were garnished with all manner of precious stones.   And
he showed me a pure river of the water of life, clear as crystal.
And there shall be no night there ; and they need no candle,
neither light of the sun ; for the Lord God giveth them light,
and they shall reign for ever and ever."   We have seen that
around a low, or selfish or impure character, there are dark and
heavy emanations, and until cleansed from such conditions, the
spirit must be too gross to gravitate into the higher realms of
being.   I have ventured to speak of this celestial realm after
which so many human hearts have aspired, and which so few
have any conception of.   And can this be called a mere speculation ?   Have I not built upon the known facts, analogies and
laws of things ? Did not the Brahminical sacred writer far back
in the misty ages of the past get a glimpse of this land of beauty,
when he exclaimed rapturously :   " Where there is eternal light
in the world, where the sun is placed in that immortal, imperisha-
ble world, place me, O Soma !   Where life is free, in the third
heaven of heavens, where the worlds are radiant, there make
me immortal !" (*Rig Vedas, 1580 B.C.*)

Let us pause a moment and see how light is used in various
ages to typify the Supreme Being, and the most exalted of all
conceivable qualities and objects.

In the portion of the Hindoo sacred writings called the
BHAGVAT GEETA, written according to Sir Wm. Jones 3000 years
B.C., occurs the following sublime passage :—" The glory and
amazing splendor of this mighty being, may be likened to the
sun rising at once into the heavens, with a thousand times
more than usual brightness. * * * Thou art the Supreme
Being, incorruptible, worthy to be known !   Thou art prime
supporter of the universal orb ! * *   I see thee without beginning, without middle, without end ; of valor infinite ; of arms
innumerable ; the sun and moon thy eyes ; thy mouth a flaming
fire, and the whole world shining with thy reflected glory !"
(*Charles Wilken's Translation.*)

" That All-pervading Spirit, which gives light to the visible
sun, even the same in *kind* am I, though infinitely distant in
degree." (*Rig Vedas.*)

" Zoroaster, whose period of life is variously estimated at from
560 to 1300 years B.C. calls God (Ormuzd) the " Self Luminous,"

" The King of Light," and says : " The soul is a bright fire, and by the power of the Father, remains immortal and is mistress of life."

" He is Life, Counsel and Light." (*Orpheus, B.C. 1200.*)

" There is One Universal Soul, diffused through all things, eternal, invisible, unchangeable ; in essence like truth, in substance resembling light." (*Pythagoras, B.C. 586.*)

" God is Truth, and Light is his shadow." (*Plato, b. 429 B.C.*)

" They that be wise shall shine as the brightness of the firmament, and they that turn many to righteousness, as the stars, forever and ever." (*Daniel, B.C. 534.*)

" The sun shall be no more thy light by day ; neither for brightness shall the moon give light unto thee : but the Lord shall be unto thee an everlasting light, and thy God thy glory." (*Isaiah, 698 B.C.*)

The following is from a celebrated poem on " Milton in his Blindness," written by Miss Elizabeth Lloyd, of Philadelphia. Its author seems to have come into rapport with this diviner illumination of the inner life just as every true poet does :

> Oh ! I seem to stand
> Trembling where foot of mortal ne'er hath been,
> Wrapped in the radiance from thy sinless land,
> Which eye hath never seen.
>
> Visions come and go ;
> Shapes of resplendent beauty round me throng ;
> From angel lips I seem to hear the flow
> Of soft and holy song.
>
> It is nothing, now
> When heaven is opening on my sightless eyes,
> When airs from Paradise refresh my brow,
> The earth in darkness lies.
>
> In a purer clime,
> My being fills with rapture—waves of thought
> Roll in upon my spirit—strains sublime
> Break over me unsought.
>
> Give me now my lyre !
> I feel the stirrings of a gift divine ;
> Within my bosom glows unearthly fire
> Lit by no skill of mine."

CPSIA information can be obtained
at www.ICGtesting.com
Printed in the USA
BVHW092322140819
555871BV00010B/499/P